Family
Skeleton

NEW HORIZON PRESS

Dear Reader,

We proudly present the newest addition to our internationally acclaimed true crime series of *Real People/Incredible Stories*. These riveting thrillers spotlight men and women who perform extraordinary deeds against tremendous odds: to fight for justice, track down elusive killers, protect the innocent or exonerate the wrongly accused. Their stories, told in their own voices, reveal the untold drama and anguish behind the headlines of those who face horrific realities and find the resiliency to fight back...

Many people have a skeleton in their closet, but the Carmichaels had one that was all too real. *Family Skeleton* tells the chilling true story of child abuse, murder, family secrets and ultimately, the power of courage. At the back of her closet, hidden inside a cedar-lined trunk filled with air fresheners and mothballs, horrified detectives found the mummified body of Mrs. Carmichael's three-year-old daughter, Latanisha. Her big sister Sabrina and twin brother Andre describe in detail how their secret ate at them like acid through their entire lives and what it took for them to come forward with the awful truth.

The next time you want to read a crackling, suspenseful page-turner, which is also a true account of a real-life hero illustrating the resiliency of the human spirit, look for the New Horizon Press logo.

Sincerely,

Dr. Joan S. Dunphy
Publisher & Editor-in-Chief

Real People/Incredible Stories

Family
Skeleton

by

Andre Carmichael, Sabrina Carmichael-Yaw
and Aurora Mackey

New Horizon Press
P.O. Box 669
Far Hills, NJ 07931

Carmichael, Andre, Carmichael-Yaw, Sabrina and Mackey, Aurora
Family Skeleton

Cover design: Robert Aulicino
Interior Design: Susan Sanderson

Library of Congress Control Number: 2007934019

ISBN 13: 978-0-88282-295-2
ISBN 10: 0-88282-295-0

New Horizon Press books may be purchased in bulk quantities for
educational, business, or sales promotional use.
For more information please write to:
New Horizon Press
Special Sales Department
PO Box 669
Far Hills, NJ 07931
1-800-533-7978
Email: nhp@newhorizonpressbooks.com

www.newhorizonpressbooks.com
Manufactured in the USA

2012 2011 2010 2009 2008 / 5 4 3 2 1

Dedication

For
Latanisha

"Three can keep a secret, if two of them are dead."

—*Benjamin Franklin*

Author's Note

This book is based on the experiences of Andre Carmichael and Sabrina Carmichael-Yaw and reflects their perceptions of the past, present and future. The personalities, events, actions and conversations portrayed within the story have been taken from their memories, court documents, interviews, testimony, research, letters, personal papers, press accounts and the memories of some participants.

This is a true story. No names have been changed. The events and conversations in this book have been described as carefully as possible and as they actually occurred. There are, however, two sections that require clarification. Prior to the trial, Andre and Sabrina had numerous conversations with detectives and prosecutors from the district attorney's office; for the sake of clarity, those conversations have been compressed and presented here as one.

Table of Contents

Introduction   xi

PART 1: Chilling Past   1

Chapter 1   A Horrific Memory   3

Chapter 2   Andre's Understanding   23

Chapter 3   Sabrina's Secret   47

Chapter 4   Ensuring the Silence   55

Chapter 5   The Ripple Effect   65

Chapter 6   Shock of a Lifetime   77

PART 2: Terrible Revelations   89

Chapter 7   The Agonizing Decision   91

Chapter 8   The Secret Revealed   107

Chapter 9   Sins of the Mother   121

Chapter 10   Terror and Scars   127

Chapter 11   Awful Truths   139

Chapter 12   Presumed Innocent   151

PART 3: Fitting Judgment   157

Chapter 13   The Mills of Justice   159

Chapter 14   A Sister's Testimony   195

Chapter 15   A Brother's Testimony   215

Chapter 16   The Verdict   235

Chapter 17   A Reporter's Search for Andre   251

Chapter 18   Connection   267

Chapter 19   The Shadow of Doubt   275

Chapter 20   In Jesus' Arms   293

Epilogue   299
Afterword   301
Acknowledgments   317

Introduction

The three-year-old twins, Andre and Latanisha, are sitting on the rug in front of the TV when Sabrina, their eight-year-old sister, comes home from school and sits down beside them. Their older brother Gregory, seventeen, is standing next to their mother in the kitchen.

"Do you have homework?" Mama asks.

"Yes'm," Sabrina sighs.

"Well, shouldn't you be doing it then?"

Sabrina gives a big sigh and starts to get up. But Mama and Greg both suddenly bolt toward her, so she stops in her tracks. She's riled them for sure, maybe sighed too loudly. But then she realizes it's not her they're after. Reacting behind her, Greg grabs Latanisha by her shoulders and then Mama grabs her too, starts shaking her with both hands.

Sabrina doesn't know what Latanisha did, what happened to set them off. But her little sister is screaming now, which makes Mama even angrier. She's slapping Latanisha's face, hitting her back and her head, while Greg holds the little girl down. It's the first time Sabrina has ever seen Greg lay a hand on Latanisha.

"Are you listening to me?" Mama screams. "Are you?"

Mama and Greg are both hunched over Latanisha now, slapping her as if someone wound them up and they couldn't stop if they wanted. Then Mama balls up her fist. In a moment that will be burnished into Sabrina's memory forever, as if the scene had been captured on video and constantly replayed in slow motion, Sabrina sees Mama's knuckles arch through the air and end with an audible crunch into the side of Latanisha's head.

The little girl falls onto the rug with a *thwump*.

Andre and Sabrina are still in front of the TV, but they're both looking at Latanisha, waiting for her to sit up or start crying again. Sabrina is too scared to move, terrified that Mama will come for her next, but Mama, she realizes, is doing the same thing she is. She's waiting for Latanisha to move or start crying again, too.

Mama lifts Latanisha's shoulders and shakes her.

"Tish?" she says.

She lays Latanisha down again and Mama puts her ear against Latanisha's chest. And then Mama's eyes widen, as if she can't believe what she's hearing. She puts her mouth over the child's and in between puffs she tells Greg to pump on Tish's chest, to push down when she says to, but not too hard. The two of them do that over and over—Mama puffing into Latanisha's mouth, Mama barking instructions to Greg, Mama puffing again—until finally they both stop. They stand up, stare at Latanisha and then walk into the kitchen, begin whispering and waving their hands.

Suddenly Mama starts moving really fast—into her bedroom, into the kitchen again. When she comes back into the living room, she's holding a large black plastic garbage bag in one hand, a little white box in the other. Mama and Greg don't say one word. Greg holds the garbage bag open and Mama lifts up Latanisha and puts her inside. Then Mama tears open the box she's holding. Before Sabrina sees any of the glittery white balls rain down on her little sister, she smells them: the dead stench of mothballs.

Mama twists the top of the garbage bag closed. Sabrina sees the outline of Latanisha's leg, her bent knees stretching against the plastic, as if her little sister is trying to break free. But Mama doesn't pay any attention. She walks into her bedroom and comes back dragging her old blue metal trunk, the one she always keeps inside her closet. Greg unlatches it, Mama scoops up the garbage bag and puts it inside, then she closes the lid. Together, Mama and Greg drag the trunk across the rug into Mama's bedroom.

Sabrina doesn't know what makes her dare move, what makes her dare follow them, but she does. From the doorway of Mama's bedroom, she watches as they shove the trunk into Mama's closet. *But my sister is in there*, she thinks as she hears the closet door shut.

Sabrina has already scampered back in front of the television set when Mama and Greg come into the living room and sit on the sofa. Mama is breathing hard; Greg is blinking rapidly, as if someone just shined a spotlight in his face. It stays like that for a long time: the television flickering, Andre sucking his thumb, Sabrina staring straight ahead of her, frozen.

No one says a word.

"Mama told the few people who ever asked that Latanisha was living somewhere down south," Sabrina recalled many years later. "That was the story she told Aunt Dorothy and Sonny and a few others and maybe it was even the story she tried to believe herself. But I knew the real truth about where Latanisha had gone, because I was there. I saw with my own eyes where Mama and Greg packed her off to. For more than twenty years, I never told a single soul. Even after I grew up, got married and had kids of my own, I still thought Mama and Greg could send me to the same place if they fixed their minds to it.

"I'm not trying to make an excuse for what I did," Sabrina continued. "Or maybe I should say, for what I didn't do. Still, the vision of Mama and Greg grew so big inside my head that even after Greg got sent to prison for robbery, I pictured him and Mama finding some way to send me off to join Latanisha if I ever said a word.

"But to tell you the whole truth about what happened in our family, I need to confess something else that kept me quiet during those years," Sabrina went on. "All this time, I thought of Latanisha as Mama and Greg's terrible secret and that I was just keeping it. What I didn't know was if you keep someone else's secret long enough, after a while it belongs to you. It's like buying a house when you don't know the foundation is rotting and about to cave in, but then one day it happens and you realize you're the new owner. Suddenly you don't want to live there anymore, yet you can't get rid of it and have to keep making mortgage payments on it. And the worst part is, by then you can't afford to move and have nowhere else to go.

"But I didn't know any of that back then," she explained. "And maybe more importantly, I don't want to live in that rotting house anymore. I don't want to own any part of what Mama and Greg built around me, either. That's why I have to go back now, to the very beginning, to tell you everything I remember. It's the only way I can think of to finally get free of it."

PART 1

Chilling Past

chapter 1

A Horrific Memory

Before the twins were born, when it was just Mama, Greg and me living at our apartment in Castle Hill, Mama was very sweet at times. I'm not saying she didn't always have some strangeness, like running around covering up the mirrors whenever it thundered or hiding knives and meat cleavers all over the apartment in case anyone ever broke in or tried to sneak up on her. But back then, she also had a lovable side.

Every morning, she braided my hair, never tugging too hard, and in the afternoons she read me stories and helped me with my ABC's. Mama was still happy then, too. I remember watching her dance while dinner was cooking, with some Motown turned up on the stereo and her eyes closed and she'd sway back and forth, her mouth curled into a half-smile, like she was thinking about something nice. She was still pretty then, too. Even if she was just staying home all day, Mama always dressed carefully, with lipstick, dangly earrings and a short, straight wig. She looked like one of the record covers we had of Diana Ross and the Supremes.

Every night before Greg and I went to bed, Mama laid out our clothes for school, making sure they were spotless and ironed. Mama said a person had to take pride in their appearance, no matter what. "Just because a person's living on public assistance don't mean they've got to look like gutter rats," she told us.

But there were other predictable things, too. Every Saturday, even if Mama was short on money, she sent me down to the corner market to buy fresh flowers for the kitchen table. And every Sunday, even if it was raining, Mama walked Greg and me over to the Catholic church a few blocks away to thank the Lord for all His blessings. Mama used to say that no matter how little you had in life, there were always people with a whole lot less.

"If you don't let the good Lord know you're grateful for whatever He gave you," she said, "He's likely to start reminding you."

* * *

Andre and Tish—that was what we all called her—didn't look like twins. They didn't even look like brother and sister. I was five and Gregory was fourteen. We had been living in separate foster homes for the last part of Mama's "time," as she'd called it, because she'd been too sick to care for us. I don't know how long we both had to stay away, but I lived in a strange house and was not allowed to phone Mama, not even to tell her I missed her.

When the social worker finally led me into Mama's bedroom and took me over to the white crib at the foot of Mama's bed, I looked first at the tiny girl and then at the pudgy boy. Andre had a head of black curls, with arms like thick sausages and skin the color of a dark chocolate bar, but Tish was skinny and the color of Mama's milky coffee. Her hair was reddish brown and straight as a pin, too, and she had little gold freckles all over her nose and cheeks like someone threw cinnamon on her face.

"Are they both yours, Mama?" I asked.

Mama looked more tired than ever before. Maybe it was because I couldn't remember her without her page-boy wig and big earrings, or seeing the real color of her lips.

"The girl looks like her daddy," she said. She lifted one hand and waved it in the air like she was shooing away a slow fly. And then she turned her head toward the wall, as if maybe she was crying and didn't want anyone to see it.

In the beginning, Mama took good care of them both. She changed their diapers and kept them clean and fixed their bottles. But it wasn't long before she started acting like someone else. Like someone we didn't even know. First, Mama stopped going out of the apartment. She wouldn't answer the phone, wouldn't even crack the door for neighbors, and before long it seemed as if Mama didn't talk to anyone except us. People saw Greg or me out doing one of her errands, to the corner store or the mailbox, and sometimes they'd ask how she was doing. I never knew what to say.

"Tell them it isn't their business how I'm doing," Mama said.

The twins were about a year old when Mama stopped caring for Tish, stopped paying any attention to her. Half the time Mama wouldn't even feed Tish. We'd all be sitting around the table and I'd wonder, "Why isn't she with us?" One time Tish was crying so hard in her crib and I felt so badly for her, that I sneaked into Mama's bedroom with a bottle of Kool-Aid. But Mama caught me. "You just mind your own business," she told me.

It was right around then that something happened to Tish's hand. Mama was in the bathroom cleaning when suddenly Tish started screaming. I ran back and the skin on top of Tish's hand was white and raw, completely burned off. Andre was standing next to me, wide-eyed, with one fist stuck in his mouth.

"She stuck her hand in the cleaning solution," Mama said. She looked down at Tish angrily, as if whatever happened was her own stupid fault. And then Mama opened the cabinet door under the sink, pulled out her nursing kit and started medicating Tish's hand, calm as can be.

Pretty soon, it seemed as if all Mama wanted to do was lie in bed all day, or else clean the apartment. Whenever she got into that cleaning mood, she'd scrub for hours and go crazy mad if there was even one speck of dirt anywhere or one toy out of place.

When she wasn't cleaning, she was cooking big pots of food she heaped high onto our plates. For breakfast she'd make oatmeal and toast and eggs and bacon, and dinner would be collard greens and rice and fried chicken and cornbread and sweet potato pies. She'd sit there and watch us eat and if we didn't finish every last bite, she said we were disrespecting her. Didn't we know how much trouble she'd gone to? Greg was a teenager, so he didn't mind a bit, but I had to force myself. I was a fat kid and Andre was getting there, but Tish had it worst. She never liked eating that much, but Mama acted as if she pushed away the food just to spite her.

* * *

People living month to month, paycheck to paycheck, don't just pick up and move their families to a new apartment building, especially if they've been living in the same place for almost ten years. Someone like that needs a good reason to uproot, something that outweighs all the trouble of packing up and starting over.

Mama told us we were moving because of her family. We were going over to St. John's Apartments, not very far away, she said, because we'd all be living in the same building with her own mother and sister, our grandma and Aunt Dorothy. We had cousins living there, too.

"You're all going to have a really nice big family now," Mama said. "Things are going to be a whole lot better there."

Hearing that was some kind of surprise. Until then, we didn't even know she had a family and we sure didn't know that Mama was the oldest in a big family. In all the years we'd lived at Castle Hill, Greg and I had never met anyone related to Mama, much less heard one word about them, but all that time they'd been living just a subway ride away.

Maybe Mama thought that being around Grandma and Aunt Dorothy could help her, maybe protect her from herself.

Grandma lived right next door to us on the second floor and Aunt Dorothy and her three kids, two girls and a boy, lived downstairs. In the beginning, Mama let me take the twins downstairs and play with our cousins for an hour or so and Grandma would come next door to visit.

Grandma was a big, kind lady with thick gray braids wound around her head and gold-capped front teeth and whenever she laughed, which wasn't that often, she'd go "heh-heh-heh" in a way that reminded me of a truck tooting its horn. "Come here, child, and come sit on my lap," she said, and patted her big, jiggly thighs. Then she told me that I was the prettiest girl she'd ever seen.

"What are you going to be when you grow up, pretty girl?" she asked me.

"A nurse."

"A nurse!" she exclaimed, and slapped one thigh like she was hearing that answer for the first time ever. "Well isn't that something! Did you know that your Mama used to be a nurse in South Carolina?" I loved this story, so I always shook my head.

"Well, she was. One of the best nurses around. Made us all proud, too. You should have seen your Mama in her white uniform and little white cap, the way people looked at her when she got on the bus. Yes ma'am. Like, *there goes a lady with a really important job!* Back then, your Mama was *somebody.*"

Grandma always stopped right there in the story and looked away, as if she was remembering something sad.

"And then what happened, Grandma?"

"Oh baby girl," she said, and then sighed. "Life is so hard."

I didn't like being called a baby, so I'd fill in the rest, the story Mama told to Greg and me before the twins were born. "Then Mama came to New York and one day a bunch of guys mugged her." I didn't know what "mugged" meant, except it was bad. "They hurt her back really badly and then Mama couldn't work anymore, ever again."

"Yes baby girl," Grandma said, patting me. "That's what happened."

But one day there was a big confrontation between Mama and Grandma. I was sitting on the living room rug playing Jacob's Ladder with Andre. It was one of his favorite games. I looped the string through my fingers, showed him again which string to pull and then I caught his little hand in my net. He was laughing when we both jerked up at the sound of a thud. It came from Mama's bedroom, where Tish was supposed to be napping.

There was a crash, another thud and then Tish started shrieking. Andre had the same look on his face as he did back at Castle Hill when Tish put her hand in the cleaning solution.

"What did I tell you?" Mama screamed. There was another thud, a brief silence and then Tish shrieked again. "Are you listening to me?" Mama yelled. "Are you?"

Then came pounding on our door. Grandma was out in the hallway, screaming through the door to Mama.

"Madeline! What are you doing in there? Open this door!" Grandma waited a few seconds and then pounded some more. "What's going on in there, Maddy? Open this door, right now!"

Andre and I didn't dare move. Tish kept screaming and Grandma kept pounding and kicking at the door and suddenly the door burst open, the lock broke off and Grandma marched straight back into Mama's bedroom.

"What are you doing to that child!" she screamed at Mama. "Look at that child, what are you doing to her?"

"What I do with my kids isn't your business!" Mama screamed back. "You just mind your own damn business!"

"It's my business if you're treating your kids like dogs!" Grandma yelled back. "No *dog* deserves that!"

"Get out," Mama said. "Get out of my house and don't come back. This is my house, and you're trespassing. I don't want to see your face here again. You hear? You come back, I'll call the police."

Finally, Grandma came out of the bedroom. She walked into the living room and stared at Andre and me sitting on the rug. I thought she was going to say something to us, but she just let out a deep sigh, shook her head and then walked out the door.

Right after that, Mama told us we weren't allowed to talk to anyone in her family. "Grandma and Aunt Dorothy, they both need to mind their own damn business," Mama said. "I don't want you associating with any of them anymore."

I had no way of knowing it, but it would be the last time I ever saw Grandma.

* * *

We moved again, this time to an apartment on 96th Street in Brooklyn. "It's going to be a whole lot better here," Mama said.

When I saw it, I thought it was the darkest apartment of them all, the smallest too, which didn't make sense. At three years old, the twins weren't exactly babies anymore and five people did take up some space. But Mama, I figured, must have had her reasons.

Andre and Tish still slept in the same crib next to Mama's bed. Andre's head went at one end, Tish's at the other and neither of them seemed to mind that they were crowded together and sleeping with two little feet stuck in their faces. But maybe, I thought, Greg would leave for good and then Andre and Tish could come stay with me. That was the prayer I whispered every night.

Even though I was eight and Greg was seventeen, he and I had to share a bedroom. Sometimes it wasn't so bad though, because a lot of times Greg didn't come home. He started doing that right after we moved to St. John's, going off at night without telling anyone. But at the new apartment, Greg started disappearing for days at a time. Even though it made Mama crazy mad, made her actually put on a coat and leave the apartment to go hunting for him, it made me happier than I could say. At least he wasn't around there beating on me.

Beating on me was Greg's hobby, how he amused himself. At least, that's how it seemed to me. There certainly wasn't any rhyme or reason to what he did. There were many nights like the one he just walked in the door, dropped his keys on the little side table and yelled, "Mama says you aren't helping her like you should." A heartbeat or two went by and then he grabbed me and started hitting me, kicking me, stomping on me, throwing me against a wall and slamming my head against the floor. The whole time he had a little smirk on his face.

But the worst part was, Mama just watched, didn't do one thing to stop it. I was screaming, the walls were shaking and thudding and out of the corner of my eye I saw her leaning against our bedroom doorframe, seeing everything. "What did she do now, Frog Eyes," she said.

That was her pet name for Greg. *Frog Eyes*. Maybe it was because of the way his eyes bulged out like a river toad's. Mama had nicknames for all of us. Sometimes I thought that if she called us what was printed on our birth certificates, none of us would ever turn around.

Never once had Mama called me Sabrina. It was always, "Shawn, go fix the twins their bottles because I'm watching my story." And never once had Andre been anything but Boy. "Boy, go over there and give your twin her toy so she'll stop crying." Only Latanisha had a nickname we all called her— Tish—one that suited her just fine.

The only time Mama called Greg by his real name was when she was mad at him. And mostly, at least ever since we'd moved, that was when she couldn't find him. She mumbled a lot of angry words about him when he was gone. None of us knew where Greg disappeared to or what he did while he was away, but we got hints. We got information. People came looking for him and they had stories to tell.

One day a woman from across the hall showed up at our door screaming at Mama about how Greg stole her boy's bike right under her nose and then rode off on it, waving his fists in the air when she called after him. Another time, the man who had given Greg a part-time job at his corner market told Mama that Greg and a bunch of other boys robbed his store and walked out laughing. There were other stories, too—people saying Greg threatened them with a knife or that they saw him selling drugs or that they'd seen him hurt people for no reason.

Mama always stood there in the doorway, one hand on the doorknob, and gave all of them the same answer. "My son doesn't do that kind of stuff," she said. "You must have the wrong boy." And then she closed the door in their faces. She kept her angry words about Greg being gone to herself.

Whenever Greg finally did come home, all the "I'm going to kill that child" stuff disappeared the second he walked in the door. Suddenly Mama acted as if Greg were her long-lost prince, coming back to rescue her. She'd wrap her arms around him and kiss his face and go, "Oh Frog Eyes, why do you want to worry your Mama that way? Where have you been so long?" And Greg would just stand there and grunt, like it wasn't any of her business. "Out," was all he'd say.

But sometimes Mama tried even harder to get him to feel badly about being gone so long. "Don't you know you're the man of the house, the one in charge? Don't you know you're like my husband and I depend on you?" Even though it sounded like crazy talk to me, her calling him her husband, Greg always puffed up hearing it. I could see pride on his face, too: *Yeah, I'm the man, I'm in charge now.*

Maybe Mama was only treating him that way because she was getting scared of him. Maybe all her sugary talk was just looking for protection. A year or so before, while we were still living at the St. John's Apartments, Mama wouldn't have let him off so easy if he came home after being gone all day. Back then, if Greg came in just a half hour late, Mama would have used the extension cord on him and Greg would have put his hands over his head, the same way I did now.

But at this point, Mama must have realized that Greg was practically a man. He was more than a head taller than she, wide across his shoulders, and he was stronger than Mama. Angrier, too. Greg could fight Mama back and win in a second, unlike me and certainly unlike the twins. So Mama must have figured that Greg's cowering days were gone. Maybe she started to think that she could use Greg to discipline us, that if she fixed it right, Greg could save her a whole lot of trouble.

I could see how Mama had been coming to that idea, too. In our other apartments, the minute I came home from school, even before I had a chance to get a drink or a snack, Mama would tell me to empty my backpack. Then she'd take my school work, sit down with me on the sofa and drill me on any mistakes marked in red pen by the teacher. But once we moved away from St. John's, Mama didn't seem to care about my schoolwork anymore. She gave the job to Greg. She told him to look in my backpack and see what the teacher wrote; and while he was dumping everything out on the coffee table, pawing at my papers and crinkling them all, Mama told him everything I'd done wrong that day. There was the lazy job of cleaning I did, or the long time I spent at the Laundromat or the disrespect I showed at dinner by not eating every single piece of okra or my other vegetables or chicken on my plate.

Turning his bulging eyes on me, Greg said, "Are you giving Mama trouble, Sabrina? Giving her grief?"

Mama answered, "Oh Lord, you can't believe the grief she gives me."

And then Greg grabbed me by my neck before I even had a chance to run, even though there wasn't any place to run to, and he threw me against the wall like he'd discovered a new role in life. He dragged me by my hair into the hallway, into the bedroom we shared and kicked me over and over in my ribs until I couldn't breathe, until I thought I was going to die right then and there.

"Are you disrespecting Mama?" he yelled, kicking me some more.

Greg seemed to have forgotten that until just a short time ago, everything he was doing to me was exactly what Mama did to him. Until just recently, *he* was the one having to tell teachers how he fell down the stairs or fell off his bike or fell into a door. He forgot, because it wasn't happening to him anymore. Getting free by doing the beating—if that was the deal he and Mama made between them—must have seemed like a pretty good trade-off.

I hated him for what he was doing to me. To me, he was the Devil himself. At night, I lay in my upper bunk bed and it made my spine feel stronger to think that no power on earth could make me do what Greg was doing to me, that nothing in this world could ever turn me into a beast like that.

* * *

The only times Mama didn't act red-hot about Greg being gone was when Sonny was around.

Sonny, whose real name was Charles, was Mama's new boyfriend. At least, I thought he was her boyfriend, even though Mama said he was married. I had no idea where or when Mama could've found the time to meet him, especially since she almost never left the apartment anymore and I did all her errands, to the drug store and copy machine store and whatever else Mama needed. But Sonny had been showing up off and on for a few months now, ever since we moved there.

Sonny was from Jamaica. He'd only been in New York a few years, which was why his voice went up and down when he talked. He was a tall slim man with big hands and perfect white teeth and Mama said he worked in construction. Whenever he came over, he brought us all a big bag of fried chicken and lots of times he gave Mama money. Some days he even brought candy for me and the twins.

"Tank you mistah Sonny," Tish said, whenever Sonny gave her something sweet. Sometimes Tish even gave him a kiss on his cheek and wrapped her skinny arms around his neck. "I love de choc'late. And I love you too, mistah Sonny," she'd say.

Tish got shy around Sonny, only said a few words here or there, but normally she talked up a storm. She and Andre had one white bear toy they shared. It lay in the crib between them at night and during the day, Tish liked to sit on the living room rug, making up story after story about what Mr. Bear had been doing. As she rattled on about what Mr. Bear had been eating and thinking and the latest trouble he'd gotten himself into, Andre sat across from her silently, completely still, staring into her eyes like she was the best storyteller on the planet.

Sonny already knew not to expect hearing anything from Andre. Mama said Andre must be slow because, unlike Tish, he hadn't started talking yet, hadn't even said one word. But Sonny told Mama that a lot of three-year-olds don't talk yet and it didn't mean a thing. One time, Sonny even took Andre on his lap and said, "I didn't say one word either till I was good and ready. And that's just like you, little man, isn't it?" Andre broke into a big wide grin, like he'd understood every word.

Just then, Tish ran over to them. "Ahn-day talks to me wit his toes!" Tish gave Sonny a huge smile. "He wiggle them in my face, tell me stories at night!" We all laughed when we heard that, the idea of Andre telling Tish stories with his toes, even though we had no idea what she was talking about.

Whenever Sonny was around, Mama was on her best behavior. She didn't smoke so many cigarettes and she didn't say bad things about me to Greg, either. In fact, I don't think Sonny ever heard her raise her voice to any of us even once. The two of them would sit on the sofa laughing and talking with the stereo on. And while Sonny was there, it seemed like everything would get better, that maybe everything wasn't going to be that way forever, after all. Maybe, I thought, Mama would change back to her old self again. Maybe it really wasn't too late for someone to help us.

But Sonny could only help us while he was there. And each time he left, it seemed like Mama just got worse, like the Devil took Sonny's place on the sofa.

Sometimes it was like Mama had some kind of light switch inside her head—one second off, one second on—and you never knew what was going to happen. One minute she'd be knitting on the sofa and talking nicely to you, or standing at the stove asking, "You want a taste of what I'm making for dinner?" And the next thing you'd be lying on the floor seeing stars. You'd have blood coming down your face or hot stripes down your back from the extension cord or a hazelnut popping out of your arm where the iron struck. So you had to be really careful what you said, what you did.

And if I could go back in time, if I could travel back twenty years and pull Andre and Latanisha into my room and warn them, I'd tell them:

You've got to eat every last bite she puts on your plate, no matter how much she heaps on it and never leave a speck. You've got to learn your letters and numbers perfectly and don't ever get any red-pen notes from your teacher. And the second she tells you to pick up the toys, even if there's only one or two of them, you've got to do it really quickly, run over there really fast, so she sees you jumping the way she likes it.

And another thing. You've got to say, "Yes'm" to her every time she asks you to do something, so she doesn't think you're disrespecting her.

Most of all I'd say, the best thing, though, is just to stay out of her way. When Mama's sitting there smoking her cigarettes and watching her soap operas, don't cross in front of the television. And as soon as Greg walks through the front door, just go straight back and hide in your room. She and Greg together—oh Lord. You don't want any part of that.

But I didn't tell any of that to Andre or Latanisha. And to this day, even as a grown woman, that's part of my greatest guilt, that I was too busy thinking about myself, about how I was going to survive Mama and Greg, to think about protecting the twins.

* * *

I don't know how long we lived at the same apartment after Latanisha disappeared. Everything from that day forward is murky in my mind, as if someone had closed a trunk lid down on top of me, too. The place my memory starts up again is the day we left that apartment.

Sonny loaded all of our furniture onto a flatbed truck. In the middle of it was our sofa and on top of that was Mama's blue metal trunk from her closet. We were moving again, this time to a first-floor apartment over on Rockaway Parkway.

"Things," Mama said, "are going to be a whole lot better there."

At the new apartment, Sonny unpacked the flatbed one item at a time. Looking down from the new apartment window, I could see Mama outside on the sidewalk, waving her arms and telling Sonny where everything should go. Sonny hadn't mentioned my little sister for a long time now, ever since Mama told him that Latanisha had gone down south to live with relatives.

I watched Sonny carry that blue trunk like it was just another chair or lamp and saw him take it inside Mama's new bedroom and drop it inside her new bedroom closet. And then he closed the closet door and went back to the truck for a coffee table.

Latanisha had come with us.

* * *

I never saw the spirit that lived with us at Rockaway Parkway, but I knew it was there. It made itself known. Almost every night, lying in bed, I heard it—little feet creaking up and down the wood floors, back and forth, back and forth. It wasn't the heavy sound you'd hear when Mama or Greg walked, but more like a little kid padding around in socks. First I'd hear it in Mama's bedroom, then out in the hallway, then sometimes in the kitchen, like it was wandering from room to room, looking for something.

Mama kept a few nightlights on so the hallway wasn't pitch black, but usually I was still too scared to even go to the bathroom. A few times I got up the courage to peek around the corner, but whenever I did, there'd be nothing—no one there, no more sounds. And then as soon as I went back to bed and pulled the covers around me, the footsteps started right up again. Andre told me much later that he had heard things too, that he had even seen shadows moving, but no one there to make them.

At our apartment on Rockaway, Mama started waking us up early every morning and taking us to church. She started doing voodoo, too. She bought all this stuff from a special religious store—different colored glasses she filled with water and put everywhere, candles she placed all over the floor and sometimes she even put snippets of reddish-colored hair into the candles. The smell of hair shriveling in the wax filled the air. That, and incense burning. Mama used special potions to mop the floors, stuck feathers on lamps, did anything the voodoo woman told her to do. Mama must have been hearing the same things I was, those wood floors creak-creaking at night.

Mama's bedroom closet had been sealed shut a long time before, probably right after we moved there. To this day I'm not certain whether someone could have opened it, but once Andre tried to pry it open with a spoon. That was my fault—I told him Mama had hidden his new toys in there. It was an awful thing to have done, but I said it because of all the night sounds. Part of me wanted to know if there was a ghoul living inside Mama's closet—but if there was, I sure didn't want to be the one who found it.

It was Andre who caught Mama's fury for being "nosy" when she caught him with the spoon. Even though he could have put the blame on me, could have told her what I said about his toys being hidden in there, he didn't. He just lowered his head and took Mama's blows for both of us.

Right after that, though, Mama and Greg moved a big heavy wardrobe in front of the closet. If strangers had walked into Mama's bedroom, they never would have known a door was even there.

But the wardrobe blocking the door also helped me forget what was behind it.

Whenever I was home, which was less and less as I got older, the mental job I set for myself regarding Latanisha was: *Don't dwell on it. Don't even think about her name.* But as time went on, Mama made that harder and harder for me to do. Every time Mama sent me down to the copy machine store, I knew exactly why she was doing it.

For years, Mama had been sending me to make Xerox copies of my old school report cards and medical bills. But instead of "Sabrina" being written on those official documents, Mama erased my name and carefully substituted "Latanisha." Every time I walked to that fax store and saw my sister's name written there, I felt as if I was carrying a death certificate that no one except me could see.

Mama always told me to copy each paper over and over so that the words on each one got fainter and harder to read than the last, "until you have to look really hard to see it." When the printed copies were faded enough, that's when she sent them off to the welfare office. Every month she got money for my sister, who'd been dead for years. The welfare people must have though Latanisha was a student at PS 398 with pretty good grades, but also a little girl who had lots of medical problems that made her concerned Mama take her from doctor to doctor.

Most people in Mama's position would have thrown all those papers away, gotten rid of the evidence. But not Mama.

She never threw anything away. Even if a receipt was a decade old, she still put it inside a grocery bag labeled with dates and then she flattened the grocery bag and slid it under her mattress. She did that just in case the welfare people ever claimed they didn't get what she'd sent them, or in case anyone ever asked her for proof of something from five or ten years back.

According to Mama, the welfare people were even worse than the IRS. They could ask you for anything, at any time, so you always had to be prepared.

"You have to keep everything," she said.

chapter 2

Andre's Understanding

Sabrina used to get a strange look on her face when we were kids, like she wanted to tell me something but couldn't. Usually it would happen when we were alone. She'd start glancing around like someone was going to sneak up on her and yell "boo!" She'd chew on her lip like she was trying hard to decide something.

"Come on, what is it?" I'd ask her. "Just *tell* me."

"I can't. You're going to tell Mama."

"I won't! I promise!"

But she always kept biting her lip, shaking her head, like she couldn't risk it, like she couldn't trust me.

There was only one time I really thought she was going to tell me something secret. I must've been about five or six, and we were sitting at the kitchen table while Mama was in the next room on the sofa watching her television soap operas. It must've been near my birthday because I was thinking that Sabrina knew what I was getting for a present.

Usually when Mama was watching one of her soap operas, you could've set the house on fire and she wouldn't have noticed. In fact, one time Greg did just that, set fire to a pile of newspapers in the kitchen and the whole heap was blazing before Mama roused herself off the sofa. Everyday she got so glued to the TV—to *General Hospital* and *All My Children* and all the rest—that she didn't move for hours.

On this particular day, Sabrina whispered from across the table, "You have to promise not to tell." Her back was to the living room and she glanced over her shoulder to make sure Mama was still in front of the TV. All I could see was one of Mama's ankles and one fuzzy slipper hanging over the edge of the sofa.

"I won't tell anyone!" I whispered back.

"Cross your heart and hope to die."

I crossed my heart and waited. Sabrina squinted at me and then she leaned across the table really slowly. Just then, quietly and quickly as a cat, Mama walked in, grabbed Sabrina by her hair and yanked her off her chair onto the floor.

"You're plotting against me!" she yelled. She dragged Sabrina by her hair into the living room and started slapping, punching and kicking her. "I know what you're doing and don't think I don't!"

Plotting about what? I didn't know what she was talking about. All I knew was, one minute Sabrina and I were talking about my birthday present and the next thing, Sabrina was getting beaten up. I wanted so much to run over there and help her, to save her, but I knew if I did, Mama would come for me next. I felt ashamed, being so worried about saving my own skin that I didn't even try to help my sister.

After that day, though, it seemed as if everything changed, everything got worse. After that, when only the three of us were there in the apartment, Sabrina and I were never left alone, never allowed to play together, always kept in separate rooms, always watched. If we didn't have anything to do, Mama told Sabrina to clean the kitchen and told me to clean the bathroom, or else she came up with some other kind of errand to keep us apart.

"Go down to the store, Boy, and buy me some licorice." Or, "Shawn, I need copies of this paper. Go down to the copy machine store and get me five of them. If anyone asks you, tell them, 'Oh, my Mama lost the original.'"

From then on, Mama listened to everything that went on, paid attention to every place in the apartment we went. If I went into the bathroom she was right behind me, watching. And even if she was sitting on the sofa watching TV, it still felt like she had ears all over the apartment. Eyes, too. But then, I guess she got all that information by using each of us against each other.

Almost every day she told me to go spy on Sabrina. "Go on down there and see what she is doing," Mama said to me. "Go tippy-toe."

I only did it so I wouldn't get beaten. But usually Sabrina would be doing nothing, just writing in a notebook. Even that made Mama jump up, march into Sabrina's room, grab her notebook and flip through all the pages. I never knew what Mama was looking for, but, whatever it was, she never seemed to find it.

"Oh, aren't you the poet?" she said, throwing the notebook down. "Those words don't even rhyme." Sabrina glared at me like she hated me for ratting her out.

Of course, Sabrina only knew I'd ratted her out because she was doing the same thing to me. Sometimes I'd see her poke her head around the corner and then disappear and right afterward Mama would show up and say, "What are you drawing, Boy?" She'd grab my crayon pictures, squint at them and then toss them back. "Well, aren't you the great artist? Can't even draw a tree."

But Sabrina and I weren't just separated at home. At about that time we were sent to separate schools, too. Sabrina was going to PS 398 and I could have gone there with her, but Mama said I had to go to the Catholic school and learn about sin and the Devil's ways. Every morning, Sabrina walked a few blocks to school, but I got picked up in a bus, wearing a uniform that Mama had washed and ironed the night before.

I hated that school. And I felt the nuns couldn't stand me either. During prayer time, I always asked God to please make Mama change her mind and let me go to the public school, but there didn't seem like much chance of that, especially since Mama had the church so much on her mind.

Mama started getting us up early every day and making us go to morning Mass. She'd sit in front of the priests and nuns and I could tell they all thought she was a sweet lady, this loving and caring mother, crossing herself and bowing her head and saying all of her amens. If I had seen her, I probably would've thought the same thing, too.

I sat near the altar and prayed, *Please God, let somebody save us. Please God, let someone find out what's going on.* But there were only a few times I ever thought God heard my prayers.

One time was when I got thrown out of the Catholic school for my bad attitude. The other times were whenever Mama said to me, "Go get my stuff from the drawer, Boy, and make my feet look nice and soft." I was always happy to scrub Mama's feet and put polish on her toes because that's how I knew Sonny was going to come over.

Whenever Sonny was around, we never got beaten and it was the only chance Sabrina and I ever got to talk to each other alone. Even if it was just for a few hours, it seemed to me Sonny was sent by God, an angel from heaven to save us from just a little bit of hell.

Mama would even brag about me to him. "Look, Boy did this to my feet." And Sonny always said, "Oh he did a very good job," and gave me two or three dollars.

In front of Sonny, Mama put on her sweet mother act, same as she did with the priests and nuns. But the minute Sonny walked out the door, just like the minute Mama walked out of the church, Mama did a complete attitude change. If we even dared to talk back to her, we'd be beaten.

The worst change, though, was that Greg started coming over more often. By then he had a girlfriend and was living somewhere else—we didn't know where exactly—but the minute we heard his keys in the door, Sabrina and I both began running and trying to hide, even though there wasn't any place to hide. Greg was Mama's foot soldier. She's snap her fingers and say, "This person is bothering me," and Greg would go out there and do whatever she told him to. The two of them were bosom buddies, like Bonnie and Clyde.

At that point, another unbelievable thing happened. Mama and Greg started calling themselves husband and wife.

"Frog Eyes is my husband, he's going to take care of me," Mama said. Or Greg told us, "Mama's my wife and no one is going to mess with my wife."

I always thought they were joking. Still, it always seemed like Mama had Greg on a dog leash, telling him what to do like he didn't have a mind of his own. And for some reason I never understood, Greg always did it. It was almost as if she had something on him, some secret way of controlling him.

* * *

When he was told to attack us, Greg always went for Sabrina first. He picked her up over his head and slammed her to the floor. If she tried to fight back, it just got worse for her. One time he hit her so hard you could actually hear the punch and her eyes turned so black and blue she didn't go to school for weeks. After he finished beating Sabrina, Greg came for me. Mama turned up the stereo loud so the neighbors wouldn't hear, because by then both of us were crying for our lives. While Greg was beating on me, Mama was beating on Sabrina. The two of them were like a tag team.

Sometimes Mama and Greg put Sabrina and me in the bathtub and made us sit there naked while they beat us with extension cords and belts. They knew it hurt more when our skin was wet. After a while, though, Sabrina and I started to get used to the wet whippings and learned how to hold in our pain. That made Mama crazy mad. She used broomsticks, plates on our heads, anything else she and Greg got their hands on. He and Mama beat us harder and harder.

"Oh, so you're trying to get bold now, like you don't feel the pain," she said. "Well, let's see you *now*."

After the beating was over, Mama used her nursing skills, fixed us up with creams and bandages from a kit she kept under the bathroom sink. She was nice and gentle about it, too.

"Is that better? That hurt? Is the bandage too tight?" And then, after enough time went by and we looked good enough to go out in public again, she took us to doctors. But it wasn't for us. *She* was the one with the problem, she said.

Mama sat in front of the doctor and trembled, explaining how she had a bad nervous condition and needed a certain medicine really badly. Then she went to another doctor and said the same thing, or else told them that Sabrina needed the medicine, or that I needed it. We weren't allowed to say a word. The doctors all did the same thing. They sat there looking at Mama's sweet-lady smile, listening to her talk about how she used to be a nurse before she was mugged one day and injured her back, and then they wrote out the prescriptions she wanted.

Before Mama left their offices, she always stole stationery off their desks and stuck it in her purse. She did the same thing with school papers, welfare papers, anything else she could get her hands on. At home, she wrote things on the letters, signed someone else's name and then took the papers to another office. She always made sure Sabrina went to the copy machine and made copies of everything. I can't remember a single time anyone ever questioned her. Mama probably could've conned the Devil himself if she'd gotten the chance.

Mama ended up with medicine bags all over her bedroom, under her bed, in kitchen drawers, anywhere she could think to hide them. Maybe in the beginning she hid everything so Greg wouldn't discover them and sell those drugs on the street, but later on Sabrina took whatever medicine bags she could find and threw them out the window or flushed them down the toilet.

But there were always more pills coming.

Mama told us the pills were vitamins, but Sabrina and I both knew that vitamins don't make you feel like you're walking around on the bottom of the ocean, or make you so tired you can't keep your eyes open. And we tried everything not to take them, too. But one day, Mama caught Sabrina spitting them out and from then on she sat there and watched us swallow them.

If we didn't, she told us Greg was going to come over and *he'd* make sure we took them.

* * *

By then, everyone in the neighborhood was scared of Greg. He always showed up with a black hat tilted over one eye, a shiny black leather jacket, gold neck chains thick as my thumb and pockets full of hundred dollar bills. Later on, I found out it was Greg who paid for my Catholic school, that he was the one who gave Mama the money. When I learned that, I thought Greg must've cared about me to do that, to spend his own money so I could go to a better school, even if I did hate it. I don't know why, but whenever I thought about that, it made his beatings a little easier.

Easier, that is, until Sabrina started disappearing when I was around seven or eight. In the beginning, Sabrina just took longer doing Mama's errands—going to the Laundromat, or making copies of the papers Mama needed—but then she didn't come home for hours. When Sabrina finally did come back, when she first walked in the door, it was clear as day she knew she was going to get beaten again. However, her face conveyed an attitude of, *Okay, go ahead and do whatever you're going to do. But it was worth it.* Whatever taste of freedom Sabrina had gotten in the outside world gave her the kind of boldness that Mama had always tried to whip out of us. And the amazing thing was, no matter what Mama or Greg did to her, no matter how many scars she ended up with, Sabrina's boldness didn't go away. The more they beat her, the stronger she got.

Deep down, I think that's when I started to realize that pretty soon I was going to be on my own, that Sabrina wasn't going to be around much longer. Even though the thought of being alone terrified me, part of me was rooting for her like when you're watching a horror movie. You're watching the killer sneaking through the shadows with a long shiny knife, and the pretty girl is doing something like painting her toenails with the stereo turned up, not hearing a thing, and you're yelling at the television, "Get out! Get out!" That's how I felt about my sister. I wanted her to escape.

Once, when Sabrina was gone, Mama and Sonny decided to take a weekend trip to Atlantic City. They left me with Aunt Dorothy and our three cousins while they were gone.

At her place, Aunt Dorothy took me into her kitchen. I sat at her glass table with the heavy iron chairs and she leaned against the wall holding a can of soda and stared at me.

"So what happened to your sister, Andre?" she asked. I shook my head, "I don't know where Sabrina is."

"No, I mean your twin sister," she said. "Where is your twin?"

I was so shocked I didn't know what to say. I thought she was just messing with me. But she kept telling me she wasn't.

Then she said, "When you were little, you all used to live right upstairs, next door to Grandma." She told me Sabrina used to bring my twin sister and me downstairs to visit her and our cousins. She even thought she had pictures of me and my twin in our crib and she went hunting for them. But she couldn't find any. And even without the pictures, she didn't change her story. She kept on saying, "Andre, you *do* have a twin sister."

Later, I thought about what she said. It made little pictures start forming in my head. For years, I'd had flashes of things I didn't understand—two hooded snowsuits, one pink and one blue, hanging on hooks by a door. A little girl's hand with the skin burned off on top. Two small feet touching my chin at night. A toy bear.

All that night as I lay in bed, I kept asking myself, *why would my own aunt tell me that kind of thing if it wasn't true?* Of course, I was just a kid and I knew I didn't understand all the ways grown-ups could twist things. Still, I kept wondering— why would she lie?

That weekend after Mama and Sonny got back from Atlantic City, they picked me up and took me home. Sonny was outside parking the car, but Greg was already inside our apartment when Mama and I walked in the door. Mama was in a good mood. She was taking off her coat and smiling and so even though I was scared, I said, "Mama, there's something I want to ask you." She was still smiling, like she was remembering something nice, and then she said kind of off-hand, "Well go ahead then, Boy. Ask me your question."

As soon as I did, it was like all the lights went out and the air got sucked out of the room. "Get ready for bed and don't move an inch out of your bedroom," she said angrily. Then she marched over to the phone and started yelling at Aunt Dorothy to mind her own business. Then she slammed down the phone and through a crack in my door I saw her whisper something to Greg.

Suddenly, Greg marched into my room and started beating on me. Pounding on my head, kicking me, stomping me, punching me. Beating the hell out of me. He was screaming that I was trying to kill Mama with all my questions, trying to make Mama sick with stress. And then he grabbed a hammer—I swear to God that's what it was—and swung it at my head.

Not long after that, just as I had been afraid of, Sabrina stopped coming home for long periods of time. Of course, Mama didn't have any easy way to find her—it wasn't like she knew Sabrina's school friends and could call up their homes and talk to their parents. Except for the days Sonny came over, Mama didn't talk to anyone but us. She didn't answer the phone, wouldn't even crack the door if a neighbor knocked. She was like a hermit, didn't know a person. The only one she had was Greg. But Greg knew people, how to get information. And for a while, Greg managed to track down Sabrina and drag her back home again.

The last time he did that, Greg grabbed Sabrina's baggy sweatshirt and lifted it up. Her stomach looked like she'd swallowed a little watermelon. Seeing that made Greg and Mama go crazy mad—both of them went at her like I'd never seen them do before. Right after that, Sabrina started wailing and clutching her stomach. Then she lay on the living room rug with her legs spread and Mama was on her knees yelling at Greg to go get her some hot water and towels and yelling at me to get in my room, to mind my own business.

But I didn't go in my room. Even though I couldn't see everything, I hung back and watched from around the corner.

I heard a baby cry. And then the ambulance came.

Mama and Greg were both scared when Sabrina was taken to the hospital. After Sabrina and her baby got loaded onto a stretcher and carried out, I saw them whispering in the kitchen with their heads together, their foreheads scrunched. To me, that was a good sign. It felt the same way it did when I found out that it was Greg who'd been paying for my Catholic school. The way I saw it, Mama and Greg wouldn't be so worried about Sabrina if they didn't really care for her deep down inside.

I wish I could explain everything in a straight line—first this happened, then that—but the truth is, big parts are missing. If the truth is told, I've got memory holes so big that sometimes it seems like maybe I wasn't even there.

But I *was* there. And the parts I do remember, the parts I can tell you about, are the ones I have to figure stuck with me for some kind of good reason. If you can't make sense of what happened in between them, if the holes in my story make a lot of things like a jigsaw puzzle missing lots of pieces, then maybe what's happening is that you're standing in my shoes.

Sabrina came back from the hospital, alone. I don't know if she stayed days or weeks or months. But then she disappeared.

Mama told me that Sabrina made the choice to go live in a foster home. For a while, I tried to convince myself that Sabrina would be coming back again, that she'd walk in the door and hug me the way she always did, even though I really didn't believe it. In my heart, I knew this time she was gone, she wasn't coming back, and everything started turning worse just like I'd been afraid of.

It might've had something to do with Sonny.

Over the years, Sonny had put up with a lot, especially from Greg, and lately Sonny had been coming around less and less. One day, though, Mama pushed him over the edge. For the first time ever, she couldn't hold it inside her. She started whipping me with a long extension cord and when Sonny tried to stop her—*Maddy! Maddy! Stop! What are you doing?*—She spun around and screamed at him.

"You just mind your own business! They aren't your kids. They're mine! You keep your nose out of it or I'll tell Greg."

Sonny already knew what kind of man Greg had turned into, what Greg was capable of doing. Not long before that, Greg had even tried to choke Sonny in an argument. By then, Sonny was getting older and Greg had the size on him, the strength on him, too.

Sonny wasn't the kind of man who would ever start an argument, who ever wanted a fight. For as long as I'd known him, everything about him made you want to light a candle and put on some soft music and relax. Just looking at Sonny made life seem easier, like life had a gentler side.

But when Mama started beating on me that day, when she threatened to tell Greg if Sonny didn't mind his own business, I guess even Sonny got scared of both of them. Because right after that, he stopped coming over at all. Sonny had been in our lives for years and years, but I guess he finally had enough.

Mama was probably the last one to figure out that he wasn't ever coming back. I saw it dawn on her the way thick, dark rain clouds sometimes move in really slowly, like maybe they're going to pass you by, but then they drop down and rain pour and pour for days on end.

After that, I started to pray every day. At night, I got down on my knees next to my bed, folded my hands and bowed my head, just so God would know I really meant every word.

Please, God. Please let Sonny come back. Please don't leave me all alone. If you can hear me, if you know I'm still here, please show me, give me some kind of sign. God, if you're really there, if you really exist, please help me.

But every day it was just Mama and me. And Mama's behavior got worse than ever before. She acted like it was my fault that Sonny wasn't coming over anymore.

To this day, I don't understand what could make any mother strip her ten-year-old son naked and throw him into a hallway. I don't understand how a neighbor knocking on the door saying, "Mrs. Carmichael, what's your boy doing out here with no clothes on?" could make her whip that boy so badly he bled in places no boy should ever bleed. And I can't understand, either, what would make any mother take an empty mayonnaise jar, urinate in it and then make her child drink the liquid in front of her. What did I ever do to make Mama hate me so much? *Just tell me God*, I prayed, *and I'll stop doing it.*

And what did I ever do to make Greg hate me so much? Some days, my big brother showed up the same way nightmares do. He walked in like a king coming to visit, took off his leather jacket, draped it over the sofa and then suddenly he spun around and came on me like he'd been planning it all along.

One day, I came home from school and started looking for something to eat. Mama was watching one of her television stories and wasn't paying attention, so I went hunting in the kitchen. I knew Mama liked to stash food around the house, so I looked in all the cabinets and found a sandwich-size plastic bag that was hidden behind a few Tupperware bowls. The bag was filled to the brim with the kind of sugar they sprinkle on doughnuts. I opened it, stuck in my finger, took a taste and right away my whole tongue went numb.

I got scared. "Mama, my tongue feels like it's going to fall off," I said.

"What have you been messing with?"

I told her I got into the sugar. She got up, opened the bag, took one small taste of it and then she marched into the bathroom and poured it down the toilet. When Greg showed up a few hours later, the two of them were arguing, fighting.

"I don't want any of your drugs in this house," she screamed at him. "The child welfare people are coming back pretty soon to check out whether Sabrina can come back home again and if they find anything, they could take Andre out too. So you just get out of here now. And take all your drugs out of here, too."

A couple of hours later, Mama stepped out to go to the store. I was in the front room when Greg came back. He didn't look at me as he set his house keys on the little table, didn't say anything to me either. He walked straight back into the bedroom we used to share and then a few seconds later he called me to come back there. Even though I was scared, I decided to go back anyway, to show him no fear.

He was holding a hammer.

"You went up there touching my stuff, didn't you? And you showed Mama, didn't you?" I didn't have time to answer. He swung the hammer into my head. I was lying on the floor and his face was swimming in front of me. Lying there, I really thought I was going to die, that Mama would come home and find me lying there dead.

"You wanna touch my things?" he said. His face was one inch from mine. "You wanna mess with things that don't concern you?"

He was sitting on top of me now and I couldn't move, couldn't even see straight. I felt him take one of my hands and hold it down against a piece of wood. And then he picked up a nail and hammered it through my palm, from the top of my hand to the bottom. Then he took my other hand and did the same thing. I don't know how long I was lying there, both my arms stretched out, with my hands nailed to the floor.

I still hear the echo of my own voice screaming. I'll never forget how my hands were bleeding all over everything or how Mama came back from the store, walked in and took one look at me stretched out and didn't say one word. She just looked at Greg like, *good job*, and walked into the kitchen.

But maybe I'll never forget that day because it also was the first time I heard the voice.

Greg had gone away. Mama was watching TV. I was washing my hands in the bathroom. The holes were so big I could've put a thin rope through them.

"*Don't go through what Sabrina went through,*" the voice said.

It was strange, because it wasn't my own voice, or anyone I knew either. It was higher, like a young girl was standing right behind me and talking right into my ear. I looked around me, behind me, thinking maybe someone was joking with me. That, or else I was going crazy.

But then the voice talked to me again, *"Andre, you have to survive."*

Part of me knew that the voice couldn't be real, that maybe my brain was inventing a little angel. Still, right then I made up my mind. Whatever it took, whatever I had to do, I was going to do what that voice told me. No matter what, I was going to survive.

When Mama and Greg showed up at my school not long after that and accused me of stealing the rent money—I had tucked it in the pocket of Mama's raincoat because Greg had come over to steal it to buy drugs—and when Greg hung me upside down by my feet in the school cafeteria in front of everyone and told me he'd finish with me when I got home, I knew I couldn't take it anymore. Something deep inside me knew that if I didn't leave that very day, I'd never come to school again, that I was going to end up dead.

I went to the principal and told her everything. And then a social worker showed up. "Are you sure you want to live in a foster home?" the social worker asked.

I didn't even blink. "Yes, I'm sure."

I was ten years old and I finally escaped.

* * *

My foster mother, Mrs. Lewis, was the kindest lady I'd ever met. Right from the start, she treated me like I was her own son. The first night I was there, I sat at the dining table with her and another foster child and Mrs. Lewis lowered her head and said, "We thank you, Lord, for bringing Andre into our lives. We are truly blessed to have him as part of our family." No one in my entire life had called me a blessing, much less treated me like one.

Not long after I arrived there, Mrs. Lewis asked me about my family, what it was like for me at home. She seemed pretty shocked when I told her that Greg was the enforcer and that Mama always watched while he beat Sabrina and me.

It was then that I also told her that I thought I maybe had a twin. She didn't quite understand what I meant.

"Do you remember having a twin?" she asked.

"Not exactly," I said. But I did have little flashes of things in my mind sometimes—two snowsuits hanging by a door, another baby's burned hand, two feet sticking in my face in a white crib. I also told her what Aunt Dorothy said when Mama and Sonny were in Atlantic City, how she even tried to find pictures of us.

"Well, if you did have a twin, wouldn't she be in foster care with you?" Mrs. Lewis asked. I told her I didn't know. "Well," she said, "if you do have a twin, let's find out where she is."

Mrs. Lewis tried really hard. She must've called the social workers ten or twenty times, until finally they called her back. "There's no twin there," they told her. "He's lying or else he's making it up for attention."

Mrs. Lewis never said she didn't believe me, but after a while I guess she figured there wasn't anything more she could do to find out one way or another. And so finally, I just stopped talking about it. I pushed the idea of having a twin out of my mind.

Still, every once in a while, I'd hear that strange voice talking in my ear, the same one that told me I had to survive. Usually I'd hear it when I was about to do something stupid, like getting into a fight on the school yard.

"*Just walk away, Andre,*" the voice said. "*Don't be messing with those guys. It isn't worth it.*"

Every time I heard that voice, I spun around, expecting to see some girl talking right into my ear. But every time I looked, I saw the same thing—empty air. The only thing I could figure was that it was just my leftover craziness from living with Mama and Greg. That, or else it was what Mrs. Lewis talked about.

She told me that we all have a little voice inside us, but not everyone can hear it. Sometimes, she said, it's our conscience, but other times, if we're truly blessed, it also can be the Holy Ghost trying to reach us. Mrs. Lewis said the voice was nothing to be afraid of, that it was there to show us the right way, to protect us from evil, to save us from going astray. The worst thing, she said, was to ignore it.

* * *

I lived with Mrs. Lewis until I was eighteen. During that time, I only saw Mama and Greg one time and I didn't see Sabrina again for nearly fifteen years. A social worker collected me from Mrs. Lewis's house and took me over to the same restaurant in Brooklyn where Mama used to take all of us on special occasions.

Mama looked heavier, bloated and tired and got out of breath just squeezing into her seat. Greg, as usual, was wearing a shiny black leather jacket with clunky gold neck chains and he kept staring at me with a smirk that always used to mean he was planning to do me serious harm. But I wasn't afraid of my big brother that day. Or of Mama either. It had been more than two years since I saw them and I was bigger now. Stronger, too. But the social worker was also there to protect me, so I felt safe knowing that Mama or Greg couldn't hurt me even if they wanted to.

We all had cheeseburgers. Between bites Mama asked, "How's school going?" and "Are you getting enough to eat at Mrs. Lewis's?" and questions like that, ones I knew she didn't really care about, so I answered with just the same amount of caring, with just a few words. Every now and then the social worker tossed something into the conversation—"Mrs. Lewis says Andre has been making a real effort in math" or "Andre's teacher says he's a real pleasure"—and Mama nodded, pretending she was really interested. The entire time, Greg leaned against the wall, silently dipping one French fry after another into a squirt of catsup on his plate, never once taking his eyes off me.

At one point, I asked Mama how she was doing, if she was taking care of herself. When I'd left home, she had high blood pressure and heart problems and now she didn't look so well.

"I have a pacemaker," Mama said. "That old heart of mine's doing just fine now." Greg still hadn't said anything and the way he hunched in the corner, staring at me, reminded me of a coiled cobra. Finally, I kept nodding at Mama and said things like, "That's good." It seemed as if we all had run out of things to say.

After that, the social worker got up to buy me a birthday dessert. Suddenly Mama sprang to life, as if she'd been waiting all along for the woman to go away. She leaned forward, her big chest smushing up against the edge of the table, and she hissed at me through her gold-rimmed front teeth.

"Listen here, Boy. Greg, Sabrina and I, we washed our hands of you, understand?" She pointed a finger at me. "We want nothing more to do with you. So the social workers can just quit calling me. I don't care anything about what you do anymore. You've made your bed, Boy. So now you can just lay in it."

It was strange, but hearing those words out loud—instead of just having the *feelings* of the words swirling around inside me—was almost like a weight taken off me. The idea of never seeing Mama or Greg again didn't even hurt me. I'd been glad to leave Mama's house, glad to be living with Mrs. Lewis, who was the kindest lady I'd ever met. And at that moment, I realized deep down I'd probably known all along that I could never go home again.

Sometimes at Mrs. Lewis's, I had actually pictured going back, getting cornered and having to kill Mama and Greg if it came down to my own survival. I'd already made up my mind that I'd never go through the kind of suffering that Sabrina did. She had it even worse that I did and for years and years longer, too.

But now that Mama had said it out loud, I realized I could go back to Mrs. Lewis's house and stop wondering if maybe I'd made a mistake by telling people at school how badly I was getting beaten up at home, that I could finally stop thinking, the way I sometimes did at night under Mrs. Lewis's big fluffy comforter, that maybe Mama and Greg could change.

But Sabrina? What did I ever do to her? Why would *she* want to wash her hands of me? That was the only thing Mama said that hurt me. It was the idea of never seeing Sabrina again, that my big sister was throwing me away just like they were, that made me feel like someone just punched me in my heart.

Suddenly, I saw the social worker halfway across the room digging in her purse for her wallet to pay the cashier. She'd soon be back. I knew it was the only chance I'd probably ever have to say my piece.

"Mrs. Lewis is very good to me," I quickly said to Mama. "I'm very happy with her and I don't want to come home again." Then I stared at Greg. "And I don't take crap anymore, either. I don't let anybody hit me anymore." Greg knew immediately what I was talking about, because he started laughing. Mama grinned too, like I was being really amusing.

"And one other thing," I looked back at Mama and blurted out the one question I had left. "Do I have a twin sister or twin brother out there?"

This time I knew she couldn't beat me for asking, the way she did after she and Sonny went to Atlantic City. I knew Greg couldn't beat me either. The social worker would be coming back to the table at any moment.

The grin left Mama's face really fast. She glanced over to where the social worker was standing in line.

"I'm not going to tell you now! But I will say that I know somebody who walks like you, talks like you, even sat on the paint bucket like you."

The paint bucket. That was where Mama used to make me sit, sometimes for hours and hours as punishment.

"I'll tell you when you get old enough," Mama said, nodding as the social worker slipped her wallet back inside her purse. "When you are older, then you can know."

When I heard Mama mention that other person who sat on the paint bucket, all I heard was something inside me saying, *See, I wasn't lying.* That's what mattered most to me—that I hadn't been making anything up or lying just to get attention.

When the social worker came back to the table, she was smiling. She held out a small plate with a slice of cheesecake and in the middle was a single red candle.

"Well, go on Andre, make a wish," the social worker said, like we all were having a nice party.

I knew inside that she was trying to be kind and trying hard to make me believe I still had a family, and so even though I had no wishes left, I blew out the candle anyway.

chapter 3

Sabrina's Secret

I never thought I'd see Andre again. I had accepted that a long time before. No one had ever told me why Andre left home, what had happened.

I was fifteen the year he disappeared. For Andre, I was sure it had seemed like the other way around: that I was the one who had disappeared from *his* life. One day, I was in the emergency room getting patched up and the next thing I knew I was in a foster home. A few weeks later, when I finally got the courage to call home, the only information I had was what Mama told me.

Mama said Andre had gone to live in a foster home, too. That he'd washed his hands of us all, so I could forget about trying to contact him. "The social worker already told me that Andre doesn't want anything more to do with any of us, ever again," Mama said. For a long time afterward, I wondered if he really was in foster care somewhere, as Mama said. Maybe, I thought, it was another one of Mama's stories, just like the one about Latanisha living somewhere down south. The idea of that terrified me—that Andre and Latanisha might be together.

Not wanting to ever see Mama or Greg again, that part I could understand. And Andre running away, or else getting taken away—I never knew how it really went down—that part I could understand, too. But Andre didn't want anything to do with *me*? For a long time, that had hurt more than what sent me to the hospital. And then all those years, nothing. As if Andre had simply been erased, as if he'd never existed.

If anyone had told me that Andre would show up at my door out of the blue thirteen years later, I never would have believed it. And if anyone had asked me before that day, I would have said that the little world I was living in had turned out to be a pretty good one. I'm not saying it had been easy— but then again, nothing in my life had been easy. So I was used to that. Still, I considered myself lucky.

At that point I was twenty-eight years old and had a husband I adored, a man who still made my heart flip just looking at him, even after almost ten years of marriage. I had five children, one of whom I'd had before I met Chris. They all knew I loved them. I also had a part-time job as a nurse's aide that reminded me every day to be grateful for all my blessings. There were so many people in the world, I realized, with burdens so much heavier than my own: people who were sick, people who had no family members, people who had no hope the next day would be any better.

Sometimes on the subway going back home, I'd think about the people I took care of, bathed or cooked for, people living in a city with millions of others, and that's when it would hit me: *I'm their only connection to the outside world. Just me.* And that's when I truly understood what having no family could do to a person. In the evenings, even when I was exhausted and the kids were hungry or fighting or tugging at me for something or another, I kept that thought in mind: *None of my children are ever going to need some stranger to look after them. My kids and Chris and I, we're a real family.*

From the start, Chris and I had made a conscious decision that our struggles would only be as hard as we made them out to be. We both knew we'd have them, of course, but Chris made it seem as if everything was just a matter of how you looked at a thing, that perspective was what determined how well a person did in life.

"There are people who're always looking at the dark side, and so the dark side is always what they find," Chris once told me in his beautiful Jamaican accent, the one he later worked so hard to get rid of. "You have to have the right attitude. If you do, then you can survive most anything."

He had a strong character. There weren't a lot of twenty-six-year-old men who would have taken on an eighteen-year-old girl who'd been living in foster care the last three years and had a small daughter. Most men would've run for their lives from a single mother like me—especially if they hoped to go to law school one day like Chris did. But Chris didn't run. He took my little girl and me in and found us all a small apartment. And that by itself was some kind of miracle.

When I first met him, Chris could barely scrape together enough money for his own little room at the YMCA. He and his mother had come to New York from Jamaica and even though he could have kept living with her in her small apartment, he moved out to prove to himself he could make it on his own. And Chris struck me right off as someone who mattered. Someone people listened to. Maybe, I'd think sometimes, he'd become a famous defense lawyer who could prove to the jury how his client got framed, or a prosecutor like on TV, who could talk so convincingly that every guilty guy ended up in jail. Even in jeans and a plain white shirt at the YMCA, Chris was the kind of man I could picture walking down Fifth Avenue one day in an expensive suit and three hundred dollar sunglasses, with women stealing glances at him and men wondering where he bought that fine leather briefcase.

Chris's ideas were as big as he was. He was six-foot-one with big broad shoulders, skin darker than midnight and hair shaved into a flat top. Everything about him reminded me of a beautiful, black, penned-up stallion that knew he could leap over that fence any time he pleased, as if Chris were just gathering strength, pawing at the ground temporarily and waiting to pick his own time.

"I'll tell you something I've learned," he told me one time. "Back in Jamaica, people don't worry so much about getting everything right now, right this minute. They can wait for things. That's the problem with so many people here. They take what they can get right now, instead of working for what they really want."

As I listened to him, his Jamaican accent making words go up and down like fluttering birds, I felt hypnotized. During the days, he had a job as a security guard and at night he was enrolled at City College. The way he worked so hard at everything made me believe every word he'd told me about how we'd both make it, if we just stayed focused on what was important.

He made me believe that what wasn't important was my past. He said he didn't care about it, that he didn't need to know the details. He said we all had to come from somewhere and what mattered most was how we shaped our futures. The way Chris said it made me think that maybe there was something in his own past he didn't want to talk about—that maybe he was set on starting out from scratch, too—but I also wondered if maybe he was just sensing a whole lot of shadows in my own life that he'd rather not know about. Either way, though, was fine with me. I didn't need to go digging around into his past, into whatever came before me, and I sure didn't need him doing that to me.

Still, part of me wanted to tell him everything—about Latanisha, about what Andre and I had gone through—even if it was only so I could finally confide in at least one other human being. But I also loved that man and loving him made me want to share the truth with him. I wanted Chris to know what I had been carrying around inside me for so many years.

But I also had another part of me, the part I wanted to forget and get on with my life. Hearing Chris talk about shaping our futures and staying focused was like being given permission to cram every awful thing that had ever happened inside a metal box and then bury it six feet under. And I knew he'd let me do that, too, from the first time we ever slept together.

That night I took off my clothes in the dark, I braced myself for the awful moment when his fingers would first feel them: the raised lines all over my back, like embedded pieces of a kid's railroad track; the hazelnut-like bumps on my head, my arms, my legs. I tensed, waiting for Chris's "What happened here?" or "How'd you get that?" But there was nothing. In the dark he was like a blind man and I was like a woman written in Braille, but my future husband's fingers moved over me gently. Gentle, or else reading my skin in a language he didn't recognize.

In all the years we'd been married, Chris had never once asked me to explain, to translate the marks on my skin, to cast off the sheet in the mornings. All those years, the clues were right there under his nose if he'd wanted to unravel them, but he was looking the other way, trying to look forward and not back. And I let him. Lord forgive, but I did. All that silence, all that talk about the future, was like the key to my freedom, to my new life. What it meant was that the whole text of my past, the one etched into my skin, could be erased as quickly as flicking off a light switch, as easily as putting on a dress.

I really could forget everything awful and get on with my life.

There was only one time when I wasn't sure I'd be able to do that. A few years after Chris and I got married, on one of the rare occasions I went to visit Mama, I asked again about Andre. Did Mama know anything more about him? Had she heard anything else? Was it possible to maybe call him?

"I tried calling him again not long ago," Mama told me. "But Andre's set in his mind. The social worker said there isn't anything we can do about it." And then she let out a long sigh, as if it were a difficult thing to accept. "Maybe it's just better if we pretend he's dead."

When I heard that, it was as if someone dropped an ice cube down my back. It was the only time in my marriage that

I ever came close to telling Chris the whole truth, when I really didn't think I could keep the secret inside me anymore.

Not long afterward, Chris and I were lying together one night, all our kids were finally asleep and my face was against his chest. I was listening to the steadiness of his heartbeat, the rhythm of his breathing, and being next to him with everything quiet made me feel safe. I was going to tell him. I *had* to tell him. Maybe he would know what to do.

"Chris?"

"Mmm." His hands were folded under his head and he was staring at a candle's dancing shadow on our bedroom ceiling.

I thought about how to say it. There was never going to be a good way, an easy way. "I never told you this before," I said to him. "About my little sister. But it's been weighing on me, what happened. I've wanted to tell you for a long time—"

Just then, one of our kids started crying in the next bedroom. Chris sighed and said quickly, "Can this wait?"

It was almost as if he sensed something bad was coming, as if he had to stop me from saying it out loud before it became real, before neither one of us could take it back.

"Can you go see what he wants?" Chris said. "Because I have to be up early. I can't deal with this now." He flipped over on his side and buried his face in the pillow.

But Chris also did other things that helped convince me that I could leave my old life behind. He helped me as he improved himself. Chris's favorite place in the world was the New York Public Library. I swear that he would have lived there if they had let him. He read books the way other people eat French fries, and every day he tried to use new words he'd learned. The landlord, by not fixing our plumbing problem,

was creating a *conundrum*. If we had to pay for the repairs ourselves, we'd have to seek *redress* or *restitution*. Sometimes, I'd
hear him practicing one word over and over until he got rid of
the Jamaican sound to it. Pretty soon, Chris's college classes
got even more difficult and time consuming and he spent even
more time in the library, even more time reading books.

Meanwhile, I kept working as a nurse's aide and raising
our kids. Chris and I had never discussed what size family we
wanted and neither of us had taken steps to do anything about
it, so every two years another child came. Even though I was
usually frazzled and so exhausted that it felt like I was sleep-
walking, I wouldn't have given it up for anything. All my life I
had dreamed of having a big loving family and finally I had
one. Sometimes it felt like I'd created a whole new world.

But other changes were going on, too. I didn't realize it at
first, but it wasn't long before I started to imitate Chris's
educated way of speaking. By the time Chris was about to
graduate from college and start teaching English at a junior
high school—he had given up on the lawyer idea years
before—we'd had four children together and I had managed,
just like Chris, to make myself into a better, more self-
educated person; someone I hoped he was proud of.

For ten years, I let myself believe that none of what
happened before Chris entered my life mattered anymore,
that the past really was dead and gone.

And then, out of the blue, Andre arrived at my door.

chapter 4

Ensuring the Silence

I never planned to see Mama again. It had been ten years since I last saw her at the restaurant with the social worker. I'd moved on with my life. I was twenty-three years old and a married man now. The last thing I wanted was to begin thinking and reliving what my life used to be.

There was only one thing in the world that ever would've made me go to see Mama again and that was my three-year-old daughter. If it hadn't been for Andrea, I never would've gone to that Rockaway apartment again, the one I ran away from when I was ten, the one that to me was always like a jail cell. But Andrea kept asking me if she had a grandma like all the other kids at preschool and then when I said she did, she asked why couldn't she go to see her grandma?

I only did it for my little girl, I only *would* have done it for her. No matter how I felt about Mama, I decided it wasn't fair to make my daughter suffer, too.

Andrea was so excited when we stood outside Mama's apartment that day. She was moving from foot to foot and I squeezed her hand when I answered Mama through the door.

"It's me," I answered, staring straight ahead into the fish-eye lens. "It's...Boy."

What else in my entire life, after all, had Mama ever called me? But either Mama didn't recognize me straight off or else she wasn't going to let me in. It seemed like forever that my little girl and I stood there, neither of us saying a word, until finally Mama ordered me from the other side of the door to smile. I pulled up the corners of my mouth like it was for my driver's license picture.

"Yeah," Mama said slowly, "only your father had that smile. You and Sabrina both have that smile."

She unbolted two locks, slipped the chain and opened the door. Even though it was late afternoon, she was still in a dirty pink bathrobe, her gray hair flying out all over like she hadn't brushed it for days. She was barefoot and I noticed that her yellow nails were so long they curled under her toes.

The apartment was even darker than I remembered it. All the same furniture was there—the plaid sofa Sonny bought Mama fifteen years earlier, the wood and glass coffee table, the green velour recliner—but everything was so worn and dirty that it was like seeing it through Vaseline. It seemed like it had shrunk, too. For a second I felt like I was inside a kid's playhouse.

But what surprised me most was the piles of junk every-where. The whole living room was crammed with stacks of yellow newspapers, unopened mail and stinking garbage bags.

Twenty years earlier, Mama was such a neat freak she wouldn't have stood for one speck of dirt or mess anywhere, and would've whipped me or Sabrina if every toy wasn't in its proper place or if every jar on her kitchen counter wasn't in a perfect row after she scrubbed it with Clorox. But now here she was, living like one of those filthy pack rats you saw pushing their junk around in rickety carts near Times Square.

Mama kept saying that I sure had changed, had grown into a man. "If you had been on the street, Boy, well, I wouldn't have even known you," she told me. "I would have walked right past you and that's the truth."

When I asked, she told me she hadn't seen Sabrina in, oh, maybe a couple of years, same thing with Greg. "Don't know where either of them is anymore," she said. All she knew was that Sabrina was married and had a whole bunch of kids, but none of the kids had ever visited her. She'd never met any of them. Only the good Lord knew where Greg and Sabrina were anymore. Yeah, it was just her now and she'd been kind of sickly, with diabetes, asthma, high blood pressure and all her heart problems.

Keeping the conversation going was hard work. I tried a few times to talk about my little girl, about what Andrea had been learning in preschool, but Mama wouldn't even look at her, wouldn't even say one word to her. That didn't make any sense, Mama acting like her granddaughter wasn't even there.

Maybe, I thought, that was why Andrea hung onto my arm the entire time we were there, scared out of her mind.

I'd never seen my daughter like that. Usually she's always curious, always liking to meet new people and go to new places, but that day at Mama's she wouldn't even go to the bathroom by herself.

"Go on, it's right down there," I told her, pointing. But she just shook her head. Finally I had to walk down the narrow hallway with her, past the bedroom Sabrina and I used to share after Greg moved out and then past Mama's bedroom. The whole time, Andrea was clinging to my leg, trembling.

"She's not usually like this," I said to Mama after we came back into the living room. "I guess something must've spooked her." Mama just nodded and looked away.

Not long after that, I told Mama we probably should get going, that my wife would be waiting on us with dinner. Mama walked us to the door. It was only then that she let on she knew that Andrea was even there.

"Boy," Mama said, "if you ever want to come back here, that's fine with me. But if you do, don't bring that child." For the first time she looked at Andrea. "I don't want that child coming back here ever again, you hear?"

I stared at Mama, too shocked to say one word back to her. I held Andrea's hand as we walked down the hallway past Mama's neighbors and onto the sidewalk outside Mama's brownstone. Andrea's lips were trembling. I got down on one knee and cupped her face in my hands.

"Grandma's sickly, Andrea. And being sickly makes Grandma say things she doesn't mean. She wasn't angry at you. Grandma's just really angry about being sick, just like the way you were the time you got sick and couldn't go to that birthday party. Remember that?" She rubbed her eyes with her fists, leaned into my shoulder and then let out a long wail before she started sobbing.

The truth was, I had no idea why Mama said what she did. Andrea hadn't done one thing wrong in there, hadn't messed with anything. When Sabrina and I were little, Mama never let any other kids come around because she said they'd mess up her clean house, so all I could figure was that maybe Mama had taken one look at Andrea and went back in her mind, automatically, like old people sometimes do. Maybe, I thought, all her medicines were messing with her brain.

But whatever the reason, one thing I knew for sure. My daughter wasn't ever going back there again. And without Andrea, I wasn't going back there again either.

Still, visiting Mama had gotten me thinking. If Mama couldn't be part of my little girl's family, who else could? The only person I could think of was Aunt Dorothy. Even though I hadn't seen her since that time I stayed with her while Mama and Sonny were in Atlantic City, I tracked her down a few days after I saw Mama. This time, though, I decided to go there without my little girl.

Aunt Dorothy acted really glad to see me. She said a lot of things like Mama did, about how much I changed and how grown up I looked. And then she leaned back on her old tattered sofa and took a sip of iced tea.

"So where's your sister?" she asked.

"Don't really know," I answered her. "Sabrina and I kind of lost touch. Mama said she doesn't know where she is either."

Aunt Dorothy leaned forward, smiling. "Oh, you must have heard your Mama wrong," she said. "I can tell you right now where Sabrina is." She set her glass down on the table. "But I'm not talking about Sabrina. I'm talking about Latanisha. Your twin sister. Where is Latanisha?"

At that moment it was like all the clocks in the world stopped ticking, like a blindfold was taken off. Until that moment, I really believed I'd invented my twin sister, that I'd imagined her. But I *hadn't* been crazy! All my life I'd had blurry pictures of her darting through my head like little fish and I'd even heard her voice talking to me. But right then I thought, maybe the same thing happened to her.

Latanisha. She had a name.

Maybe Latanisha never was told about me. Maybe she never was told my name. But then, maybe she found out about me as well and maybe she was telling *herself* that *she* hadn't been crazy either.

Aunt Dorothy wrote down Sabrina's address. My hands were shaking so badly I had a hard time slipping that piece of paper into my pocket.

* * *

I decided to walk from the subway station instead of bothering with a bus. I was too hyped up to wait for one—I could almost hear Mrs. Lewis calling me "antsy"—and besides, I figured walking would do me good. Give me time to think. On the train from Brooklyn, I'd looked at a map of the Bronx and found Sabrina's street, so I knew how to get there. It was early evening, the summer sky was a dull silvery blue and it was still wicked hot outside.

Sabrina was going to be plenty surprised to see me - that was for sure. She probably thought I'd dropped off the planet. But hopefully she was going to be glad, too. And really, I thought, there was no reason she shouldn't be. After all, there'd never been anything bad between the two of us, had there?

It wasn't like with Mama or Greg. Sabrina and I had always gotten along fine. Even though she was five years older than me, it had always been her and me against Mama and Greg, both of us watching out for the other the best we could. At least, that's how it was until I was ten years old and couldn't take it anymore.

That, I thought, was probably the worst thing Sabrina could accuse me of—that I'd hidden out in my foster home and left her, when she was fifteen, to take everything Mama and Greg dished out all by herself. She'd be right if she said it, but if she did, I was going to tell her the truth, plain and simple. I'd only done it to stay alive.

But if it really came down to it, I also was ready to talk to Sabrina about her role in all our years apart, too. After all, it wasn't like she'd turned New York upside down to find me. For those eight years I lived with Mrs. Lewis until I "aged out" of foster care, Sabrina didn't contact me once. Same thing after I got married when I was eighteen. For almost thirteen years, Sabrina and I were living just a few miles away from each other, but she never picked up the phone one time.

I slowed my pace, sweat trickling down my back. All that was a long time ago. I couldn't let my mind wander to places that didn't matter anymore. And I had to remember that too, especially when I saw Sabrina again. We were grown up now, with kids of our own. But most of all, we were still family. That had to mean something to Sabrina, no matter what her life was like now and no matter what she thought about me for leaving and never coming back home again.

Still, as I walked past one run-down building after another, past corner groceries and liquor stores with groups of guys gathered in knots on the sidewalk, I worried about the other possibility, the one I'd been playing over and over in my head all week. I kept trying to picture Sabrina's reaction if she guessed the real reason I was coming to see her after so long, if she realized I was hunting for information more than anything else.

Asking her my question was going to be hard enough. But I also knew I was going to have to pick the right moment. I couldn't just blurt it out, much as I knew I'd want to. No, I had to lead up to it gradually, put it to Sabrina in a way that made sense. I'd tell her first about how I went to see Mama. That was, after all, where it all started. But maybe I wouldn't tell Sabrina about how Mama treated my daughter, the pain it caused. Sabrina and I both knew how Mama used to be and maybe it would just stir up a lot of things we'd both rather forget. But I knew there was no way I could leave out telling Sabrina about seeing Aunt Dorothy, about how my whole life got turned upside down. How I'd finally learned the secret.

Every time I thought about it, part of me wanted to go out and buy a bottle of champagne, but another part wanted to punch my fist through a brick wall.

A few blocks away from Sabrina's apartment, I knew I couldn't show up there looking angry. No matter what, I couldn't let Sabrina think that any of what I was feeling right then was aimed at her, especially since it really wasn't. Except for Mama—*she* obviously kept the truth from me my whole life—the person I was maddest at was myself. Because deep down, a part of me had always known. *Known.* And as hard as I'd been trying to block that out ever since Aunt Dorothy revealed the truth, I couldn't.

After I was put into foster care with Mrs. Lewis, I tried to get someone to believe me. But obviously I didn't try hard enough. As I got closer to Sabrina's apartment building, that was what nagged at me. I kept thinking that I could've kept pushing for the truth, could've kept saying over and over what I remembered. But finally I got worn down. After enough years went by and nothing changed and no one believed me, I let myself think what all of them probably wanted me to think all along.

That I'd been crazy. That I made her up.

I came to another curb, slowed for a turning car and then crossed another street. I'd already been walking for more than twenty minutes and I was sweating heavily under my t-shirt. Outside a grocery store, a group of teenagers were smoking and sipping cold drinks. The way they stood there, with their cigarettes held out in front of their faces like a challenge, reminded me of guys on practically every corner in my old neighborhood. I nodded as I went by, careful not to look too long into their eyes, to give them any reason to mess with me.

Across the street was a small fenced-in park with a sandbox and swings. It was empty now in the fading daylight. Sabrina's neighborhood, I thought, didn't look so bad.

About halfway down the block I saw what I knew had to be my sister's building. It was more than twenty stories high. Inside the lobby, my finger shook as I ran down the list of occupants. But my heart didn't start pounding until I stepped off the elevator and started walking down the hallway.

"Are you sure you want to do this?" my wife, Bronsetta, had asked me that morning. I was sure then, but I wasn't so sure now. I stopped at Sabrina's door and stared at the bronze number.

Breathe, I commanded myself. I inhaled and exhaled as deep as I could. *Look relaxed.* But then Aunt Dorothy's words came flooding back, the words that had been echoing inside me all week.

I stared at Sabrina's door. *Your twin sister.* Somewhere out there, I had a twin. No matter what it took, no matter what I had to do, I was going to find her. I clenched my fist and raised it into the air. And then, after one more deep breath, I knocked three times on Sabrina's door.

chapter 5

The Ripple Effect

When I opened the front door to see Andre at my apartment, I felt like I was seeing a ghost. A ghost of a child I had once known, who, in one second, had been transformed into a man. A handsome, kind-looking man, too. Gone were the long curls he'd always had as a kid and gone was the baby fat from his cheeks, but his eyes were exactly as I'd always remembered them. My hand flew up to my mouth so fast I actually hurt my lip. I threw my arms around him, led him into the living room and I must have told him at least twenty times I couldn't believe it was really him.

Andre was grinning as I pulled him onto the sofa and introduced him to all my kids. When I came to my oldest, Madeline, Andre's head gave a little jerk.

"My husband Chris is at school, but he definitely should be back any time now," I told him. "I can't wait for you to meet him."

Four of the kids quickly gathered around Andre like ants on a sugar cube—on either side of him, at his feet, climbing onto his lap. Only Madeline stood in a corner, staring at him and smiling shyly. I could tell that Madeline was thinking that Andre wasn't like the other brother I'd told her about. Still, I was glad she didn't mention Greg at that point—the other kids were too young to understand that their other uncle was a very bad man.

After a few minutes, Madeline herded her little brothers toward a back bedroom and said, "Come on, we can go play anything you'd like. Mama and your uncle want to sit and talk." She made it sound as if they were going to have a big treat.

After they left, Andre and I both sat and stared at each other. Neither of us said anything right off. I couldn't find the right words and I guessed that Andre felt the same way. Where do you start after so many years? What blanks do you fill in first? I wanted to know everything that happened to him and I also wanted him to know everything that had happened to me.

Minutes passed silently, then we started with the simple things. Yes, I answered, the kids were all mine and yes, it sure was hard work with so many. And him? Andre said he had five—well, actually, he added, four of them were his wife Bronsetta's—but they might as well all be his own, he said, because that's how he felt about them. He pulled out his wallet and showed me a picture of his wife, surrounded by her kids from before she and Andre met. She was pretty, with long straight dark hair and a wide smile with big white teeth. Andre volunteered that she was six years older than he was.

"Mrs. Lewis, my foster mother, thought I was making a huge mistake taking on a ready-made family, especially because I was so young," he said. "She told me I had my whole future in front of me and why would I want to go saddle myself with such a burden?" He looked at Bronsetta's picture again. "Usually Mrs. Lewis was right about everything. She's always had a way of reading me, as if she could see things inside me long before I could. But that time, Mrs. Lewis was wrong. When you love someone, you can't just pick and choose what you want. You have to take the whole package, you know?"

I nodded. I had been that package once, too.

Then Andre handed me another picture of Andrea, the three-year-old daughter he and Bronsetta had together. I looked at the picture and instantly it was as if someone had electrified me. I felt a jolt, the shock of some kind of recognition—the child's light skin and freckles, her straight brown hair—but I didn't understand where the vision came from.

I didn't know it was the past and that the past was coming for me.

"She's beautiful," I said, handing the picture back.

He looked at it again before slipping it into his wallet, almost as if he'd never seen it before. "Yes, she is, isn't she? Sometimes I can't believe I am so blessed."

That was the moment I think that our real dialogue began—and not just the conversation I later learned that Andre had intended to have with me all along. Andre and I didn't know it, but that moment was the start of our journey together, of an ordeal neither of us could have imagined. And maybe, that was the real blessing: that neither of us could have foreseen the events that were going to follow or the price of the past on both our lives. If we had, I truly don't believe either of us would have willingly gone through the hell we did—or ended up being so graced later on.

"I went to see Mama," Andre said.

I was surprised to hear it, especially when he said he'd taken his little girl and hadn't even phoned Mama first. "I guess I was afraid she'd hang up on me," Andre explained. "How about you? When did you see her last?"

I shrugged. "The last time was probably about two years ago," I replied softly.

I remembered how I had gone to her Rockaway apartment and at some point Mama and I had walked into her bedroom. Without thinking, I sat down on her bed and instantly I felt the lumps. I hadn't wanted to think about it then, hadn't wanted to think about it afterwards either, but the memory of all those stuffed grocery bags, of all those times I'd carried Latanisha's name around with me to copy stores haunted me anyway. Under Mama's mattress was her filing system, the way she'd managed to keep Latanisha alive, at least on paper, all those years.

"I'd seen her off and on before that, but never regularly," I went on. "But I never once took the kids. Chris was reading the Bible a lot and he kept telling me I should honor my mother and father, stuff like that, so I only went to make him happy."

We both smiled and let the silence settle. It wasn't at all uncomfortable, at least not from my end.

"I couldn't believe how Mama was living," Andre said. "Stuff everywhere."

"Mama sure is a keeper. Been that way for years now. She doesn't throw anything away."

Suddenly, I glimpsed my current life as nothing but a façade, as nothing but something I had invented. It made me think back to the little photo studio where I once took the kids and they all put on orange life jackets and held paddles and sat in front of a fake background of a mountain lake with canoes. The photographer was snapping away, telling us all to smile and asking things like, "You all having a good time now?" All of us did what the man asked, pretending we really were away for the summer at a lake, that it was cool and quiet and beautiful and there wasn't a bus or traffic light for a hundred miles. And then we all stepped back outside the studio, onto the city sidewalk, as if we'd just walked out of a dream.

"A few days after I saw Mama, I went to see Aunt Dorothy," Andre went on. "I'm not sure why, except I didn't know where you were and I needed to find out if I still had any family left. But anyway, that's how I found you."

"Then I'm glad you went there," I said. I truly meant it.

"Have you ever seen Greg?"

I shook my head. "He's in prison for robbery, been there for years. But even if he wasn't, I wouldn't have a reason to see him. Not after everything that went down between us."

Andre nodded. Not wanting to see Greg again didn't need explaining. Andre clasped his hands together in his lap, lowered his head and then looked up at me.

"Sabrina, there's something else." He took a deep breath and then began blurting out, "Aunt Dorothy said something that shocked me. I really need to talk to you about it."

It was then that I felt a sudden sickness rising up inside me, a lurching of dread. Maybe it was because when you're used to things coming at you out of nowhere—things like plates crashing down on your head because you didn't move fast enough—you get a feeling for things you can't see. Someone once told me that blind people can tell when they're walking up to a wall because they can feel the darkness on their faces. Shadow vision, it was called. That's how it was with Andre, too. I could tell that I was coming up against whatever Andre was planning to say.

"People say all kinds of things," Andre said. "And at first, when I left her house a few days ago, I didn't know whether to believe her or not. But after I left Aunt Dorothy's, I remembered something else that happened a long time ago, when I was around seven or eight. It was a couple of years before I went to live with Mrs. Lewis."

He began telling me about the weekend he went to stay with Aunt Dorothy while Mama and Sonny were in Atlantic City. The whole time he was talking I kept nodding, bracing myself. It was the same way I braced myself all those years earlier against Chris's fingers, against whatever he might discover on my skin, against whatever he might ask me. And just as with Chris, I waited, hoping everything would pass and go away.

But this time, somehow I knew it wouldn't.

"Aunt Dorothy is aware of things you don't know about," I said, interrupting him. "She knows of and was part of problems you never knew. Bad memories she played a part in. You remember when my baby Madeline was born? When you were ten? When Mama and Greg beat me so badly they had to deliver my baby themselves on our living room rug?"

Andre's eyes moved back and forth and then focused on one spot in front of him. I knew he was remembering, that he was seeing it all play out again.

"You never knew what happened later at the hospital," I said. "A doctor took one look at all my scars and asked me right off where they came from. He asked it like he was with the police, so I told him everything. And right after that, a social worker showed up. She came to my bed and calmly, almost casually said, *Your home environment clearly isn't suitable for a child.*

"So they just took my baby Madeline away from me," I went on. "They wouldn't even tell me where they took her, either." The memory still made me so angry that I felt like crying. "They sent me home. The 'home environment' wasn't safe for my baby, but the social worker thought it was safe enough for me. Go figure that, Andre. Even after everything that doctor saw on me."

"Before today, I never knew what you named your baby," Andre said.

Suddenly I understood why his head had jerked when I'd told him Madeline's name. Obviously it was because I named my daughter after our mother.

"Well, there's a reason you didn't know that," I said. "You remember how I came back from the hospital, but I didn't have my baby with me?" Andre nodded slowly. "Well, I didn't know for a long time that they put my baby girl with Aunt Dorothy. She was Madeline's foster mother. A few months after she was born, I was put in a group home—I don't even remember if you saw that last beating I got or not—and then you were put into a foster home, too. That was the last time you and I saw each other. You remember that?"

Andre looked as if he wanted to interrupt, to stop me from going on. But I had to get it all out. I couldn't stop, not now.

"When I got out of that group home, I was eighteen. And straight off, Andre, I went looking for my baby girl. I'd met Chris by then, and he was willing to help me, to take us both in if I could get my daughter back. That's when I found out that Aunt Dorothy had Madeline. But Aunt Dorothy didn't want to give her back. "You had your chance, girl," she said to me. Like she really thought I was just going to go away without my daughter, just walk away. I finally had to fight her in court. She made up all kinds of lies about me being unfit, but I guess even the judge didn't believe her."

I stopped and stared at him. "What I'm saying is, you can't trust everything Aunt Dorothy says, Andre."

What I told my brother was the truth—if you looked at it one way. Aunt Dorothy did try to keep Madeline and she also tried to make me look unfit in front of the judge. But Andre also seemed to sense what I was trying to do: to throw him off the track, to make Aunt Dorothy look bad so that he would just forget anything she might have said to him.

But Andre clearly wasn't buying that version.

He looked at me and then picked up his own story as if he hadn't heard a word I'd said about our aunt. He was telling me about his latest visit to Aunt Dorothy the way he might have told a bedtime story to one of his kids, soft and even.

I knew the past was coming and there was nothing I could do to stop it now.

I got up off the sofa. I couldn't just sit there, couldn't just do nothing. I walked into the kitchen and started scrubbing a counter that didn't need scrubbing, listening to Madeline's voice as she said something to the other kids in the back bedroom. Andre came and stood next to me.

"Sabrina," he said softly. He stood there a long moment without moving. And then he said what I'd been dreading. "Do you know where my twin sister is? Aunt Dorothy said the only thing she knew was that Latanisha went to live somewhere down south when she was really little. Do you know how I can find her? Where might she have gone to?"

I couldn't look at him. I rinsed the sponge, started scrubbing the spotless sink. There was a roar in my ears, as if my whole life was like a waterfall flooding down on me. *Oh God*, I was thinking, *oh God, oh God, help me.*

I could have told him the truth right there, the truth he had a right to know. But I could not say the words. I could not tell my brother that there was no use looking for Latanisha, that she was dead, that she was murdered twenty years before.

"Just leave it alone, Andre." It came out as a whisper, as a plea. "Some things are just better off unsaid."

He stepped closer to me and shook his head.

"I can't do that Sabrina, not anymore and I don't think you should either. I need your help, Sabrina. There's no one else. I'm willing to beg you if that's what it takes. All I need is anything you remember, anything about where she might be. I'll do all the rest, all the hunting for her. I won't bother you about any of it. I just need a starting place."

I heard the kids' voices in the back bedroom. Madeline had her hands full and wasn't going to last much longer. In another few minutes, they'd all come out wanting dinner.

"I can't help you, Andre."

"You can't?" He put his hand on my arm to stop me from scrubbing. "You can't, Sabrina? Or you won't? Which one is it?"

I bit my lip. I didn't dare say another word, didn't dare look at him. I was certain I'd burst into tears or collapse if I did.

"Sabrina," Andre said, louder now. "You think I don't have a right to know where my own twin sister is? A twin I didn't even know I had for sure until just a few days ago? I come here looking for help and you are shaking your head and shutting your mouth and I don't know why. And you don't give me any reason why. And then you think that's going to be okay with me? You think I'm just going to say, *fine, Sabrina doesn't want to say anything, Sabrina doesn't want to tell me whatever she knows?* You think that's going to be just fine with me?"

I bit my lip so hard I tasted blood. I don't know how long he stood there, but finally I silently followed him as he walked to the hall and then he turned to face me.

"You know what? It isn't fine, Sabrina. And this isn't over." His voice was low but strong. "Maybe you think it's over, but I'm not done yet. I'm not finished." He walked to the front door, opened it and then quietly closed the door behind him.

Slowly I went back to the living room. When Madeline and the younger kids came back there, I was huddled on the sofa, shaking. "Everything is fine," I kept saying. "Fine. I'm just a little hungry," and, "I'll fix dinner in a few minutes or so. Daddy will be home soon, but I just want to sit here for a few seconds if that's okay. Andre had to go, but he asked me to say goodbye for him."

As I sat there, thoughts crowded my mind. Andre was wrong about me thinking it was over. Inside my bones, inside every inch of my soul, just the opposite was happening.

Everything, I knew, was just beginning.

During the next few weeks, for the first time ever, I was glad the kids were out of school for the summer with nothing to do, glad they couldn't stand it in the sweltering apartment, glad they needed constant distracting. Finding ways to amuse them kept me from worrying about Andre, from wondering what he was going to do. Whenever Andre did enter my thoughts, I shoved him right back out again. *He couldn't possibly remember Latanisha. The first ten years of his life were spent making sure of that,* I told myself over and over.

Besides, I knew that Andre could look all he wanted, search the entire south, but he'd never find a single clue as long as I kept my mouth shut. That was what got me through each day: the certainty that the past would stay buried as long as I kept silent, that I was the only one who could make the dead come back again.

But nights were different. No matter how exhausted I was when I crawled into bed, every night was the same. My mind simply would not shut off. As time passed, in fact, everything just got worse. It was as if Andre had set off some kind of slow-moving avalanche inside me, one that made every memory, every image that I had kept frozen in time, start rolling down on top of me. And the worst part was, I couldn't talk to anyone about it.

Whatever chance I'd had to tell Chris was long gone. Maybe if I had told him right after Andre came to our apartment, if I had sat Chris down and told him he had to listen to me, that he had to let me tell him about my sister, it might have been different. Maybe that had been my one window of opportunity to let go of the secret.

But that window, I knew, had closed. If I said anything to Chris now, something inside me whispered that our marriage would never survive it. What I'd kept from him wasn't like a dress you buy secretly and hang in your closet and don't want your husband to find out about. It wasn't even like some old boyfriend you never told your husband about who shows up one day and starts throwing shadows where they never were before. What I kept from Chris all those years was something entirely different. And if I couldn't forgive myself for doing that, how could he?

Chris obviously sensed that something was troubling me. But he also must have been figuring that if it was something really bad, something he needed to know about, I'd tell him eventually. Besides, that had been our pattern, the one we'd had for almost ten years and I was the only one who could have broken it. Still, even if he had prodded me more—if he'd urged me to confide in him about whatever was going on inside me—I can't honestly say I would have done it, that I would have trusted him. To this day I'm not sure why, except that lots of people say they want the truth, but when you give it to them, it turns out they didn't really mean it. Some people only want to hear their own acceptable versions of the truth.

And so the only choice I saw was to keep everything bottled up inside me and hope it all went away. But I really no longer thought it would. I could feel the truth boiling up, ready to explode. I was expecting to go through everything alone, just like I always had. What I wasn't expecting was to hear a knock on our apartment door a few weeks later and to see Andre, once again, looking straight into the peephole.

This time his jaw was clenched.

chapter 6

Shock of a Lifetime

Ever since I'd left Sabrina's apartment a few weeks earlier, I'd been trying to figure out what to do, where to go next. I couldn't force my sister to tell me whatever she knew or remembered, but one thing I was sure of. Sabrina was holding out on me. One look at her face the night she kept scrubbing that sink, chewing on her lip the same way she did when we were kids and I knew it as certain as my own name.

But, what I couldn't figure out was why. All those years with Mama and Greg, Sabrina had gotten beaten so much worse than I had. So much longer, too. So why wouldn't she tell me whatever she knew now, when all of that was over and in the past?

Mama, I knew, must've had all kinds of pressures on her, trying to take care of four kids all by herself. Still, the one thing

I kept coming back to was that nothing in the world could ever explain what she did to me and Sabrina. Bronsetta and I had hard times too, for a few years right after we got married. But I never once took out any of my stresses out on our kids. Neither did Bronsetta. If my wife even laid a hand on one of our kids, that would've been it, too. Stress or no stress, it wouldn't have made any difference to me. Your kids are like part of your heart you didn't know you had. They're God's gift to you. Something very wrong, something very sick, would have to make my mother treat us the way she did.

I'd been thinking about that for a long time. Even before I took my daughter to see Mama and even before I went to see Aunt Dorothy, there still were times I couldn't help wondering why Mama hated me and Sabrina so much. Some mornings I stepped out of the shower and got a glimpse of myself in the mirror and I just broke down and cried. That's how badly I'm scarred. Looking at my body is like staring at a photo album full of memories you never want to remember.

But at least, I thought, my twin sister didn't have to go through what Sabrina and I did. Wherever Latanisha was sent to, it couldn't have been as bad as staying with Mama and Greg. *At least my twin got out in time.* And maybe, I thought, Latanisha even got blessed with someone like Mrs. Lewis. Maybe she grew up in a house full of love and gentleness and kindness and maybe she didn't have a single scar on her.

But that's where I got confused. If Latanisha went some-where good, why wouldn't Sabrina tell me? And even if Latanisha ended up in some kind of group foster home, why wouldn't Sabrina tell me *that* so I could find Latanisha? When Sabrina and I were kids, it made perfect sense for Sabrina to clam up. She didn't want to get beaten any more than I did. But now we were grown up and things were different. Mama was just a sick old lady, couldn't hurt us if she tried, and Greg was hundreds of miles away near the Canada border in jail. So how come Sabrina *still* looked like someone had a shotgun aimed at her head when I asked about my twin?

That was the question that kept gnawing at me. Why was Sabrina *still* so scared? And if Sabrina wouldn't tell me what I needed to know, who would?

Aunt Dorothy was the only one of Mama's thirteen sisters and brothers I'd ever met. Mama's family had all grown up in South Carolina, so maybe, I thought, Latanisha went to live with one of them. If I got their names and where they lived, maybe I could start looking there. Sabrina told me that Aunt Dorothy used to be her daughter's foster mother, but then Aunt Dorothy didn't want to give her daughter back. Maybe the same thing happened with Latanisha. Maybe my twin went to live with one of Mama's siblings and they didn't want to give her back?

And then I saw the problem with that kind of thinking. Aunt Dorothy knew where her brothers and sisters lived and she also would've known if Latanisha went to stay with one of them. It wouldn't make any sense that she'd be talking to her family, but then she'd still be in the dark about something like that. Not, of course, unless they all hid my twin from *her*, same as they all did from me.

Then I thought about Greg. *"Maybe one day y'all will meet Gregory's kin."* Mama's words from a long time before came back to me. She'd never made any secret of the fact that Greg had a different father than Sabrina and I. So maybe Latanisha went to live with one of Gregory's kin? Greg was fourteen years old when Latanisha and I were born, so he'd have to remember something.

But the problem was that Greg wouldn't have a reason in the world to help me. And even if I was willing to ask him, I'd have to travel to the prison he was in near Canada and that would mean taking days off my job with no pay and maybe even getting fired. I was just a security guard. My job wasn't much, but it sure was a whole lot better than before. Could I really risk losing it just so I could talk to a brother who probably would've killed me, a brother who probably wouldn't even spit on me now if I was on fire?

Greg, I decided, would have to be my last resort. I'd only go to see him if there wasn't any other way, if no one else could help me.

I thought about maybe going back to see Mama again. Maybe I could go there alone, sit down and talk with her. Mama was the one person in the world who had to know the truth about Latanisha, so maybe if I put it to her in the right way, if I asked in the right kind of voice, she'd tell me.

But then my mind got all tangled up again. If Mama hadn't told me all these years, why would she tell me now? Something must've made her want to hide Latanisha from me.

"Only your father had that smile." That's what she had said when my little girl and I showed up at her door. *"You and Sabrina have that smile."*

My father. I'd never met him, never even heard Mama talk about him except on that one day. But if I had his smile, maybe Latanisha did, too. And if I could find *him*, maybe my father would know where my twin had gone to. Maybe my father even had something to do with where she went. Maybe I could try finding him, asking him, maybe he would tell me.

Pretty soon, each time I tried to figure out how to get the answers I yearned for, my head would start spinning so fast I couldn't think straight. Mama, Aunt Dorothy, Greg, my father, my aunts and uncles—everyone was jumbled inside my head like they'd all been put in a bowl and whipped around with an egg beater.

I kept trying to figure things out over and over again. I always ended up just as confused as the day before.

After weeks of feeling like a dog chasing its own tail round and round in circles, I realized there was only one place I could go for answers.

I didn't want to go see Sabrina again, but I finally realized I had no other choice.

* * *

This time Sabrina had a scared rabbit look on her face when she opened the door. The first thing she did was tell her daughter to take the other kids outside into the play area and to stay where she could see them all from her balcony. She didn't ask me why I came back, didn't have to. Clearing the apartment the way she did and then walking over to the sliding door and sitting down on a plastic chair on the balcony, she had to know I wasn't going to go away until she told me what I'd come for.

Her hands were clasped in her lap, like she was either praying or else trying to stop them from shaking. Maybe it was something of both.

There was no point telling Sabrina everything I'd been through those past two weeks since I last talked with her, how every idea for finding my twin sister was like coming up against one brick wall after another. So I just launched into saying what I had practiced.

"I know you have information about Latanisha," I said. "And I know you don't want to tell it to me. I haven't been able to figure out, Sabrina, what you're so scared of. But whatever it is, I have the right to know. I have the right to know where my twin sister went. And you have the obligation to tell me."

Sabrina covered her face with her hands, hunched over, and then she burst out sobbing.

"Sabrina," I put one hand on her shoulder. "It's me. Your brother. Remember all the hell you and I went through together? Remember how we always watched out for each other, took care of each other the best we could? I wanted to keep on doing that. And I would've, too. But when Mama said you didn't want to see me anymore after I went to live with Mrs. Lewis, when she told me that you washed you hands of me, I felt there was nothing more I could do. But I'm here now. And whatever it is, you can trust me. You *can*."

Sabrina suddenly stopped crying and looked up.

"Mama told you *I* washed my hands of you?" I nodded. "But she told me *you* didn't want to see *me*. She said *you* washed your hands of *me*." I shook my head. Her eyes suddenly got wide, like she'd just figured something out. "Oh God," she blurted out. "Oh *God*."

I waited. It was the hardest thing I ever did, because I wanted to turn her face towards me and make her tell me what I needed to know. But something inside told me to just sit there, that if I said even one word, I'd scare her off again. Then I'd never learn the truth.

She had a strange look on her face. It was almost like she was hearing some kind of music she recognized playing in the distance, like she was listening to sounds that no one else but she could hear. And then, all of a sudden, her face changed and her shoulders dropped. Finally, she turned and looked at me.

"You can't tell anyone what I'm going to tell you. Andre, you have to promise me that."

"I'm not going to tell anyone, I promise."

"No, that isn't enough." She was talking differently now, almost like the way she used to talk when we were kids. "Andre, I need you to sign a paper. A confidentiality paper that promises you're not going to tell a single soul on earth. Because if you did, Mama could come after me or worse my children, Greg could come too. Greg could get someone—"

"Sabrina, Greg's in prison. He can't do anything to you now—"

"Just listen to what I'm saying! You have to listen to me, Andre! If you told anyone—I mean *anyone*—Greg could get his friends to harm me or my family. It doesn't matter that he's in prison. He's always had people. And any one of them could come kill me or come kill my kids. And maybe even Mama could get someone to do that. So I need your word that no matter what, you won't say a word to anyone."

Suddenly, listening and looking at Sabrina's frightened face, I was scared too. "I promise," I said. "I give my word of honor as a man. I won't tell anyone."

Her hands were trembling as she wrote out the confidentiality paper. She signed it and dated it at the bottom and then she handed the pen to me. After I signed it, she laid the paper on a little plastic table.

And then she took a long deep breath and told me everything that happened twenty years ago. Everything Mama and Greg did to Latanisha right in front of her and me. "You never remembered any of it," she said. "You were too young, you hadn't even started talking yet. But that's why we always got beaten the way we did.

"Mama and Greg had to make sure I never told you, that you never found out. And Andre, I was afraid that if I *did* tell you, you might go crazy and do something stupid. I wanted so much to tell you, I thought about doing it so many times, but I was afraid we'd *both* end up in a trunk if I did. And Mama and Greg could *still* do that, Andre. They could *still* put us in a trunk if they wanted."

All the air went out of the room, like a lid closing down on top of me. I sat there for a very long time, saying nothing. I was trying to picture everything she'd just told me, trying to imagine Mama and Greg doing that to my sister, but I just couldn't. I don't think anyone's mind can get around something like that.

And that's when another thought hit me. Sabrina was probably making it all up.

"I don't believe you," I said.

"Andre, everything I said is true. Mama and Greg both—"

"You know what I think, Sabrina? I think you're lying, just like I've been lied to all my life. You tell me Latanisha's dead so I'll go away, so I'll stop asking questions. I think that's your strategy."

"Andre, that's not it. I swear. I've even got letters if you don't believe me. Letters proving what I'm telling you."

"Twenty years go by and you never say anything to me, never contact me once, never say one word to me about having a twin sister and then all of a sudden you can prove you're telling the truth? Sabrina, can you explain to me why this all sounds like a big pile of bull?"

She stared at me, then she got up and went back into her bedroom. The piece of paper she'd written out about keeping everything confidential was on the table. I picked it up, folded it and stuffed it into my jeans' pocket.

Sabrina came back onto the balcony holding a small stack of letters. She sat down next to me and opened one envelope.

"All of these are from our father," she said. "He wrote to Mama looking for me and he found me when I was nineteen. He was in the merchant marines and I met him one time when he was in New York."

She took out a picture of a man in uniform and handed it to me. He had light skin, freckles and light brown hair. I squinted at the picture. He didn't look a bit like Sabrina or me. But there was something familiar about him. Something that looked a bit like my daughter.

I didn't know where Sabrina was going with any of this, so I just sat there.

"After that, our father started writing to me. He was try-ing to find you and Latanisha. In this letter here, he told me he wrote to Mama but never got any answer back, so he wanted to know if I knew anything." She handed me a second enve-lope. "In this one, he asked me the same thing, if I knew how to find you or your twin sister."

I was trying to put together everything she was saying. It was like a bunch of jigsaw pieces, but every piece felt like a chunk of cement dropping down on me.

"So what you're saying is..."

I didn't want to believe that my father could've found me when I was fourteen years old. "So what you're saying is that Mama wouldn't tell my own father how to find me, because if she did then he would've asked me about my twin sister." Sabrina nodded. "And the reason you didn't write back to him," I said, "the reason you didn't tell him how to find me, was because you knew he'd ask about my twin and then..."

She burst out crying again.

I gripped my hands together and stared down at my feet. Each breath felt like a ton of bricks was pushing down on my chest. It was taking all my strength just to keep sitting there.

"And our father, Sabrina?" Each word was hard for me to say. "Where is our father now?"

It went silent for too long. I looked up at her again.

"He died," she said really softly. "About three years ago."

Part of me wanted to cry, part of me wanted to punch my fist through a wall. Right then my mind was so messed up I hardly knew where I was. All I knew was that I had to get out of there. I couldn't take it anymore. I stood up to leave.

"Andre." I stopped and turned around.

"What, Sabrina? Are you going to tell me someone else is dead too?" I was breathing hard. "Do you have someone else to tell me about? Because if you do, you might as well just get it out now. I guess you figure that one more dead person won't make any difference to me, right?"

Her lower lip was trembling. "There's something... something else."

"Just say it, Sabrina. Because I'm leaving."

She twisted her hands in her lap.

"I think Latanisha is still there."

I froze. What was she saying? Sabrina never looked anyone straight in the eyes whenever she was lying; she was a bad liar so I expected her to look away from me. But she didn't.

"Andre," she said. "I'm pretty sure Latanisha is still locked up in Mama's closet."

PART 2

Terrible
Revelations

chapter 7

The Agonizing Decision

Bronsetta clasped her hands over her mouth when I got home that night and told her everything Sabrina said to me.

"But are you sure it's true?" she asked me.

That was the thing. I wasn't sure. All my life I'd been lied to about having a twin and maybe, I thought, this was just another lie. Even though Sabrina showed me my father's letters, that still didn't prove that Mama and Greg killed my sister. And it sure didn't prove that my twin's body was still there inside Mama's bedroom, inside the same place my little girl walked past just a few weeks earlier and trembled and shook the entire time she was there.

I showed Bronsetta the confidentiality paper I'd stolen off Sabrina's table. Having it didn't make things any easier for me because I'd still given Sabrina my word of honor. That was something I took seriously—a man, I'd always believed, has to keep his promises.

But Sabrina was also scared for her life. Scared for her family's lives, too. And what if I went and told someone what she said to me and then Greg or Mama really did end up doing something bad to her or her kids? Sabrina might've been lying about whatever happened to my twin, but if she was lying about being scared, she should've gotten an Oscar for acting.

All that night, I thought about what to do. The way I saw it, if I went to the police and they found out that none of it was true, then nothing bad would happen. But if Mama and Greg really did do what Sabrina said, then there was going to have to be some kind of justice. Either way, it seemed like I only had one choice.

I told Bronsetta what I was planning. "If you don't feel like staying with me anymore, I'll understand," I said to her. "But let me know now so I can be ready."

But Bronsetta said she'd stick by me no matter what. "However you want to do it, I'm behind you," she said.

It meant everything to hear my wife say that. I also believe she truly meant it. But I don't think she had any idea what was going to happen to our whole family anymore than I did.

The next morning I was supposed to have jury duty. My employer had already let me off work for the day, but I needed to continue my search for the truth, so I went to the jury office and gave an excuse why I couldn't do it that day. Then I left the building and headed across the street to the office of the FBI. Gathering my courage, I walked up to a guard sitting at the front desk.

"Where can I go to report maybe a murder?" I stumbled over the words. Then went on, "I'm not too sure it's true."

The guy looked me up and down like he was trying to figure out if I was crazy or not. Finally he picked up the phone and called upstairs to one of the agents, explained my story, and an agent told him to have me write it down and sign my name. Not long after that, the agent came downstairs and sat next to me in the lobby.

"I'm afraid we can't help you," he said. "You have to go to the police office in Brooklyn and fill out a missing person report to get this investigated."

I left the building and sat outside on the steps. My sister had been missing twenty years, so what good would a missing person report do? It needed something more, something that went deeper. When I got home, I told Bronsetta how the FBI didn't help me and then for the rest of the day I sat there, not moving out of my chair, just staring at the wall and thinking. Later on, I called Sabrina. I didn't let her know what I'd been doing. She told me everything with her was fine and she asked me how I was holding up. I told her I was okay, but that it was very hurtful to hear the things she told me.

The next morning, I went to work as usual. But there was no way I could keep Sabrina's news inside me, keep everything to myself. A lot of times I talked to a friend of mine who worked at the same place I did about personal things. Bobby was sixty-two and a person I could trust not to blab things all over. When we were alone, I told him how I tracked down Sabrina and what she told me.

Bobby said, "The best thing to do is to call someone to investigate it."

"But I don't have any money for an investigator."

"Then search around and see if it's true," he said. "If you feel in your heart it's true, then do whatever you have to do."

I went back to my desk and right there was a newspaper lying open with a big advertisement for a criminal the police were looking for, along with an 800 number for anonymous tips. It was for *America's Most Wanted*. It was strange, almost like someone put the newspaper there for me to find.

I picked up the phone and called the number from my desk. "My name is Andre Carmichael and I have a problem," I said to the man who answered. "My sister told me my mother and brother murdered my twin sister."

The man was very polite and nice. He said, "How long ago?"

"Twenty years ago. But my sister said my mother might still have the body in the closet inside her apartment."

There was silence. After a minute he said, "Are you sure?"

I told him I wasn't, but I wanted to find out.

"Can you hold on a minute?" he asked. "I'm going to connect you with a detective who might be able to help."

A few minutes later, a detective named Danny came on the line. He was with the Brooklyn police department. I repeated everything Sabrina told me.

"Can I set up an appointment to meet with you and your sister?" Danny asked.

"She told me I shouldn't tell anyone. But I can't have this on my conscience, because if I did, it would be like murdering my twin myself."

"Well, would it be possible for you to call your sister and tell her what you just told me? Do you think she'd understand that you need to know the truth?"

"She's scared that my brother and his friends will come after her and her whole family. And I don't know—maybe he could."

"If this is true," Danny said, "we will have protection for her. We will guarantee that her life and her family's lives won't be in danger. Andre, would you be willing to trust me about that?"

The way I saw it, I didn't have any other option. I had to trust someone.

After I hung up, I practiced over and over what I'd say to Sabrina, the right words to tell her I'd broken my word of honor. But the minute Sabrina heard my voice on the phone, she didn't even give me the chance to tell her what I had planned to say.

"Andre, I have something to tell you," she said. "I've been thinking hard about this ever since you left here. And I want the two of us to go to the police. I think it's time for this to be known, for people to know what happened."

I was in shock. It was like she read my mind.

"Why have you changed your mind?"

"I've carried this secret my whole life. And it's been eating me alive. Killing me inside. But even more than that, I don't want the people who did this to our sister to be walking around and not paying for their crimes." She couldn't even use their names.

Then I told her what I did. I said, "I'm sorry, but I broke my promise to you. I already went to the detectives. They want to meet us this evening at your apartment if you're willing."

She wasn't angry with me. She didn't even tell me that having the detectives come that evening was too soon.

"I'll be here," was all she said.

When I got to Sabrina's, Chris and all the kids were home. I'd never met Sabrina's husband before, but I thought she'd probably told him and he might be expecting me. However, Chris acted surprised when Sabrina introduced me as her brother, almost like he didn't know she even had one. I had no idea what she'd told him about what was going to happen, so I just kept my mouth shut.

When the doorbell rang, Chris opened the door. Three detectives were standing there and they showed Chris their badges. I could tell by his face that he was really frightened.

"What's going on?" Chris asked.

"Could we speak with your wife, please?" one detective asked. It turned out this was Danny, the detective I first talked to on the phone.

Chris disappeared into a back bedroom. I think he might've heard the part where I was explaining that Sabrina was my sister and that she had told me what happened to my twin, but right after that we all left the apartment. Chris stayed home with the kids.

As we walked outside, I said to Sabrina really quietly, "Does Chris know?" She shook her head. "About anything?" I asked. She shook her head again.

No one spoke on the drive until we pulled up to the police station. I was scared—in the back of my mind I was thinking, don't let her be lying or we'll be in big trouble for making a false report. But as we stepped out of the car, Sabrina looked terrified.

"Are you going to make sure we'll have some protection?" she asked. The detectives promised her they would, that nothing would happen to either of us.

"I'm not worried about me," I said. "I'm worried about Sabrina and her family."

At first, Sabrina and I were together in one room with Danny and the other two detectives. I focused on telling them what happened. I told them again what Sabrina said to me and how both Sabrina and I got beaten all our lives just to keep us quiet or in the dark. And then the detectives took turns telling us how important it was to tell them everything we knew, everything we could think of and how they wanted our "independent recollections" so she and I wouldn't be influenced by what the other one said. I guess that was a fancy way of saying they didn't want us comparing stories.

But then, one detective turned to Sabrina and said, "We need the full truth about whatever happened. No matter what you already told your brother, we need the absolute truth, starting at the very beginning."

Until then, Sabrina had been sitting quietly, looking from one guy to the other, nodding every now and then. But as soon as the guy said that about giving them the full truth, she bolted out of her chair.

"You think I'm lying?" Her knees and hands were shaking as badly as her voice, but she kept glaring at the man straight in his eyes. "You think I am? Because if you do, I can take off all my clothes right here. Prove to you what Mama and Greg did to keep me quiet." Never once had I ever seen my sister angry like that.

I don't care if that man was right out of *Law and Order* or *NYPD Blue*, there wasn't any way he wanted a woman stripping down naked in front of him and all the other police officers. Sabrina looked like she was ready to do it, too.

"That won't be necessary," he said, trying to soothe her. But when she kept standing there breathing hard and trembling, he dropped his voice. "Please sit down Mrs. Carmichael." He nodded at her chair.

Suddenly, Sabrina looked like she didn't know what had come over her. Her hair was pulled back from her face and she was wearing a loose summer dress with sandals and for a second it hit me that she looked just like when we were kids, scared as a rabbit and willing to do anything in the world not to have something bad come crashing down on her.

"Excuse me, I didn't mean any disrespect," she said as she sat down. "It must sound crazy hearing all this, but it's just that—" She cleared her throat and then, when she realized they were listening to every word, she clammed right up again. "Actually, I would like to clear up one thing," she went on. "My last name isn't Carmichael anymore."

The detective who talked about telling the whole truth smiled at her. "My apologies," he said. And then he offered us both something to drink. A minute or two later he came back with two sodas. With a little jerk of his head he said to Sabrina, "How about if we go down the hall and have a talk?"

I watched as Sabrina took small steps, one hand holding the soda can and the other clutching her purse to her chest. Right before she turned the corner to step into the interrogation room, she stopped and glanced over her shoulder at me. The cops were looking at both of us, I guess trying to size us up.

I couldn't say anything more to her then. All I could do was pray. *Please don't make up any stories in there, Sabrina. Please don't tell any lies.*

And then, suddenly, she was gone.

* * *

They asked Sabrina things she'd never told me, things I didn't ask her then. *How do you know the body is still in the closet after all these years? What did the trunk look like? Where was Latanisha killed? How did it happen? Why did it happen? When was the trunk moved to the Rockaway Parkway apartment? Why wouldn't your mother have gotten rid of the evidence? What did your mother do to make it appear that Latanisha was still alive? What kinds of documents did she fill out for Latanisha over the years? If your mother kept any of those documents, where do you think they would be?*

Sabrina told me later that she explained everything—her old report cards that Mama changed to make it look like Latanisha was in school, the forged papers Mama sent to the welfare people, the lumpy mattress in Mama's bedroom. She told them about the wardrobe Mama and Greg had put in front of the closet and how no one walking into Mama's bedroom would have even known a door was behind it. Afterwards, she told me they had a hard time believing anyone would do what she was saying. "I don't know if they thought I was making everything up or not," she said to me. "Their mouths were kind of hanging open."

At one point, while the detectives were talking to Sabrina, Danny came into the room where I was sitting. "Are you sure about what your sister is saying?" he asked. I kept telling him no, I wasn't sure and I never said I was sure about anything, either. All I knew was what Sabrina told me and how I just needed the truth. I also told him about what Aunt Dorothy told me when Mama and Sonny were in Atlantic City and the way Sabrina and I ended up in different foster homes, with each of us thinking the other one didn't want any more contact.

Danny told me they couldn't just burst into Mama's apartment based on what Sabrina and I were saying. First, he said, they'd need to go to a judge to get a court order for a search warrant. And to do that, to convince a judge that there was a reasonable cause for looking inside where Mama had been living for more than twenty years, they'd first have to find a birth certificate for Latanisha. And that, he said, would just be the starting point.

"I'm not saying I don't believe you or Sabrina," he said. "But even if we find out that you did have a twin, that doesn't mean your mother and Greg killed her. And even if we do get the search warrant, it would be pretty hard to prove a thing after all these years if your mother got rid of the evidence. I know this is probably hard for you to hear, Andre, but right now we have to pray that your mother didn't dispose of the body."

During the next few weeks, I didn't hear one more word from the police. I went back and forth in my mind between hoping they'd find what they needed and then hoping they wouldn't find a thing. When Sabrina had gone into that interrogation room, I'd been praying that she wouldn't tell any lies, but now I was praying just the opposite, that she had made it all up, that Latanisha really did go to live somewhere down south and that maybe all of this was just a bad dream. A bad dream or else just a big, awful mistake. *People remember things wrong all the time*, I thought. *Maybe that's what happened with*

Sabrina—maybe she believes what she's saying, but maybe she's just remembering everything all wrong.

And then I got a call from Danny. "We found a social security number and birth certificate on your twin sister," he said. "So at least we know that she was here once. Now we need to find out if she is still living, or if she is somewhere else."

He told me he wanted to pick up Sabrina and me and drive us over to the apartment where Sabrina said Latanisha was killed and then drive to the apartment where Mama was living now. We got into an unmarked police car, dark blue. Sabrina and I rode in the back. Danny and the same two detectives went with us. On the drive, Danny showed me Latanisha's birth certificate.

"Have you ever seen this?" he asked. I shook my head and then tears started rolling down my face. I couldn't say one word, I was so choked up inside. Sabrina looked at that piece of paper too, saw our sister's name printed there and then tears were streaming down her face just like mine. That's how I found out my twin was born five minutes before me.

We parked across the street from the building where my family had lived when I was a baby. All of us stayed in the car. The detectives asked Sabrina to point out which floor we had lived on. She was trying hard to remember, she was looking up and down, back and forth, but finally she said she wasn't sure. "All I know is that it was small and dark in there," she said.

Then they drove us just a few blocks away to the brownstone where my mother lived. Sabrina was very nervous, she slipped down low in the seat and she kept saying she was afraid someone would see her, recognize her. But this time, she knew which apartment it was. "Apartment 1D," she said. It was the same apartment where I'd taken my little girl to visit Mama just a month or so earlier.

A few days later, Danny called to say they'd gotten the search warrant. But he refused to tell me what day they were going to show up at Mama's apartment and all he would tell me was that it would be "sometime this week." I wanted to be there with them when they went, wanted to see if it was true with my own eyes, but Danny wouldn't let me. He said it could be "too upsetting" for me. At the time I thought it wasn't fair, I thought I had a right to go, but maybe Danny was right. Maybe I would have flipped out and gone crazy for what Mama did.

During those next few days of waiting, Sabrina and I didn't want to be apart. Both of us felt like a huge block of granite was about to fall down on our lives at any second and that no matter what the police found, our entire lives were going to be changed. So both of us hung onto the other, just waiting for it to happen. Chris was gone during the days at his new teaching job—I hadn't wanted to ask Sabrina anything else about what she'd now told him, whether he knew about any part of what was happening or not—and so every day I went there to her apartment and the two of us sat on the sofa with the TV and the radio turned on. Her kids were all glad to see me and I had a hard time pretending I was just there to spend time with them. But no matter where Sabrina or I went in her apartment, both of us had one eye or one ear glued to the TV or radio.

If Chris wondered what I was doing there when he got home in the evenings, he didn't say anything. He was polite to me, but after Sabrina made dinner, he usually disappeared into his bedroom while Sabrina and I sat on the sofa in front of the television. He was in his bedroom that evening, November 5, 1999, when Sabrina picked up the remote control and pushed a button.

Suddenly, Mama's brownstone was on the screen. Outside of it was a big group of news people with notepads and cameras and one news reporter was talking about a "gruesome discovery" inside the building. "Mrs. Carmichael," we heard the reporter say, hadn't wanted to open the door when the police first showed up and detectives from the Cold Case Squad finally had to get the building superintendent to let them in. Finally though, Mama cracked the door just enough that they busted it down. A few minutes later, Mama fainted and collapsed to the floor. On the television, we saw one ambulance outside her building.

Some witnesses said afterward that Mama immediately dashed back toward the closet and screamed, "Please don't let them take me! I don't want any more suffering." I could imagine Mama saying that, imagine it being true. Still, it's not what I got told later by one of the detectives who was there. He told me my mother went straight back, ran to the closet and said, "I want to go! I want to go! Thank you for setting me free." And if that last version was right, it would make sense with something else Sabrina and I found out.

People in Mama's apartment building said later that for years and years, Mama complained to the super that a screaming baby was always keeping her awake at night, but whenever they looked they never found a baby living anywhere near her. And then there was the story from one eleven-year-old girl who lived right next door to Mama. Even though the girl knew that my mother lived alone, she said Mama was always yelling inside her apartment. "She'd yell, 'Be quiet now! Stop talking to me!'" The girl said she always thought Mama was just crazy.

I thought of all the times in my life I'd heard a voice talking to me too, telling me to *just walk away, Andre,* or *don't be messing with those guys,* and how I always expected to see a girl talking right into my ear. But maybe, I thought, that voice didn't just talk to me. Maybe the voice had been talking to Mama all of those years, too.

But maybe Mama and I weren't the only ones the voice talked to. When Sabrina found out that Mama had been hearing a baby crying at night for years and years, she put her hands over her face and then looked at me, wide-eyed.

"Remember when you came to my apartment that second time, when you demanded to know the truth?" she said. "I heard something that day, Andre." Sabrina told me that while she was trying to figure out what to do, whether to tell me the truth about what happened twenty years ago, she suddenly heard a small high-pitched voice. "It was like someone else was in the room with us, talking right into my ear," she said. "The voice said to me, 'He's got to know, Sabrina. He's got a right to know!'"

Until Sabrina told me that, I had forgotten the strange look she'd had on her face that day, or how I thought it was almost like she was hearing some kind of music playing in the distance, or maybe listening to something no one else could hear.

The police found Latanisha right where Sabrina said they would. The blue trunk was wrapped in layers and layers of garbage bags and mothballs, along with a yellowed newspaper from November 4, 1979. I got a shudder when I realized that it was almost exactly twenty years to the day from that newspaper's date. Inside Mama's closet there also were piles of air fresheners and incense sticks and baking soda boxes and camphor cakes. Latanisha was wearing a white diaper.

When I saw my mother on television being carried out of the apartment on a stretcher, my heart felt like it went straight up into my throat. Until that moment, I'd still been praying that it wasn't true, that none of it was real. And maybe Sabrina had been feeling the same way. She stood in the middle of her living room with her hands over her face and she just sobbed and sobbed.

I went over and hugged her.

"This is the beginning of the end, Sabrina. Now you won't have to go through this pain anymore. I wish you had let me know this a long time ago, so this could've been found out. I wish you never had to carry this so long."

"Oh, Andre, I wanted to tell you so much," she said. She was still sobbing.

"My whole life, I had people thinking I was crazy," I said.

Sabrina kept her head on my shoulder and let me keep on hugging her. "My whole life, I was trying not to *go* crazy," she said.

Just then, Chris walked into the living room and saw us. The news reporter was still talking about "Mrs. Carmichael" and the "mummified remains" of a toddler discovered after twenty years inside a trunk in her closet. Sabrina's head was still against my chest, her eyes closed. I saw Chris stare at the TV and then at Sabrina and then I saw the horrified expression on his face.

chapter 8

The Secret Revealed

Over the next few weeks, Chris could barely bring himself to look at me, much less talk to me. The only time he spoke to me was if he absolutely had to—"Did you pay the phone bill yet?"—and whenever he was home he did everything to avoid being near me. Every evening he did something with the kids and at night he slept as if we were brother and sister, with his head at one end of the bed and mine at the other. In the mornings, he crept out early, sometimes before I even woke up.

Nothing I said to him made any difference. He acted as if I was a ghost.

I truly did want to talk to him. I truly did want to explain everything. But every time I tried to open my mouth, the words just fell silent inside me. What could I possibly say that would make him understand? How could I explain it to him if I couldn't even explain it to myself? It felt as though the words I needed didn't even exist, that no one had even invented those kinds of words yet.

The best I was able to do was to tell him over and over that I was sorry, that I never meant for any of my past to come into our life together, that I never wanted any of it to touch *us*. But each time I spoke, Chris just stared off at a wall in the distance or walked away.

What I said to Chris was the truth. After Andre and I went to the police and even after they got the search warrant for Mama's apartment, I still clung to the idea that the past could stay sealed off, that Chris wouldn't have to know about anything. Until Andre and I saw Mama's brownstone that night on the television news, I really did believe that none of my past would ever have to touch my life with Chris. Even I didn't understand how the news media would make our past a public event and it had never occurred to me that what Andre and I had decided to do would ever become known by anyone else except the police.

Obviously, though, I couldn't have been more wrong. Within just two days of Latanisha's discovery, the story wasn't just all over New York and wasn't just in newspapers all over the United States, but it also had traveled over the internet, translated into Russian, Czech, Polish and Italian. The whole world, it seemed, was horrified by my family—and that world most definitely included Chris.

And two weeks later, on November 19, everything got even worse between us. *The New York Times* ran a second big story about us under the headline, "Brother's Search for Twin Revealed a Twenty-Year-Old-Killing." The story revealed that the Kings County District Attorney's office had just charged both Mama and Greg with second-degree murder, along with hindering prosecution and tampering with physical evidence. Mama had been charged the day before in her Brooklyn hospital bed where she'd been taken right after she collapsed inside her apartment, but the story said that Greg had been "arraigned in State Supreme Court in Brooklyn" and then had been taken back to "the Cape Vincent Correctional Facility near the Canadian border, where he is serving a two to four year sentence for robbery." The Brooklyn district attorney was quoted as saying that what happened in our family was "straight out of a Stephen King novel."

As I read the article, I pictured Mama in her hospital bed finally hearing the words she'd been trying to avoid for twenty years. Once the police had broken into her apartment, she must have known that it was all over, that the truth was finally going to come out and so she couldn't have been surprised when she learned what crime she was being charged with.

Greg, though, was a completely different story. Until I read the *Times* article, I had no idea how long his prison term for robbery had been. What, I wondered, if Greg was nearing the end of his sentence, if he had been expecting to get out of jail any day? I imagined Greg's shocked face as two guys from the DA's office came to see him, unlocked his cell, took him out in handcuffs and told him that they were taking him to Brooklyn to face murder charges in Latanisha's death. And then I imagined Greg's response when he found out, since the *Times* had revealed it, that I was responsible for those charges.

I could not let myself imagine what might be going on inside Greg's mind right at that moment, what thoughts he probably was having about me. *Focus on something else,* I commanded myself. *On anything else.*

The story also went on to say that after the police started investigating, child welfare workers had gone back to old files and found out that over the years at least eight child abuse complaints had been filed against both Mama and Greg. That was news to me—but the reporter obviously had shared that information with Andre. And when Andre discovered that what happened to his twin might have been discovered years and years earlier if those welfare workers had done a more thorough investigation of our family, he told the *Times* reporter that he was going to file a lawsuit against the city.

"I blame my mother," Andre was quoted as saying. "But I also blame the system." The story ended by saying that even though Andre was working as a security guard to support his daughter, his wife and her four children, he wanted to one day open up a center for abused children. He told the reporter that he didn't want any more kids to suffer like we did.

Andre and I hadn't talked for several days, so that was the first I knew about his plans for a lawsuit or a center for abused kids. But I was glad for him—glad he could talk about everything so openly now, glad he already was trying to change everything horrible that had happened into something that might turn out to be good. *Maybe that will happen to me one day too,* I thought.

But that day, for me, wasn't going to happen any time soon.

* * *

In the beginning, I hadn't faulted Chris one bit for his reaction to everything. I had to admit that if I had found out such shocking things about him, I probably would have felt the same way—hurt and confused and furious that he hid something so important from me for so long, on top of having to learn about it just like everyone else. But then, after all of those emotions had gone through me, I honestly thought I would have tried to understand. And if my husband couldn't have told me right away, if he didn't have the words to express it to me straight off, I truly believed I would have waited for him to tell it to me in his own time.

And during those first few weeks, that's what I thought Chris was trying to do—right up to the day when he came home from work and told me he had decided to go stay with his mother in Queens for a while.

"I'll just have to see," he said, when I asked him for how long.

As I watched him folding his slacks and shirts and neckties in piles on top of our bed, I told myself that Chris was just trying to work everything out, just trying to come to terms with everything. I also figured that he probably needed to get away from all the sudden craziness in our lives, from the newspaper and magazine and television people—some of them from as far away as Europe—calling our apartment non-stop and the people in our building knocking on our door or stopping us in the hallway and asking me, "Was that your sister they found in the trunk?"

But when Chris finished packing all his clothes he turned around and looked me in my eyes. It was the first time he'd done that since Latanisha had been found.

"Chris, I know all of this is horrible now..." Searching for the right words felt like I was digging into cement. "But pretty soon, all of this is going to settle down. And then—"

He cut me off. "You know what I think, Sabrina?"

I shook my head.

"I think anyone who keeps a secret like that for twenty years has to be incredibly sick. There's no way a person can keep something like that inside their head for that long without it making them just as psychotic as the people who did it. And I think what you did was just as bad as what they did."

I tried to say something back to him, but no words came out.

"You knew, Sabrina, but you never told anyone. Not even your own brother. Not even your own husband. You knew what your mother was hiding all those years, but you didn't even care. And my God—" He shook his head. "I even told you to take our kids over there with you when you visited her! *Our own children* could have ended up going there."

He looked at me with utter disgust, with complete contempt.

"I don't even know you, Sabrina. Maybe I never did. You've obviously got enough secrets for a hundred people. And you know what? I need to get away from you. Away from you and from your whole sick family."

And then he picked up his things and left.

* * *

I could not break down.

I could not allow myself to break down.

Our children still needed a mother, they still needed a roof over their heads and food on the table and that meant that I simply had to go on. I had to keep making sure they got off to school in the mornings and back home again safely, had to make sure all their clothes were clean and ironed, had to keep working each day and cooking meals for the kids at night. Even though Chris was gone and even though my life felt as though it was collapsing, I couldn't let any of what was happening to me affect my children.

But I also couldn't break down because of Latanisha. Andre and I had put everything into motion and now we both had the obligation to follow through.

Not long after Mama and Greg were formally charged with Latanisha's murder, the two district attorneys who were going to be prosecuting the case, Ama Dwimoh and Frank Urzi, asked Andre and me to meet with them and the detectives involved in the cases in Miss Dwimoh's Brooklyn office. Even though we had already told everything to the police, Miss Dwimoh said we needed to tell them everything all over again, starting at the very beginning.

It was easy to see why Miss Dwimoh was the district attorney in charge. Everything about her, from her tasteful clothes to the way she moved, gave her an aura of professionalism, as if she was the type of person who wouldn't let even the smallest detail get by her. Andre told me later how beautiful he thought she was, too. She was tall, with long dark hair and an olive complexion that made her appear exotic. Mr. Urzi was a dark-haired, stocky man who seemed intelligent, easy going and relaxed. In his crisp suit and tie, he sat in Miss Dwimoh's office with a pen and pad of paper and the three detectives sat in chairs near the wall.

Miss Dwimoh and Mr. Urzi began by asking Andre to tell them again how he found out about having a twin, along with any times in his life he had ever mentioned the possibility of having a twin. They asked him about what types of beatings he had gotten over the years, too, and told him they needed him to be as specific as possible about what caused the beatings, along with what kinds of objects were used.

Andre held up pretty well while he talked about belts and extension cords and plates crashing down on his head and he even kept his voice steady while he was talking about why he got beaten. He said if he didn't clean the house the exact way Mama wanted it done, if he didn't eat every last bite on his plate, if the creases in his pants weren't perfect, or if he looked at Mama in a way she thought was disrespectful, the blows would start. But Andre said he still never really understood the real reasons why Mama abused him. "She beat me for everything," he said, "and she beat me for nothing."

But there was one point where Andre couldn't hold in all that pain any longer. When he came to the part about Greg pounding nails through his hands and how Mama had just watched and done nothing to help him, that's when he broke down and started crying. Miss Dwimoh and Mr. Urzi both came over, hugged him and kept telling him that everything was going to be okay, that everything would be all right. Miss Dwimoh comforted him by telling Andre he had done such a very brave thing by coming forward and now that he had, the whole world would know that Latanisha had once walked this Earth.

After Andre got control of himself again, they asked him more questions. It was important for them to understand the role Greg played over the years, Miss Dwimoh said, and possible reasons why he didn't come forward. But Andre didn't have an answer for that—he told them he would just be guessing about what had made Greg beat him so terribly for so many years.

"I guess you'd have to ask Greg," he said.

When it came time for me, it seemed as if they asked me the same questions over and over. The only difference was, each time, the wording of the question changed just a little. Did I remember why Mama and Greg started beating Latanisha that day? Did Latanisha do something that made Mama and Greg start hitting her? Do you have any idea why your mother and Greg started beating Latanisha? Over and over I told them the same thing, that I never knew what set them off.

Miss Dwimoh's voice got even softer, even gentler, when she asked me why I had never told anyone what happened, why I had never come forward earlier. I could tell she was trying not to sound as if she was accusing me, but instantly I heard Chris's words echoing in my head. *You knew what your mother was hiding all those years, but you didn't even care.* Is that what the district attorney would think about me, too? Is that what a jury would think, that I just went about my life as if Latanisha had never meant a thing to me?

I had a hard time getting the words out. A few times, Miss Dwimoh asked me if I could speak a little louder, that she was having a hard time hearing me. That was how scared I was while I was trying to explain how many times I had wanted to tell someone—how many times I had wanted to tell Andre— but how terrified I had always been. My entire life, I told her, I was afraid that if I opened up my mouth, I would have ended up in a trunk, too. Or Andre would have. And later I feared for my children.

Miss Dwimoh asked if I had believed that Gregory could have been capable of that. "I still believe he's capable of that," I said.

Then Miss Dwimoh asked whether I remembered the precise way that Latanisha had fallen. Was it backwards or sideways? Was it perhaps on her face? Was it possible that Latanisha could have hit her head on something around her, like maybe the edge of a table? Could I remember any dangerous objects around her, like chairs or maybe a refrigerator door? Was it possible that Latanisha might have just fallen down on her own and then hit her head accidentally? Again, I repeated exactly what I remembered, that Mama and Greg were slapping her and then Mama punched her on the side of her head and she fell backward.

"The only dangerous objects around her," I said, "were Mama and Greg."

Either Miss Dwimoh or Mr. Urzi—I can't remember which one—then asked me if I was completely sure, without any shadow of a doubt, that everything I was telling them was the complete truth.

At that point, I couldn't stop thinking that they probably thought I was crazy.

I jumped up from my chair and stood there, shaking. "If you don't believe me, then why did the police find everything just like I told them? If I'm lying, then why'd they find Latanisha right where I said they would? Why'd they find all of Mama's papers under her mattress, just like I said they would? And if you think I'm making up all the beatings I got, I can strip naked right now, let you see all the scars I got from Mama and Greg, what they did to keep me quiet all those years." It was the same threat I'd made in the police station, but now I was trembling like I'd never had in my life.

I don't know what I would have done if Miss Dwimoh hadn't come over and put her arm around me. It wasn't that she and Mr. Urzi didn't believe me, she said. It was just that they had to know ahead of time if there was anything I was unsure of, if there was any detail that perhaps was foggy in my mind or else a detail that could have happened in a different way than I remembered. The reason, Miss Dwimoh said, was that both Mama and Greg had gotten lawyers.

"They have both pleaded not guilty to the charges," she said.

I don't know why hearing that shocked me, but it did. I realized I should have considered the possibility that Mama and Greg would both deny everything, but ever since Andre and I had gone to the police, I had assumed that once the evidence was staring Mama and Greg in their faces, both of them would confess.

But obviously it wasn't going to be that simple. For one thing, Miss Dwimoh told us that even though an autopsy had been done on our sister, after twenty years it might not be possible to be absolutely certain about how she died. That sounded like it left Mama and Greg a huge legal opening. And then, for another thing, if Mama and Greg were convicted on just the murder count alone, both of them were facing a maximum sentence of twenty-five years to life in prison. That gave both of them a powerful reason to fight the charges.

Miss Dwimoh then told us that a detective had already gone to Greg's prison near Canada and interviewed him. Greg had admitted that he helped Mama hide Latanisha in the trunk, but he had insisted that he had no part at all in how our sister died. And the reason he never came forward, never told anyone, was that he was trying to protect Mama. When Andre and I heard that, we didn't know if that meant Greg might end up putting all the blame on Mama—if he was going to say in a courtroom that Mama killed Latanisha all by herself—or if he was going to say that Latanisha's death had been an accident and then he and Mama made the bad choice to cover it up.

Still, based on what Miss Dwimoh and Mr. Urzi were saying, it sounded as if it would be my word against theirs.

"We're hoping that after we present all of our evidence, your mother and your brother will both agree to plead guilty," Miss Dwimoh said to me. "That would spare you from having to testify."

"And if they don't?" I asked. "If they deny everything right up to the end?"

Miss Dwimoh looked as if she was searching for the right words to say to me. "Again, Sabrina, we're hoping it won't come down to that."

She didn't have to spell it out for me. I understood perfectly what she really meant. If Mama and Greg kept to their stories, the only way they could convince a jury they were both innocent would be if they made me look like a liar. A liar or else just a little girl who had remembered everything all wrong. From all the questions Miss Dwimoh and Mr. Urzi had been asking me about which way Latanisha had fallen and if she might have hit her head on some object, it seemed pretty clear that Mama and Greg might be getting ready to claim that Latanisha's death had been an accident.

"So if I have to testify, their lawyers would basically tear me apart."

Miss Dwimoh looked at me as if she was trying to gauge whether I was capable of holding up in a courtroom, especially after I had just threatened to strip naked in front of her a few minutes earlier. The truth is, I wasn't any more certain about that than she was.

She nodded. "Their lawyers would most likely try to discredit you, yes."

Andre was sitting across the table, staring at me. At that moment, he looked as if his whole future depended on what I would say. I think he was afraid I was going to tell Miss Dwimoh and Mr. Urzi that I couldn't go through with that possibility of being torn apart—that I couldn't risk having my family ripped to shreds any more than it already had been.

I looked at Andre. Latanisha had been Andre's twin and she should have been alive and part of his life. But maybe what Andre didn't understand at the moment was that Latanisha also should have been part of my life, too. The three of us should have been sitting around a dinner table somewhere, in one of our homes, with all of our kids playing together. The three of us should have been talking about where we wanted to be for Thanksgiving, what we wanted to do for the kids on Christmas, to whose house we would go. What Andre and I shouldn't have been doing was sitting inside a district attorney's office and trying to prove what happened to Latanisha and why she wasn't with us. And we sure shouldn't have been facing the idea of standing up against Mama and Greg all over again, after all that both of us had been through during our childhood.

But if that was how Mama and Greg were going to play it, I thought, then that's how it would have to be. As Andre, Miss Dwimoh, Mr. Urzi and the detectives all looked at me and waited for me to say something, I realized that for the first time in my entire life, I was not going to let myself be paralyzed by Mama or Greg or what they might do to me.

"I know what I saw that day," I said finally. "Maybe I don't remember all the little details, like whether it was winter or summer or what time of day it was. But one thing I'm sure of. Nothing that happened to my sister was any kind of accident. Mama and Greg beat my sister and then they threw her away like she was trash. And nothing is going to make me change my story."

I saw Miss Dwimoh and Mr. Urzi look at each other, as if in that glance they were sharing information.

"I've been hoping Mama would bring it up and talk about what she did," I added, "but so far she hasn't."

Miss Dwimoh did a double-take. "Excuse me?" she said. "You've talked with your mother since her arrest?"

I nodded. "She started writing to me and phoning me about a month ago. I've taken the train to Riker's Island a few times to see her."

Miss Dwimoh and Mr. Urzi both looked as if they were going to fall out of their chairs. "Sabrina, I really don't think that's a very wise idea at all, having contact with her," Miss Dwimoh said. "How do you think that will look in court? You're accusing your mother and brother of committing a terrible crime, but then you're also having contact with her and going to see her?"

chapter 9

Sins of the Mother

I could see her point of view, but I don't think she understood mine. Mama was locked up inside a tiny jail cell and the doctors had just told her she had bone cancer. As much as I hated what she had done to my sister and what she had done to Andre and me, it still was hard for me to deal with the fact that I was the reason Mama was in jail, that I was the reason the other inmates were threatening to kill her.

There was no way I could explain to Miss Dwimoh that even though I was willing to testify against Mama, I still had a lot of guilt about revealing the truth and I also had some genuine concerns about how Mama was being treated and if she was getting the medical care she needed.

But there also was something else that had been making me go to the prison to see her. For the first time in my entire life, Mama was showing love to me. In all of her letters and every time she phoned, Mama called me her "baby girl" or her "wonderful daughter," or said how I was "God's blessing" in her life. Mama had never once mentioned the fact that it had been Andre and me who were responsible for her being there in jail and she had never once given even the slightest hint that she was angry with me. She just went on and on about what a great gift from God I was and how the good Lord had graced her by putting me in her life.

Even though a part of me knew that Mama probably wouldn't be saying any of those things if she wasn't locked up in jail, another part of me needed to hear it. It struck me then that maybe it doesn't matter what kind of mother you had— you still always hunger for her love.

I did not tell Miss Dwimoh that each time I had entered the prison I felt as if I was being treated like a prisoner myself. I had to hand over my purse to a guard and then be hand searched all over my body and then go through metal detectors until I entered a cinder block room filled with tables and benches and maybe a hundred or so other family members doing the same thing as me. Finally, a woman guard would bring Mama in a wheelchair, dressed in her prison clothes.

On every visit, Mama told me I was the only one who ever came to see her. She told me how much it meant to her, too. The way things were in prison, she said, the other inmates considered your life to be worthless unless you received letters and visits. Unless you had a family, without people on the outside looking out after your welfare, Mama said, they all treated you like scum. The only way not to have people threatening to kill you was if they knew you had someone watching out for you. Mama said she'd like to see Andre if he ever wanted to come, but then she added that she wouldn't blame him if he didn't want to. All she knew was that, sure as there was a God in heaven, I was her baby girl, her blessing from the Lord.

Never once, in any of her visits, had we ever talked about any aspect of the upcoming trial. Our twenty to thirty minute conversations were limited to how my kids were doing—I stuck with telling her things they were doing in school—and then to what items she needed, things like hair supplies, candies, snacks and flip-flop sandals for when she had to go into the shower stalls. On each visit, I also gave her twenty dollars for the prison commissary.

"I sure would be grateful if you could get me a wrist watch," Mama said the last time I was there. She said she knew it was a lot to ask, especially since she hadn't even needed one before, but it sure would be nice to know how long the hours were taking to go by. When I told her I would try, she said, "And maybe a pair of earrings too? Just so I can feel a little prettier in here?"

Miss Dwimoh looked at me from across her desk. I knew she was probably thinking that visiting Mama might influence me, might get me to have so much sympathy for her that I wouldn't testify, and maybe even ruin the case she was building.

"If you're worried that Mama is going to convince me to change my story," I said, "you don't have to."

She nodded slightly. "Well, I'm glad you're holding up so well and staying so strong," she said. "But perhaps you might like to talk to someone else about what you're going through? Perhaps get some emotional support?"

Miss Dwimoh told me that the city of New York had a vic-tims' fund that would pay for me to see a therapist if I wanted to. No matter what I told the therapist, she said, nothing would ever be repeated to anyone else, including her or Mr. Urzi. "The person would simply be there to help you through this."

All my life I had thought of therapists as listening posts for rich people. I pictured them sitting next to someone lying on a couch, someone talking on and on to a total stranger who pretended to care about what was going on and then just took their money. I had always thought that if a person had a real friend or close family or strong faith in God, they'd never need to pay someone to listen to their problems.

But the moment Miss Dwimoh used the word "help," something inside me realized that I didn't really have anyone in my life to talk to about what was happening. Andre and I talked often, but he was going through his own dark tunnel, the same one I was, and so we both tried to focus our conversations on things like our kids and our work. Chris was gone—not that I could have shared it with him anyway—and the few friends I had were not the right ones to talk about the kind of private things that might show up one day in a newspaper article.

I needed someone safe to talk to. At the same time, though, I was worried that Mama or Greg's lawyers would find out I'd gone to a therapist and then try to make me out to be crazy.

But what I didn't know was that in just a few days, I was going to need all the help I could get.

I was home with the children that afternoon when there was a knock on my door. Standing in the hallway was a police officer.

"Sabrina Carmichael-Yaw?" the officer asked.

"Yes?"

He handed me a piece of paper. "You have been served."

As soon as I saw the words "Order of Protection" across the front, I assumed it was the district attorney's way of formally notifying me that they were making certain that my children and I were kept safe, just as the police had promised Andre and me when we first reported our sister's murder. But as I read further, I realized that the document had nothing at all to do with Mama and Greg's trial.

The document had my husband's name on it, along with the names of all of our kids. I was being ordered, it said, to "stay away from Chris Yaw," to "refrain from assault, stalking, harassment, menacing, reckless and disorderly conduct, intimidation, threats or any criminal offense against Chris Yaw."

I was being ordered to appear for an emergency hearing in the Bronx family court a few days later. My failure to appear, the document warned, might subject me to "mandatory arrest and criminal prosecution."

I don't know how long I stood there in the middle of my living room, staring in disbelief at what my husband had done. At what I felt he clearly was trying to do.

Chris was planning to take away my children.

"How could you do this?" I said to Chris when I saw him in the courthouse hallway on the day of the hearing. "How could you make up all those lies about me? There's not one single word on that piece of paper that's true. How could you do that to your own kids?"

Chris wouldn't even look at me. "I have nothing to say to you, Sabrina. What I've got to say, I'm going to say to the judge."

The judge obviously didn't want to take up the court's time with pleasantries. She got right to the point by asking Chris what basis he had for his petition.

"I believe that my wife is a danger to herself, to me and to our children," he said. Then he told the judge that I was the daughter of the mother who killed her child and put it in a trunk, the one in all the newspapers.

The judge's eyes widened when she looked at me. She wrote something down and then she said that she was ordering the immediate removal of my children into foster homes, pending an investigation.

By dinnertime, all of my children were gone.

chapter 10

Terror and Scars

Only my oldest child knew about what had happened to Latanisha. My daughter, who was fourteen, had been named after Mama and at school, right after the story came out, her classmates had been brutal and cruel to her. Several times she had come home in tears, telling me that she had been called a "baby murderer" and taunted about how many trunks she kept inside her closet.

Now my daughter Madeline was faced with further trauma when she and her siblings got ripped away from me and put into strangers' homes. I don't know what any of them were even told about why they were taken from their mother so cruelly or if they had any idea I could do nothing to get them back until my next scheduled court appearance, which was six days later.

During that time, while child welfare workers looked into my background, I was terrified. Terrified not for anything that might be discovered about me—but terrified for my children. For three years, beginning when I was fifteen, I had been sent to different foster homes and I knew how awful some of them could be. Andre had been blessed by being placed with Mrs. Lewis, a woman who told everyone from the start that "this is my son," and who had treated him with love and kindness all those years. But I hadn't been so lucky. Each day that my children were gone, I imagined how scared my kids must be, and at night I lay in bed, staring up at the ceiling and praying with all my strength for God to protect them.

When the investigation was finished, the child welfare people issued a report to the judge. Even though I never was allowed to see it, all I could assume was that it proved that there was nothing whatsoever to support my estranged husband's contention that I was unfit. The judge said that based on the report, she was ruling in my favor. She ordered all of my children to be returned to me immediately and for me to retain full custody.

It was the only time in my life I ever cried because of happiness.

When my children came back home again, they wanted to know why they'd had to go away. I told them that someone had made a false allegation against me, but after it got looked into, the child welfare people realized that there was nothing to it. "It was a big mistake," I told them. "But those child welfare people just needed to make certain that all of you were safe and well cared for. That's their job, to protect children."

Still, my younger sons were terribly upset. "Are we going to get taken away again?" they asked.

THE CITY OF NEW YORK
VITAL RECORDS CERTIFICATE

DEATH TRANSCRIPT

CERTIFICATE OF DEATH

Certificate No. 156-99-058412

DEPARTMENT OF HEALTH

DATE FILED 1999 DEC 14 ☐ 12:25

1. NAME OF DECEASED Latanisha (First Name)   Sanabria Smantha (Middle Name)   Carmichael (Last Name)
(Type or Print)

MEDICAL CERTIFICATE OF DEATH (To be filled in by the O.C.M.E.)

2. PLACE OF DEATH	2a. BOROUGH NEW YORK CITY BROOKLYN	2b. Name of hospital or other facility if not facility, street address 94-104 Rockaway Parkway	2c. If in Hospital or Other Facility 1 ☐ DOA 3 ☐ Outpatient 2 ☐ Emerg 4 ☐ Inpatient	2d. If inpatient, date of current admission Month / Day / Year

3. DATE AND HOUR OF DEATH OR FOUND DEAD	3a. (Month) November	(Day) 05	(Year) 1999	3b. HOUR 10:22 ☐ AM ☒ PM	4. SEX Female	5. APPROXIMATE AGE 3 Years

6.	DEATH WAS CAUSED BY:	Enter only one cause per line	INTERVAL BETWEEN ONSET AND DEATH
PART 1	a. Immediate cause Homicidal Violence, Etiology Undetermined.		
	b. Due to or as a consequence of		
	c. Due to or as a consequence of		

PART 2	d. Other significant conditions contributing to death but not resulting in the underlying cause given in part 1

7a. INJURY DATE (Month) (Day) (Year) 1979	7b. TIME ☐ AM UNK ☐ PM	7c. AT WORK ☐ YES ☒ NO	7d. PLACE OF INJURY – At home, farm, street, etc. UNKNOWN 7e. LOCATION UNKNOWN	

7f. HOW INJURY OCCURRED UNKNOWN

8. Manner of Death ☐ Pending Further Study ☒ Homicide ☐ Natural ☐ Suicide ☐ Accident ☐ Undetermined	9. Autopsy ☒ Yes ☐ No Autopsy Pursuant to Law ☐ No Autopsy	10. On the basis of examination and/or investigation, in my opinion, death occurred due to the causes and manner as stated. CERTIFIER SIGNATURE _____ M.D. DATE November 10, 1999 CERTIFIER NAME (Print) Marie Macaioux, M.D. XXXXXXXXXXX (Deputy Chief, XXX (Medical Examiner)

11. M.E. Case No. K99-5107	12a. Date Pronounced Dead (Month, Day, Year) (If different from 3a)	12b. TIME ☐ AM ☐ PM

PERSONAL PARTICULARS (To be filled in by Funeral Director, or in case of City Burial, by O.C.M.E.)

13. Usual Residence a. State New York	13b. County Kings	13c. City, Town, or Location Brooklyn	13d. Street & House No. 94-104 Rockaway Parkway	Zip 11212 (#4A)	13e. Inside City Limits of 7c ☒ Yes ☐ No

14. Served in U.S. Armed Forces No ☒ Yes ☐ Specify years From To	15. Marital Status (Check One) 1 ☒ Never Married 2 ☐ Widowed 3 ☐ Married or separated 4 ☐ Divorced	16. Name of Surviving Spouse (If wife, give maiden name)

17. Date of birth (Month) (Day) (Year) of Decedent February 27, 1976	18. Age at last birthday 3	If under 1 Year mos. / days	If less than 1 Day hours / mins	19. Social Security No.

20a. Usual Occupation (Kind of work done during most of working lifetime. Do not enter retired) Child	20b. Kind of business or industry

21. Birthplace (City & State or Foreign Country) Brooklyn, New York	22. Education (Specify only highest grade completed) Elementary/Secondary (0-12) College (1-4 or 5+) -0-	23. Other name(s) by which decedent was known Latanisha Sanabria Samantha Carmichael

24. NAME OF FATHER OF DECEDENT Joseph B. Carmichael	25. MAIDEN NAME OF MOTHER OF DECEDENT Madeline Rogers

26a. NAME OF INFORMANT Sabrina L. Yaw	26b. RELATIONSHIP TO DECEASED Sister	26c. ADDRESS 150 West 225th Street; (CITY) Bronx, (STATE) New York (ZIP) 10463

27a. NAME OF CEMETERY OR CREMATORY Rosehill Crematory	27b. LOCATION (City, Town, State and Country) Linden, New Jersey	27c. DATE OF BURIAL OR CREMATION June 4, 2002

28a. FUNERAL ESTABLISHMENT FRANK R. BELL FUNERAL HOME, INC.	28b. ADDRESS 536 Sterling Place; Brooklyn, New York 11238

VR18 (1/94)   **VITAL RECORDS**   **DEPARTMENT OF HEALTH**   **THE CITY OF NEW YORK**

This is to certify that the foregoing is a true copy of a record on file in the Department of Health. The Department of Health does not certify to the truth of the statements made thereof, as no inquiry as to the facts has been provided by law.

Steven P. Schwartz, Ph.D., City Registrar

Do not accept this transcript unless it bears the security features listed on back. Reproduction or alteration of this transcript is prohibited by §3.21 of the New York City Health Code if the purpose is the evasion or violation of any provision of the Health Code or any other law.

DATE ISSUED **JUN 3, 2002**   DOCUMENT NO. **F602202**

The City of New York

ANY ALTERATION OR ERASURE VOIDS THIS CERTIFICATE

The death certificate of Latanisha Carmichael, dated November 5, 1999, twenty years after she was murdered and crudely mummified inside a cedar-lined trunk filled with mothballs and air fresheners and hidden in a bedroom closet by her mother, Madeline Carmichael, and her older brother, Gregory Carmichael.

Andre and his mother at Andre's thirteenth birthday. It would be the last time he saw his mother for another ten years.

Sabrina and Andre as kids.

Young Gregory Carmichael on a swing near the family home in Brooklyn.

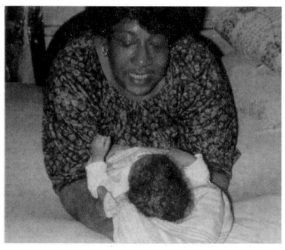

Madeline with her granddaughter who shares her name; an eerie image considering the gravity of her crime.

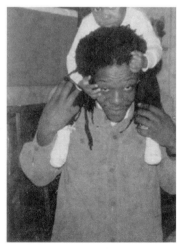

Adult Gregory with an unidentified child.

Memorial card for Latanisha Carmichael that was handed out to attendees at her June 8, 2002 memorial service.

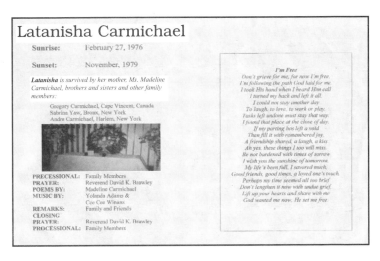

Latanisha Carmichael

Sunrise: February 27, 1976

Sunset: November, 1979

Latanisha is survived by her mother, Ms. Madeline Carmichael, brothers and sisters and other family members:

Gregory Carmichael, Cape Vincent, Canada
Sabrina Yaw, Bronx, New York
Andre Carmichael, Harlem, New York

PRECESSIONAL:	Family Members
PRAYER:	Reverend David K. Brawley
POEMS BY:	Madeline Carmichael
MUSIC BY:	Yolanda Adams & Cee Cee Winans
REMARKS:	Family and Friends
CLOSING PRAYER:	Reverend David K. Brawley
PROCESSIONAL:	Family Members

I'm Free
Don't grieve for me, for now I'm free.
I'm following the path God laid for me.
I took His hand when I heard Him call
I turned my back and left it all.
I could not stay another day
To laugh, to love, to work or play.
Tasks left undone must stay that way.
I found that place at the close of day.
If my parting has left a void
Then fill it with remembered joy.
A friendship shared, a laugh, a kiss
Ah yes, these things I too will miss.
Be not burdened with times of sorrow
I wish you the sunshine of tomorrow.
My life's been full, I savored much,
Good friends, good times, a loved one's touch.
Perhaps my time seemed all too brief
Don't lengthen it now with undue grief.
Lift up your hearts and share with me
God wanted me now, He set me free.

A plaque that was presented to honor Latanisha Carmichael on display at her memorial service.

Andre and Sabrina Carmichael arriving at the memorial service for their sister.

Madeline Carmichael receiving oxygen outside of her Brooklyn home after complaining of chest pains following her arrest for the murder of her young daughter Latanisha.

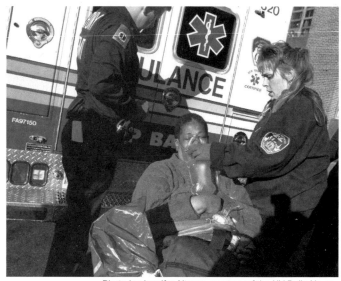

Photo by Jennifer Altman, courtesy of the NY Daily News

The Scene of the Crime: The Park Manor building in Brooklyn where the Carmichaels lived together and where young Latanisha Carmichael was brutally beaten to death by her mother and older brother and her body kept hidden in a trunk inside a bedroom closet.

Photo by Mark Bonifacio, courtesy of the NY Daily News

I looked at them, at their confused faces and I wanted to promise them that nothing like that would ever happen again. But then I thought about my husband, about how angry he was with me for everything that had been discovered about my childhood horrors and I knew that I couldn't make that promise.

"I'm your mother and I've always looked after you, haven't I?" My kids all nodded. "And you know that I will always fight with all my strength to protect you and take care of you, don't you?" My kids all looked at me and nodded again. That seemed to soothe them a little. "Now come on, let's go get some ice cream. I think we've all earned it, don't you?"

On the outside I might have looked calm to my kids, but on the inside I wanted to scream, to scream at Chris for what I felt was throwing my childhood in my face and then what he said to the judge, which I felt just wasn't true. I wanted to scream at the court investigating me because I could never be like my mother and then traumatize my kids by putting them in foster care. And I wanted to scream at Mama to quit lying about what happened.

Miss Dwimoh, the prosecutor, had called to tell me that Mama was now denying that the child inside the trunk was even related to her. Before that, Miss Dwimoh had told me that Mama had admitted that she had "spanked" Latanisha, but didn't know anything else about how she died. Mama's version of what happened seemed like it changed every day. Greg, on the other hand, was sticking to his original story that he had never laid a hand on Latanisha and didn't know "what the hell" I was talking about, that I must be crazy.

Even twenty years later—and even though they were separated by hundreds of miles and different prisons—Mama and

Greg were still terrorizing me. Still forcing me to defend myself. All I could pray for was that the whole nightmare would finally, finally, finally go away.

"I'm so sorry you're having to go through all of this," Andre said when he called a few days later to see how I was.

Andre knew that Chris had moved out, but I hadn't told him a single detail about the family court hearing. I could not bring myself to let Andre think, for even one second, that there might have been even one speck of truth in what Chris had said about me.

"I wish I could help make things easier on you," Andre said.

"Oh Andre, just talking to someone who's not judging me helps me. Sometimes I feel like I'm losing my sanity. And you know what? If one more reporter called me, and if I hadn't gotten my phone number changed and unlisted, I swear I probably would have gone crazy by now."

The newspapers and television shows all made Mama into a monster. Someone from the district attorney's office even said that what the police discovered about our family was like something straight out of a Stephen King novel.

Still, what people were told after everything came out was only one small slice in our lives. Even though there was nothing in the media I could dispute—most of the reporters got their basic facts straight—I couldn't help feeling as if all of them were writing about just a tiny part of what happened to my family, as if they were looking at a huge marble statue and then describing only the statue's big toe.

There was a long pause. "Well, that's kind of one reason I was calling you," Andre said slowly. "But never mind."

"Never mind what?"

"No, it doesn't matter."

"Just tell me, Andre. It can't be any worse than anything else right now."

Andre hemmed and hawed, but then he finally told me that a television news producer had contacted him and asked if he'd be willing to be on their program. He told them he'd only agree to do it if I did, too. But then the producer hadn't known how to get hold of me.

"I don't want you to do anything you don't want to," Andre said. "And you've got enough going on right now."

I could tell by Andre's voice that he wanted to go on the program, that he wanted to talk about Latanisha. My first instinct was to say no—but then it occurred to me that maybe that was what we both should be doing, talking about our sister. If our whole lives had to be turned upside down, then at least we could focus on the reason for it. Everything we were going through now was for Latanisha's sake—it was what Andre and I had promised each other right before we walked into the police station. Maybe the best thing both of us could do was try to make sure that no other family ever had to go through the abuse we did.

"Go ahead and call them and tell them okay," I said to him. "And besides," I added, "it's not me they want to talk to, it's you. They're all acting like they found themselves a Harlem version of Sherlock Holmes. Maybe you should show up wearing one of those funny plaid hats and smoking a big curvy pipe."

Andre laughed and then told me he'd talk to me later. It was only after I hung up that I noticed the phone number I'd left on the kitchen counter. It was for Daniel, the therapist recommended to me, along with his address.

I stood there, the kids playing in the living room behind me and right then the immensity of what had happened to my life hit me. My husband had left me and then had filed a suit alleging that I was an unfit mother. In a few months, I most likely would have to walk into a courtroom and tell a jury what Mama and Greg did and then let that jury decide if I was lying or not. And on top of that, Andre wanted me to go on national television and probably be asked one more time why I never opened my mouth for twenty years. If my life didn't fit the definition of crazy at that point, I don't know what did.

Even if disclosing all I was feeling to someone else ended up hurting me later on, even if Mama or Greg's lawyers found out and tried to use it against me, I knew I couldn't go on anymore by myself. I *had* to get help from somewhere, from someone.

The therapist ensured that anything I said to him would be completely confidential. He also told me right off the bat that he already knew a little bit about me from having read about my family in the newspapers. When he said that, I wanted to tell him that what had been written about my family was like having an X-ray taken of your whole body and then getting back a picture of just the tip of your little finger. But I didn't.

"This must be incredibly difficult for you," he said.

He had a gentle face and round wire glasses and his voice was deep and soothing. I don't normally trust people right off, but there was something about him that made me feel safe from the start.

For the next two months, I went to his office at least once a week. He didn't push me when I said I didn't want to talk about Latanisha and he didn't flinch when I told him about my visits to see Mama. It was as if he understood right away why I needed to keep going there.

"What is it that you are waiting for her to say to you?" he asked during one session.

I thought about that carefully, but I didn't have an answer. I suppose there are some things in this life that words just aren't made for. "I can't say," I said.

"You can't say, because you've never really talked about any of this to anyone, have you?" I shook my head. "And your brother, Andre. Has he ever talked about what he would want to hear from your mother?"

I shook my head again. "I think he understands why I go see her, but he says he just can't do it. He's afraid of what he might say to her. Everything is still too raw for him and he's got too much anger now."

"And what about your own anger, Sabrina?"

I didn't want to talk about anger. As far as I knew, I didn't even have any anger inside me. My entire childhood had been filled with anger, with violence and I didn't want any part of it. For me, anger was like one of those bottles with a skull and crossbones on it—poison.

What I wanted to talk to the therapist about most was how to fix things with my husband and what to do to get through the next few months. Ever since my husband told me that what I did was just as bad as what Mama and Greg did and every time I thought about Chris's face when he said those words to me, I felt as if I was falling down a deep, dark well. I wondered, *Is that what the whole world thought of me too? Is that what my kids would think about me when they were old enough to know what had happened? Was this going to haunt me for the rest of my life?*

"Chris hasn't said anything more to me about what Andre and I are doing," I said to Daniel. "But every time he comes by the apartment to see the kids, I can tell he still thinks that I'm to blame for bringing everything down on us all. Sometimes I catch him looking at me when the kids are pulling on me and he thinks I don't notice, but I see the look on his face. It's the same look he had after he first saw the story about Andre and me in the newspaper."

He didn't say anything, just nodded, so I went on.

"I'm not trying to put the blame on my husband. Chris has a lot of genuine reasons to blame me, especially how he found out about everything. So I'm not blaming him for being mad about that. And I understand why he's still upset about how everything went down with the police, too. But some of the things he's said to me lately I feel just aren't true. For example, Chris swears I never once mentioned Andre's name, that I never said one word about having a younger brother. My other brother Greg, the criminal, the one I never wanted to see again as long as I lived, that brother he remembers me talking about just fine. I've done a lot of things I'm sorry for, but hiding Andre's existence from him was not one of my sins."

The therapist sat across from the sofa in a leather chair, the tips of his fingers together in front of his face. Hadn't I told him during another session, he asked, that Chris had never once asked me about any of my scars? And hadn't I also told him that those scars were very prominent and all over my body?

I nodded, even though I didn't know where he was going with it.

"Your body wasn't a secret, was it, Sabrina? It was right there for your husband to see?"

"Yes, but—"

"Have you ever thought that Chris has the guilt of this on him too, that blaming you is his way of dealing with the fact that he never tried to find out what kind of life you had growing up?"

I could see how that might make sense for some people, but not about Chris. To me, his horror at what I did—or rather, what I didn't do—was exactly what it seemed. For as long as I'd known him, his entire life had revolved around getting an education, building a respected reputation and then becoming a career professional. And what I had done by going to the police, by revealing such a gruesome secret after so many years, was the same as if I had taken an axe and chopped up everything he'd ever dreamed of. My husband was ashamed to have any association with me. I had become a stigma to him and he wanted to be as far away from me as possible.

"The truth is, I didn't ever *want* to tell him about any of it," I said. I could hear myself defending Chris. "I didn't want him to ask me and I was *glad* that he didn't. All of my past was so dark and ugly and Chris was, he was..."

"Chris was what?"

"*Shining*," I said. "He was the only thing in my life that had ever *shined*." I burst out crying, just sat there sobbing on Daniel's sofa. I told him I wanted to end our session early.

"No, Sabrina." Daniel said it just like a gentle father would have. "You've been running from this your whole life and you're not going to run anymore. It's time to stop now."

I must have known he was right, or else I wouldn't have nodded and stayed—and then kept going back to see him every week after that.

In late May, I told the therapist that Chris had been coming by the apartment more often and that he had even called me a few days earlier to tell me he wanted to work things out between us, that he wanted for us to try to be a family again.

"And how do you feel about that?" Daniel asked. It was one of those questions I was getting used to hearing from him, but it never got easier whenever it came time to answer. I'd gone through my entire life pushing away my feelings about everything, spent years and years just trying to keep moving, trying to keep my head above water.

Part of me knew that Chris and I had never talked again about what he had said to me that day when he walked out and that nothing had been "resolved," as the therapist might have put it. We had also never talked again about how he had claimed in the court documents that I wanted to kill him or myself or our children, things I knew were completely untrue. Never had such thoughts entered my mind. I could not help thinking that if Chris had succeeded in getting custody of our kids, it was very possible he wouldn't have seen any reason to try to get back together.

But the biggest part of me knew that I was going to take him back in a heartbeat, if he'd have me.

"Do you trust him?" Daniel asked.

"I don't know," I answered. "A few weeks ago, he claimed in the court papers that I wanted to kill our kids."

"Do you love him?"

Maybe my feelings were wrong and naive, but I wasn't going to cover up and lie to someone who was trying to help me sort things out. "I'm sorry, but I still do. I still love him. I can't help it."

The therapist gave a little smile. "No one says you have to," he said.

chapter 11

Awful Truths

As the day of Mama and Greg's trial got closer, Sabrina and I spent part of every day together at her apartment. She and Chris were back together. Chris was usually gone during the days, but if I happened to come in the evenings he'd open the door, say something brief and polite like, "Hi, how are you doing?" and then he'd go in the back bedroom until I left to go home again.

Sabrina and I were both having trouble sleeping and eating. I have no idea how badly I must've looked to her, but my sister had dark circles under her eyes and moved so slowly around her apartment that it was like she was underwater. A few times, I brought some food along with me, fried chicken or pizza slices, but when neither of us ever touched it, after a while, I stopped wasting the money.

But it wasn't just the lack of eating and sleeping that was bothering us. We both were also having trouble talking about what was going on inside us to the people we loved most. Sabrina told me that she and Chris had never spoken a single word about what might happen at the trial. Chris was busy with his new teaching job, she said, and she thought he only wanted to focus on their future and not the past.

"The therapist I've been seeing says maybe Chris has the guilt of it on him just like the rest of us, that it's his way of dealing," she said to me one day. "I don't know whether that's true or not. All I do know is, most days I get the feeling that if I said even one thing wrong, he'd walk right out the door again. So I'm just trying to keep my head down, to wait for everything to settle down, for both of us to get past this."

Maybe Sabrina and Chris could do that. I didn't know. But one thing I did know was, no one except the two people in any marriage can ever figure out what's really going on between them—and that's only if they're smart and lucky. Besides, every marriage is different. What some people will put up with, others will walk away from. No one else can say what's right.

I don't know what I would have done, for example, if Bronsetta had told me it was my fault I didn't go searching for my twin sister earlier, if she had blamed me for giving up so soon. Deep down I guess that's because a big part of me felt the same way—that if I had kept on pushing, if I had kept on insisting to Mrs. Lewis and the social workers what I remembered and what got told to me when I was growing up, maybe all of this would have come out a long time ago. Maybe everyone, I thought, has guilt for something they did or didn't do.

And most people must figure out ways to carry that guilt around and still go on with their lives. But having someone you love and trust point out your deepest guilt is a whole different matter. Getting that kind of guilt thrown in your face is like having a big, dry log tossed on a fire that's already burned way too high and way too long.

That was one reason why I sure wasn't going to give any advice to Sabrina. Whether it was better for her to keep her head down or lift it up, whether she should talk things out with Chris or keep quiet and wait for things to pass, that was something between him and her.

But there was another reason, too. The way I saw it, Sabrina had already gotten enough judgment and "advice" heaped on her by other family members to last her a lifetime. Right before she got her phone number changed and unlisted, several of our cousins and two of our aunts, Mama's younger sisters, suddenly called her. Even though Sabrina and I hadn't seen our cousins since we were kids—and the two aunts who called were ones we'd never even met—they said they wanted to meet with us and talk about what was going on. Sabrina told me they were very kind and pleasant on the phone and that they asked if we'd like to come over to our cousins' house in New Jersey for a visit.

On the day they asked us to come over, Sabrina and I went there together. When we arrived at the set time, there was a big party going on.

"Oh my Lord," one of my aunts, a lady I'd never met, said to me when she opened the door. "We haven't seen you since you were a baby, Andre! And just look at you now!" But when she looked at Sabrina, right away her face tightened up. "And you," she said to my sister. "Well, you're all grown up now, too."

The house was crowded with people we didn't know, people we'd never met, and the rap music was blasting so loudly, it shook the floorboards. As Sabrina and I made our way past a long table covered with pot-luck dishes full of chicken, ribs, cornbread and salads, under our feet, over and over, it was thumping *duh-DUNK-uh-DUNK-uh-DUNK-DUNK-DUNK*. Sabrina and I stayed close to each other, she had one hand on my arm, until a door opened; the same door closed behind us and suddenly we were standing in our cousins' kitchen.

All our family members were gathered around us. It was almost as if they'd been waiting for us to get there, ambush-style.

"We had reporters coming here trying to talk with us and they were asking all kinds of private stuff," one cousin said.

"Whatever happened with you and your Mama is your business, Sabrina, but now our family business is all over the news," said another.

"Sabrina, if all of this is true, why have you never said anything about it before? Why are you bringing it up all of the sudden?" someone else asked.

Sabrina and I stood there clinging together while our cousins and aunts hammered us. Mostly, though, it was Sabrina they went after. They kept repeating, if it really happened the way she said it did, then why did she wait until now? If Mama really did cover up the truth for so long, then how come Sabrina wasn't on trial right along with her? Wasn't Sabrina just as guilty of covering it up, too? How could Sabrina look at her own face in the mirror each morning, knowing that her poor Mama was suffering with cancer in jail while Sabrina was free and going about her business as usual?

At first when they started going after my sister, I didn't say anything. Sabrina didn't say anything either. She just stood there with her head bent down, the same way she used to whenever Mama or Greg were picking up a plate or a hammer or a cane and getting ready to crash it down on top of her. It was just like all of those other times too, except that what my cousins and aunts were using on her were words.

As I stood there, I suddenly remembered the nuns at my Catholic school whenever they used to stand in front of a big chalkboard with the words SIN and THE DEVIL written on it. They'd swoosh their arms and then erase the words. *Confession and repentance are the only ways to forgiveness and absolution! If you do not want to burn in hell for all eternity, if you want your sins to be erased, the only way is to repent!*

Every time I heard those nuns say that, I wanted to yell at them, "Tell this to Mama and Greg! Don't tell it to me!" But the more they talked about sin and the devil and burning in hell, the more I'd start thinking that maybe they could see inside my soul, that maybe they knew about the times I let Sabrina get beaten and I just stood there and did nothing to help her, or how deep down in the darkest part of me I was relieved whenever Mama or Greg went after her instead of me.

"Andre?" one of my cousins said. "Why are you so quiet?"

I looked at all of them gathered around Sabrina and me like a pack of wolves. This time I wasn't going to let my sister get beaten up without fighting back for her.

"You all stand there and call yourselves our family," I said. "You stand there complaining that this is all over the news. But where were you all when Sabrina and I were growing up and needed your help? When I was put in foster care and she was, too? If you all were so concerned, you could've found her or me. And you could've asked where my twin was, too. But you didn't do anything. And now you stand here and think you have the right to tell Sabrina to basically shut her mouth and how this is a big embarrassment to the family?" My voice was shaking. "Well, you know what? Sabrina and I don't need a family like you."

I took Sabrina's arm and led her out of that house. All the way home on the train she held my hand and even though she turned her head toward the window, I looked at the reflection and saw tears streaming down her face.

And now Sabrina was sitting across from me in her living room, talking about wanting to keep her head down with Chris and wait for everything to pass. Who was I to tell her to do things any differently?

Inside I also was upset, confused and agitated about the future. "I worry about how Bronsetta's going to cope with everything," I said to her. "Not just whatever gets said in the trial, I mean, but afterwards, too. Are people going to stare at me and figure that I must be just like our mother? Sometimes I already get that feeling, Sabrina. Some people assume that because I got beaten that badly growing up, I obviously must be that kind of abuser with my own kids, too."

Sabrina nodded. "Yeah, I've had that happen, too."

"And I don't know why, but sometimes I get scared that Bronsetta's going to see me differently now, too."

She nodded again. "Chris told me a few days ago that I 'fly off the handle' with the kids. We've been together more than ten years and he never once said anything like that to me before any of this happened. I think that's why he's basically leaving the entire trial up to me, that it's something I have to deal with on my own. He doesn't want any part of it, or for any of it to touch our kids in any way." From the way she talked, it sounded like a bill she had to pay all by herself.

It was strange, but in a lot of ways the same thing was true for me, too. I told Sabrina that it wasn't that my wife didn't care—I knew that she did—it was just that the burden I was carrying inside me was so heavy and so dark, that sometimes it seemed like it scared her. Bronsetta was doing everything she possibly could to get us all ready to move into a new apartment, something both of us thought might happen any week now, and I truly believed that she was afraid that if she talked to me about how I was feeling, maybe I would just break down.

"She knows I'm going through a lot and that it's probably just going to get worse. But this hasn't been easy on her either," I said. "Today, reporters came looking for me, and when I wasn't there, they pigeonholed her instead. Bronsetta didn't have any idea that her name and what she told them was going to end up in the papers."

"Yeah, Chris was pretty upset when my married name got printed. I could tell he was worried that people might connect me to him."

"But as long as Bronsetta and I don't talk about it, it's like we both can keep acting like none of this is affecting our lives at all," I said to my sister understandingly.

Sabrina shook her head slowly. "And in the meantime, life just keeps going on, doesn't it?"

I looked closely at my sister. She had a strange expression on her face, almost like she was carrying another secret.

"What is it?" When she gave me a little smile, I asked her again. "Come on, Sabrina, don't hold out on me now."

"Well," she said, "I wasn't exactly planning on this. But Chris and I are going to have another baby." She was grinning now, and I could tell she was happy. I put my arms around her and hugged her.

* * *

The people at my job were extremely understanding of what I was going through. I was really shocked by how kind everyone was to me. They all knew about what had happened from reading the papers and they gave me extra time off and even allowed me to schedule my work hours so I could spend more time with Sabrina and go to the district attorney's office whenever it was necessary. Whenever Ama Dwimoh or Frank Urzi had information they needed Sabrina or me to explain for them, or a question that couldn't be answered in a few minutes over the phone, they sent a cab or a town car to pick us up and bring us over to their office.

One thing we had learned during one of those visits to the district attorney's office was that there wasn't going to be a jury trial after all. Mama and Greg's attorneys both decided that because of all the bad publicity about Latanisha's case, it would be better to get a trial in front of a judge. Sabrina and I took that disclosure as the lawyers basically saying that after so many newspapers and television stories had appeared, they didn't think they could find twelve people in all of Brooklyn who hadn't already made up their minds that Mama and Greg were both guilty.

But I knew others who were shocked by the case and sometimes I questioned whether Mama and Greg were really guilty of murdering my twin sister.

It was early September 2000 and the trial was only a few weeks away. I thought about that more and more each day. The question ate at me like a big, dark beetle nibbling away at a wet leaf.

It wasn't that I doubted for one second anything that Sabrina had told me or the police or the district attorneys. From day one, her story hadn't changed one single bit. When Ama Dwimoh or Frank Urzi asked her a question she'd already told them, to maybe give extra information or change what she'd already said, she never did. She never once said she remembered if it was summer or winter that day my twin sister died, never once said she remembered a single thing about what had made Mama and Greg start beating on Latanisha. Over and over, no matter how many different ways she got asked, she always said the same thing about what she remembered.

Still, there was a nagging little voice in my head that kept reminding me that people remember things wrong all the time. They might be one hundred percent certain that what they're saying is the truth and that what happened was exactly the way they remember it, but that still doesn't necessarily mean they're right. And what if Sabrina saw everything exactly the way she'd been describing it, the way it stayed inside her head all those years, but everything that happened that day still could be explained a different way? What if it really was an accident? And even worse, what if Mama and Greg really did both panic after Latanisha died and now they were facing twenty-five years to life in prison because of their bad choice to cover it up?

Each night while Bronsetta slept beside me, I played every possibility over in my head. I tried to picture Latanisha's death the way Greg told the detectives it happened, to put myself in their shoes. But the hard part was, to do that I had to imagine myself raising a hand to my daughter or one of my wife's children. That was where I stopped.

I knew there wasn't a single parent on this Earth who hasn't gotten angry at their kids at some point, gotten so frustrated that they've had a hard time controlling themselves. Still, nothing in this world would ever make me hurt one of my children. Whenever they upset me, whenever they get me angry, the first thing I always do is tell them they need to go to their rooms or finish their homework, or anything else that will give me time to calm down. And then, once I've done that, I pick out a punishment for them, something that fits whatever they did wrong. I might take away a privilege, for example, or maybe ask them to make an apology.

But Mama obviously didn't do that with Latanisha. Something got her and Greg red-hot angry with my twin sister that day—and whatever it was, my sister stopped breathing because of it. Sabrina insisted that she saw Mama pushing on Latanisha's chest and breathing into her mouth like she was trying to bring Latanisha back to life and I had no reason to doubt that memory. So I tried to picture it happening that way. I imagined accidentally hurting one of my kids, realizing that my child wasn't breathing, then trying to save her in every way I knew how.

But that's where I got stopped again. Each time I thought about it, I couldn't get any further. Because deep in my soul, I knew one thing for certain. *If I hurt one of my kids accidentally, I would immediately call 911. I would scream for help.*

But maybe Mama didn't call for help, I thought, because she was trained as a nurse in South Carolina. Maybe she thought she could handle the medical emergency on her own and then, just maybe, she panicked when she realized she was wrong. There she is, her three-year-old daughter is dead on the rug in front of her, Sabrina and I are sitting right there watching everything and Mama's brain just can't handle what she just did; can't handle what just happened. What, I thought, if it happened like that?

I flipped on my side, rousing Bronsetta a little. I was glad she didn't wake up and ask me what was wrong.

But if it really did happen like that, if Mama and Greg just went totally crazy because of the terrible accident that just happened, then why did Mama separate Sabrina and me all our lives? Why couldn't we ever talk to each other alone, why did we get sent to separate schools? And when I was put into foster care with Mrs. Lewis, why did Mama tell me that Sabrina washed her hands of me and then tell Sabrina I'd washed my hands of her?

I looked at it from every possible way I could think of. But that was when I finally realized that there was no possible way it could have happened the way Mama and Greg obviously were going to say it did when they got to court.

A lot of people who had been reading about my family in the newspapers probably wouldn't have believed it, but I didn't hate my mother. And I sure never set out thinking about putting her in jail. Could any son want that? Could any man want his own mother to go through that? But I had a twin sister I slept with in the same crib. And all my life I had other memories I couldn't explain, but then everyone told me I made her up.

If I didn't do anything now—if I let myself be talked into believing the story Mama and Greg were giving their lawyers, or let myself get intimidated about telling my own memories—it would be like saying that everything they did was okay.

You want to kill my sister? Okay.

You want to hide her body in your bedroom? Okay.

You want to put air fresheners in the closet so no one knows? Okay.

You want to beat your other children so they don't talk to each other about what really happened? Okay.

You want the truth to never come out? Okay.

I laid there in bed and I felt my fists balling up, my jaw clenching.

It wasn't okay. And it never was going to be okay.

chapter 12

Presumed Innocent

The trial was about to begin. Ama Dwimoh, Frank Urzi and a third prosecutor, Barry Schreiber, were planning to put on a lot of brutal evidence and grim testimony that they said would be extremely upsetting for us. They didn't think it would be best for us to hear it.

"There is no need to put yourselves through all that," Ama sympathetically said to us one day in her office. "What you and Sabrina are going through is already extremely difficult. There is no reason to create more pain than there already is."

"What kind of evidence are you talking about?" I asked.

She hesitated. It seemed to me that Ama wasn't sure how to answer, to spare us from being hurt any further. She was choosing her words carefully. She started describing the way juries or judges reach a decision in a case like ours.

Whenever evidence is presented in court, she said the jury—or the judge, in our case—has an obligation to assume from the very start that the defendants are not guilty of whatever crime of which they've been accused. That was true in all cases. Everyone, she went on, no matter what crimes they're accused of, is presumed innocent until they're proven guilty. She told us that Mama and Greg had no obligation to prove that they were innocent—it was the prosecution's job to prove that they were guilty beyond reasonable doubt.

Ama explained what reasonable doubt meant. The judge in our case might be inclined to believe that Mama and Greg beat Latanisha to death and then stuffed her in a trunk to hide their crime. The judge also might be inclined to believe Sabrina's memory of what happened when she was nine years old, along with how we got beat over the years so the truth never came out. But that wouldn't necessarily be enough to *prove* to the judge what Mama and Greg did beyond a reasonable doubt. If Mama and Greg's lawyers showed their clients' lack of guilt and convinced the judge that everything was a terrible accident, it was possible the judge might decide that they weren't guilty of the murder. It was possible Mama and Greg could be found guilty of a lesser charge, like just covering up Latanisha's death.

Ama said that she and the other prosecutors were going to provide other kinds of evidence and testimony to the judge. She said that a medical expert would be testifying about what happened to our sister. But Sabrina and I already knew that there might be problems with that, too. The district attorney's office had told reporters earlier that the medical examiner had called Latanisha's death a "homicide," even though the exact cause of death was listed as "unknown." Mama and Greg's lawyers had already told reporters that there was no solid evidence.

At least, those on the defense side were saying there was not enough evidence to convict Mama and Greg of murder.

Sabrina and I didn't have the courage to ask Ama if she planned on using a shock tactic by bringing Latanisha's body into court—the thought of it was almost too horrible to imagine. However, our disturbing thoughts on the fact that Ama was talking about providing "evidence" was enough to make both Sabrina and me sit there in her office without saying another word. It was obvious that Ama was in charge of how the prosecutors were going to present the case to the judge, and her strength and determination made Sabrina and me believe that she was the strong type of person who wouldn't leave even one stone unturned in revealing the truth. Besides, who were we to question her?

Ama told us that the only time the prosecutors wanted us to be in the courtroom was when Sabrina or I testified, and on the day when the final verdict was reached. For the rest of the trial, she said she would prefer it if each day during the testimony we could wait in her office, which was located in a tall office building just a few blocks away from the courthouse. Ama told us she'd make certain we got regular updates about what was going on inside the courtroom where the trial was being held. If either of us had any questions or concerns, she said, someone from her office would be available to us at all times.

* * *

The trial was scheduled to start on Monday October 10,

2000 in State Supreme Court in Brooklyn. Mama and Greg had both waived the right to a jury trial and decided to let Judge Anne Feldman hear all the evidence and then make whatever judgment she thought was fitting.

Ama was very sensitive to our fearful feelings and told Sabrina and me that when our time came to testify, we should talk to the judge like we were talking to someone who was extremely concerned about us, someone who wanted to understand what we had gone through.

"Many of the questions will be the same ones Mr. Urzi and I have already asked you," she said. "Even though it might seem as though you have already told these things numerous times before, try to answer each question as if you were being asked it for the first time."

Ama and Frank Urzi said that they planned for us to testify during the first two days of the trial. But they had no way of predicting how many days the trial would last, and they also couldn't say for sure if we might have to testify a second time. That's why they asked both of us to remain available at all times until everything was over. But what they didn't want us to do was come into the courtroom when other testimony was being given.

When I heard Ama give us that advice, I thought back to how Danny D'Alessandro, the first detective I ever talked to about my twin, refused to allow me to go along when he and other members of the Cold Case Squad showed up with a search warrant at Mama's apartment. At the time, I felt he had no right to prevent me from going along with them, to see with my own eyes if anything really was hidden in Mama's closet. Danny told me that it would be too upsetting if they found what he thought they might find, but I felt it was my twin sister we were talking about, and if I didn't have a right to be there, who did? Still, as soon as Danny said that, I realized the horror of finding Latanisha and stopped pressing him to be there.

But now, suddenly, I was feeling the same way all over again. Even though I knew that Ama and Frank Urzi might be right—that everything would be extremely upsetting for Sabrina and me to see and hear in that courtroom—a big part of me still wanted to be there, to look the truth in the face.

There was something else that bothered me, too. What was the reason, I wondered, everyone thought they knew what was best for me? Why was everyone suddenly concerned about my "emotional well-being" and our "state of mind" and all of the other things they brought up? No one in my entire life, except Mrs. Lewis, had ever bothered one bit with my emotional well-being or state of mind when I was growing up. And no one had cared a shred about Sabrina's well-being either, especially when she was getting beaten everyday and trying the only way she knew to let someone know about it, by getting someone to help her and me.

It seemed to me we still weren't being allowed to see and hear the truth for ourselves.

I looked at Ama and then at Frank Urzi. It didn't seem as if they were ordering us to stay away. If Sabrina and I really pushed to be in the courtroom—if we really insisted that we wanted to be there—I thought they might let us. But then I looked at Sabrina. Her hands were folded in her lap and her head was bent low. She had the same scared look on her face as when we were kids and we heard Gregory's keys in the door.

At that moment, I was afraid that Sabrina really couldn't go through the kind of pain Ama was talking about. Maybe there really were some kinds of truth no one should ever look in the face.

"Sabrina, do you mind waiting with me in Ama's office during the trial?" I asked.

She looked up at me and shook her head. "That's fine."

She said it so softly I could barely hear her. That's when I got really worried. Maybe, I thought, Sabrina wasn't as strong as I'd always made her out to be. I really didn't know if she was going to be able to face Mama and Greg on the witness stand, or if her courage would break down before she ever got there. I wished I could look within her and see exactly how she was feeling so I would know how to comfort her.

PART 3

Fitting
Judgment

chapter 13

The Mills of Justice

Chris watched me as I dressed carefully that morning, in a suit jacket and matching skirt. He must have seen my hands shaking as I pulled my hair back and pinned it on top of my head, but he didn't say anything. Neither did I. I went into the kitchen and fixed breakfast for the kids and told them all to be good for their father while I was gone. Then I left our apartment and went downstairs to wait for the town car, sent by the district attorney's office. When it pulled up to take me to the courthouse, I saw Andre and his wife inside, holding hands.

As we rode, Andre and I didn't talk much. He asked me if I was okay, and I nodded. Bronsetta had a breakfast muffin on her lap. The odor was so sweet I had to roll down the window a bit so I wouldn't smell it. I couldn't remember the last time I had been able to eat anything.

"We're going to get through this, Sabrina," Andre said. "And after this is over, we're never going to have to deal with these terrible events in our past again. No matter which way things go, it's going to end here."

No matter which way things go. Andre had to know, the same as I did, that there was no guarantee about the outcome of the trial. It was possible we would walk into that courtroom, face Mama and Greg and tell the judge everything that had happened to us—and Mama and Greg still could go free. Even though the judge might be "inclined" to believe the things we testified to, as Miss Dwimoh said, it was possible that there still wouldn't be enough evidence to prove, beyond a reasonable doubt, that Greg and my mother killed Latanisha.

Andre and I had both been living with that fact for months now. But now the reality of it—the very real possibility it could happen—made my stomach feel as though it was tied in knots. If Mama and Greg's lawyers were able to convince the judge that Latanisha's death had been an accident, that I was lying about what I saw or else just plain out mistaken about what happened to our sister, then Andre would be wrong about this being the end of everything. If that happened, it would only be the beginning.

The beginning of something too horrible to even think about.

I did not tell Andre that just a few days earlier I had gone up one more time to the prison to see Mama. She called me and said she needed new shoes, then asked if I could bring her some. We only talked for a few minutes—both of us avoided saying a word about the trial—and before I left, I gave her a pair of black shoes. She told me what a wonderful daughter I was, how God had blessed her.

* * *

The day of the trial finally arrived. Ama Dwimoh, Frank Urzi and Barry Schreiber, the Deputy District Attorney with the Homicide Bureau, were already there when we arrived at the courthouse.

We all stood outside the courtroom waiting for the trial to begin. "How are you holding up?" Miss Dwimoh asked us.

Andre tried to say something upbeat, probably to lighten the stress a little bit.

"I guess I'd have to say that I've had better days," he said, giving a weak smile, "but I've also had ones that were a lot worse."

I didn't want to tell her the truth that I was so nervous I was afraid I was going to be sick. I've heard some people say that, at traumatic times in their lives, they were so scared it felt as if their hearts were in their throats. Until that moment I never really knew what they meant. I never believed a person could really feel that way. Now I did.

"Hanging in there," I answered softly.

Miss Dwimoh gave me a little smile and patted my arm. "Good," she said.

At that same moment we both heard voices and turned. Two of my mother's younger relatives were standing a few feet away. I felt they were both glaring at me, scowling at me with their lips pursed, as if I were a criminal. Miss Dwimoh had already told me that investigators had interviewed various members of Mama's family to find out what they knew about Latanisha, so I figured they must have talked to these relatives, too. But I didn't know if the two women were going to be testifying or not.

Miss Dwimoh glanced at them, and then looked back at me. "Don't let them intimidate you," she said. "Just focus on going in there and telling the truth of what you remember. They have no bearing in this case."

"Are they going to be witnesses?"

She shook her head. "Come on," she said, jerking her head in the direction of the courtroom door. "Why don't we go inside now."

For the last several weeks I had been preparing myself for this moment, when I would walk into the courtroom and have to see Gregory and Mama together. I couldn't remember how many years since I'd last seen my older brother, and in truth, I didn't even want to remember when it had been. Every memory I had of him was filled with something painful, something violent and awful; and just the thought of seeing him again made me feel physically ill. What would he do when he saw me? How would "Frog Eyes" look at me while I told the judge what I had come there to say? Worse, what if I told the judge the truth, but she didn't believe me and then Mama and Greg were found not guilty of Latanisha's murder? An even scarier thought, what would Gregory do to me then, especially if he was getting out of jail soon for his robbery conviction?

But it wasn't just Greg who terrified me. It was Mama, too. In prison, it was different; we talked about anything except what had put her behind bars, anything except what Andre and I had done by contacting the police, anything, I suppose, except what really mattered. Somehow, for eleven months Mama had managed to avoid ever bringing up the subject of Latanisha, as if my little sister had never even existed. And I had let her avoid it. Just as I had done with Chris all those years, I still had been trying to hold the past as far away from me as I could, and I had done that by being silent. Something inside me – something I couldn't wrap my conscious thoughts around – had been looking at Mama in prison and inwardly saying, *If she brings it up on her own I will give her whatever she needs of me, even my forgiveness, but if she doesn't say a word we will pretend it never happened.*

But going into the courtroom wasn't like going into the prison. Now I would have to get on the witness stand and face her, and Mama was going to have to listen to me say what I had never said to her before I was going to call her a murderer and child abuser. What I had seen and heard the night Latanisha disappeared. I was going to reveal everything she had tried so long and hard to hide forever. All of her life, Mama had told us over and over that it wasn't anyone's concern what our family did, that all of them should just "mind their own business." But now here Andre and I were, ready to tell the whole world her business. And it was Mama who was forcing me to do it, too. If she and Greg had been willing to admit what they had done, even to their lawyers; if they hadn't denied what really had happened to our sister right up to the end, I wouldn't have had to be here today.

Miss Dwimoh had already told me that Mama and Greg's lawyers were going to do their best to "discredit" me, to make it my word against theirs. That, too, made my heartbeat rise frantically. I felt as if I was walking into the lion's den. Mama might have been sweet to me while she was locked up in prison and while I was bringing her snacks, hard candies, stationery and stamps, and whatever else she needed. But once the trial began, I knew she would do anything to save herself. I felt that in my bones. Maybe Mama wouldn't be the one tearing me apart—her lawyer would do that for her—but I didn't have one speck of doubt that as soon as the judge appeared in court, as soon as the trial got underway, Mama would fight for her life.

Even if that meant taking me down, ripping me to shreds in the process.

"Ready?" Miss Dwimoh asked with her hand on the courtroom door.

I lowered my head, took a deep breath, and then nodded.

The room was much smaller than I had imagined it. Still, it was laid out much like courtroom scenes in any number of television shows I've seen over the years; the judge's bench at the front, two tables for the attorneys and prosecutors on both sides of the aisle, and chairs for spectators lined up in the back.

I looked around the courtroom. I recognized a cousin, whom I hadn't seen since we all lived in the same apartment building. She was sitting on the other side of the courtroom, a few rows behind Mama and Greg's lawyers, and beside her were my two female relatives. They all turned at the same time and glared at me. Then they began whispering among themselves as I walked to the row where Andre and Bronsetta were and sat down. Looking around I saw the female relatives near a woman holding a small child on her lap, although at the time I didn't know who they were. Later, I found out it was Gregory's ex-girlfriend, who was the mother of their daughter. The child was Greg's one-year-old grandson.

I also recognized Detective Daniel D'Alessandro, along with another detective from the Cold Case Squad. The two detectives were sitting in front of us in the row behind the prosecutors. They both glanced at Andre and me, gave us a little nod and tight smile, as if they both knew how hard this was on us and were trying to give Andre and me a bit of encouragement.

In the back of the room, several reporters from major newspapers and syndicates had notepads on their laps. I saw them look attentively when Mama was brought into court in her wheelchair. She was pushed next to the table where her lawyer, Joshua Horowitz, was sitting. Mama wore a summer dress I had sent her, along with a sweater and the black shoes I had taken to her a few days earlier. I saw her look at Andre and then me. Then she leaned over and whispered something in her lawyer's ear.

Soon, Greg, wearing a long-sleeved shirt and slacks, was led in. I had expected that he would be in handcuffs, but he was carrying a Koran instead. I had heard that he had become a Muslim while in prison. He sat down next to his lawyer, Jeff Adler, slouched in his chair and looked down at the table, the Koran in front of him.

From where Andre, Bronsetta and I were sitting, I could see the deep creases along the side of his face and pouches under his eyes. In two years he would be forty, but to me he looked a decade older. I realized then that I did not know this man, that I had never known him. He had never been a brother to me. All of my life, he had been the person who tormented, tortured and battered me all the time I was growing up. He had been the enemy then, and he was the enemy now.

Andre, Bronsetta and I sat silently, none of us saying a word. We were too nervous to speak. We waited anxiously for the trial to start. Finally, Judge Anne Feldman entered the courtroom, sat down at the bench in front of a large American flag and called the proceedings to order. Suddenly, the air inside the room felt heavy and scarce, as if we'd all just been vacuum-packed. I don't know if I was the only one who felt it, but to me it seemed as if everyone in the room sat up just a little more, as if everyone realized that Latanisha's trunk might have been discovered a year ago, but this was where the real lid of truth would be opened.

I had expected that Ama Dwimoh would present the prosecution's opening statements, but it was Barry Schreiber who stood up and began the case. He spoke in a deep, resonant voice, which occasionally rose for emphasis.

"At the outset, since Your Honor will serve in this particular case not only as the judge of the law, but the finder of fact in both of these cases, I respectfully beg the court's indulgence and respectfully ask that you bear with me as I take some time to try and tell you what it is that we intend to prove and the context in which we intend to prove it.

"If Your Honor wouldn't mind, my intention is basically to provide an opening that talks about both defendants' actions, although I am understanding of the fact that not all the evidence is admissible against each defendant, and I will try and draw that distinction, although I know that Your Honor will clearly do so as the finder of the fact.

"For the next few days, Your Honor, it is our hope to take a journey to go through time, as basically we go back and turn back the clock almost twenty-five years to February 1976. Our journey will take us, among other places, to their Apartment 4D and to Apartment 4A, both apartments in which the two defendants, Madeline Carmichael and her oldest son Gregory Carmichael lived. During the course of our journey we hope also to discuss, and you will hear about, Madeline Carmichael's other children, also those who are Gregory Carmichael's siblings.

"During the trip I think you will see, Your Honor, that a bizarre and tragic tale will unfold as we relive the memory and the horror of the violent death of one of those children in 1979, when then three-year-old Latanisha Carmichael, Madeline Carmichael's youngest daughter, Gregory Carmichael's youngest sister, was brutally killed, beaten to death by both of them, a mother and older brother, stashed in a trunk and then stashed away in closets at both of the locations that I mentioned to you. And they were there for more than twenty years until her small skeletized body was found and finally discovered in a bedroom closet in the Rockaway Parkway address on November 5, 1999. And that was the apartment that Madeline Carmichael was still living in.

"The events underlying this tragic murder will be brought to life through the eyes of a child. The testimony of Sabrina Carmichael, the oldest daughter of Madeline Carmichael and sister of Gregory Carmichael, who is now thirty years old, but who at the time she witnessed her younger sister being beaten to death by both of these defendants was eight years old, and I suggest Your Honor will see and understand that it is the memory of that eight-year-old that she calls upon when she testifies before you.

"You will also, Your Honor, hear from Andre Carmichael, that's the dead twin's brother. You will hear that he was the twin brother of Latanisha Carmichael and despite the fact that he has absolutely no recollection regarding the existence of this twin and therefore has no information to provide relative to her death, you will see how he nonetheless, in a way that you will learn, kept her memory alive and basically got Sabrina Carmichael to come forward after twenty years of silence, eventually resulting in the discovery of Latanisha's remains in that closet.

"You will also see and hear from relatives and friends of the defendants, representatives from various agencies, Social Security, Board of Education, HRA, Bureau of Statistics, as well as hear from detectives, and you will get an opportunity hopefully to see exhibits, if you decide to allow them into evidence, and photos.

"All of this, Your Honor, we trust, that when you put it together, the testimony and the exhibits Your Honor allows into evidence, will help you to know and understand that there was once a baby girl named Latanisha born on February 27th, 1976, born to Madeline Carmichael, when she was a twin, who sometime in 1979, after these defendants beat her to death, basically disappeared from the face of the Earth."

Mr. Schreiber had found his stride. It continued.

"You will hear, learn this homicide occurred at the East 96th Street address; that both the defendants lived with the balance of the family and that after this death, Latanisha's lifeless body was stashed away in that trunk just like useless clothes placed in a closet in that apartment and then was subsequently moved to a second apartment.

"You will also come to see how this horrible crime, its concealment and its cover-up became a deep, dark, family secret; that Sabrina kept quiet until October of 1999, for almost twenty years, which I believe Your Honor will see is natural when an eight-year-old sees her youngest sister beaten by her mother and older brother.

"You will also learn how, during those twenty years as Latanisha laid entombed in the closet, the defendants covered up this horrible taking of that young life. By telling others that the infant was either down south in a home, in foster care or by ignoring requests regarding the child and how they made HRA, insurance companies, child service agencies unwitting partners in perpetuating the hoax that Latanisha was still alive and living at home as those agencies accepted representations by one or other of the defendants and this cover up continued up to and including the discovery of Latanisha's remains on November 5th, 1999, and even continued as the police questioned Gregory Carmichael on November 6th and 7th of 1999.

"You will be privy to how and why this bizarre and unthinkable murder finally came to life after twenty years that Sabrina Carmichael came forward, spoke to the police and how, as a result, Latanisha's badly decomposed skeleton of a body was discovered in the trunk when the police executed a judicially issued search warrant.

"I suggest, Your Honor, you will see this isn't a 'who done

it.' Madeline Carmichael and Gregory Carmichael are the two people responsible for Latanisha's death, and I think you will also see, Your Honor, that this is not a 'what happened.' As you will see, they basically beat this poor child. You will hear an explanation offered by the defendant Gregory Carmichael in the statement that he made, but I suggest to you, you will still be scratching your head and asking yourself how could this be, how could this child have died, what excuse or justification could there possibly have been."

Mr. Schreiber stepped back. He took a breath, then went on.

"The evidence will recount the actions of the defendant on that fateful day in 1979 as Latanisha took her final breath and then will go through the time that they disposed of this body and covered it up for that full twenty years. And ultimately it was resolved only because of two people, Your Honor. It was resolved because of Andre Carmichael, who prodded Sabrina Carmichael, and because Sabrina Carmichael finally came forward to provide the evidence necessary to solve the case.

"As I told you at the beginning, Your Honor, the trip will take us back to February 27th, 1976 at Brooklyn Jewish Hospital, now known as Interfaith, where the defendant Madeline Carmichael, then thirty-seven years of age, gave birth to two healthy twins. The boy was named Andre and the girl was named Latanisha. The defendant had two other children at the time, Sabrina, who was then aged five, and the defendant Gregory Carmichael who was thirteen, going on fourteen. Relatives saw the twins potty trained when the family lived at a St. John's address. Friends saw the twins at the time they approached three years of age when the Carmichaels lived in Brooklyn. That takes us to 1979 when the two defendants, Sabrina Carmichael and the twins, Andre and Latanisha Carmichael, were living at Apartment 4D in Brooklyn. There was no father living in the home and you will come to learn that the defendant Gregory Carmichael assumed the parental role, occasionally disciplining the children and often at the behest of Madeline Carmichael.

"You will hear also from the defendant's own statement, and I refer to Gregory Carmichael, where he talked about occasionally disciplining his younger siblings. You will even hear that in a meeting that was attended once Andre Carmichael was placed in foster care, that the defendant Gregory Carmichael referred to Madeline Carmichael as his wife, and in statements made at the time of Madeline Carmichael's arrest she basically referred to the defendant as someone who had saved her, her savior, such was that, the strange relationship that existed between the two of them.

"At any rate, one day in 1979 – and Sabrina cannot with specificity, Your Honor, place the date or particularly the time, although other evidence later recovered would help narrow down the time frame for Your Honor – one day in 1979 while the family was at the East 96th Street address, Madeline Carmichael, who was then forty years of age, in front of Sabrina Carmichael, who was then eight, and Andre, who was then three, both defendants beat a screaming and crying Latanisha with their hands, and you will hear they beat her until such time as she fell backwards unconscious.

"You will see photos of the defendants as they looked then, to get an appreciation of the two people that beat that little child."

Mr. Schreiber paused and then went on in that deep voice which held attention.

"Nothing was said by the defendants and Sabrina has no idea why the beating took place, although, as I suggested, Your Honor, relative to the defendant Gregory Carmichael in statements he gave to the police he did pose a reason to why that happened.

"But after the efforts by both defendants to revive the child either by pumping on its chest or breathing into its mouth failed, they then took the diaper-clad infant Latanisha and took her lifeless body and put it into a plastic bag, put it into a dark-colored trunk with metal edges, which had been emptied by the defendant Madeline Carmichael, put moth balls in the trunk and then put the trunk in the closet. As I told you, Andre Carmichael, while there at the time, has no memory of his sister much less a memory of her death. These events are recounted by Sabrina."

Mr. Schreiber was in no hurry to cut short the opportunity to build the prosecution's case. "Shortly afterwards, in March 1980, the family moved to Rockaway Parkway and the defendants moved the trunk to their new apartment and put it in a closet there. And you will hear Gregory Carmichael's statements admitting to that fact. But Latanisha Carmichael would never be seen or heard from again after that day in 1979 when she was placed in that trunk.

"Relatives and family members would see Andre and Sabrina and Gregory in 1980, but no Latanisha. When relatives or friends would ask the defendants about the whereabouts, they were told she was in a home or foster care or ignored or put off, but Latanisha's Social Security card issued at birth was never used. The Board of Education had absolutely no record of her. She was never enrolled in any school. A bank book was opened by the defendant Madeline Carmichael in 1980 in trust for her children; those children being Gregory, Andre and Sabrina, not Latanisha. All of the other family members, including Sabrina, Andre and the two defendants, were baptized in 1981, but not Latanisha. And the search of the defendant's apartment, and in this case Madeline Carmichael's apartment in Rockaway Parkway after the remains were discovered, revealed photographs of many members of the family, including Andre, Gregory, Madeline, but none of Latanisha. She had disappeared for all practical purposes, with only the defendants and Sabrina knowing where she was.

"Sabrina and Andre continued to live with the two defendants long after Latanisha's death. Sabrina never told anyone about the murder, never questioned either defendant about it and was, as a matter of fact, abused and beaten when she approached the closet that served as Latanisha's tomb.

"In the years that followed Latanisha's murder, Andre was also abused. He remembers one particular defining event when he was eight years old, five years after Latanisha died, he was being baby sat by an aunt who asked him how his sister was, and he told her Sabrina's fine. And she said 'I don't mean Sabrina. I haven't seen your twin in a number of years.'

"Well, as I suggested, Your Honor, Andre didn't know exactly what she was talking about but waited until his mother got home that night and posed to her for the very first time when he was eight years old, 'do I have a twin?' His answer came in the form of a beating that Madeline Carmichael told

Gregory Carmichael to administer to him. He would never ask Madeline Carmichael again for another five years about that twin and never would ask Gregory about it.

"In order to satisfy HRA of Latanisha's continued existence and continue the flow of public assistance, Madeline Carmichael copied phony Board of Education records and said that Latanisha was attending the same school as Sabrina. That was a lie. It worked until 1990, until HRA checked and found out there was no Latanisha in school. They wrote a letter to defendant Madeline Carmichael who then wrote back saying, well, take her off the family list, she's moved out.

"You will also hear how Latanisha continued to be listed up until that time as a member of the household for purposes of child services and then you will also hear how long after the victim had died, Your Honor." Mr. Schreiber leaned toward the judge, his eyes asking for understanding. "You will hear how basically the defendants continued to cover this up, not only by what they told relatives and friends, but clearly there was no death certificate on record, as there could not be, and that the defendant Madeline Carmichael actually continued paying premiums on a life insurance policy issued in the name of Latanisha. She had taken out life insurance policies at their birth for all the children, obviously could not just cancel one and couldn't cash in on the death of Latanisha with no death certificate and continued to pay premiums up until 1999, trying to keep this lie alive.

"Latanisha's immunization cards were docketed. You will see that they existed up until a certain time when both the twins were taken, both of them weighing approximately twenty, twenty-one pounds, and then you will see in 1981 how they both weighed forty pounds, how it still shows a visit to the doctor by Latanisha two years after she was buried in that closet. So the outside world was deceived into believing Latanisha was either down south, in foster care, in a home or living at home attending school and getting regular medical care.

"I mention the abuse of the defendants in the two instances I suggested. Both of the children, Sabrina and Andre, wound up in the foster care system, both voluntarily placed there by their mother. Andre was removed from the family home in 1988 and he was removed when he was twelve years old following an incident at school where both defendants came up, accused him of taking money from the home, and Gregory Carmichael beat him in front of school administrators and teachers. Andre would never go back to the family home again. He was removed to foster care, where through nineteen years of age, he stayed with foster parents, went to school, he was in special education classes, and worked.

"During that time he saw the defendants at most twice, as both refused to take any part in his upbringing. While in foster care, Andre continually told his case workers he believed he had a twin sister that he was separated from at birth. He didn't know this. He put together, as he will tell you, from what his aunt had asked him and the way his mother had answered him that he had such a twin, but when Madeline was questioned about it she said: 'No, she's living at home, Latanisha had actually lived with him up until 1988 when he was removed from foster care.' Sort of a sick truth to that, Judge, because obviously the body was there and only feet away from Andre and he just didn't know it.

"It was shortly after Andre entered foster care that he would, at age thirteen, for the second and last time, approach his mother and ask about his twin sister. It was on his birthday. It was only one of two times that he saw his mother during the entire time in foster care. And he once again asked her, do I or don't I have a twin sister? This time she said, well, there is a baby who looked like you and talked like you and played like you, but I'll tell you when you are older. He would never ask her again. And, as a matter of fact, would not see her for another ten years after that.

"Sabrina, in the years following Latanisha's murder, while living at home, continued her silence, never told anyone about this horrible crime. She had continued attending school, became pregnant at age fifteen, had a child, was temporarily placed in foster care, signed in by her mother as she would three years later sign Andre in, but Sabrina's absence, unlike Andre's, was short lived.

"Sabrina kept ties with her mother. She even named that first child after her mother, naming the baby Madeline. She stayed with her mother until the summer of 1987, months before Andre went into foster care, and then she left to set up her own household.

"You will hear from her, she now has six children of her own and is expecting a seventh. However, even after moving out she would keep the secret for twelve more years until October of 1999. She never cut the ties with her mother and you will hear she even speaks to her, writes to her, has seen her while she has been in jail, provided money to her, clothes and toiletries.

"Gregory Carmichael, meanwhile, was never far from home and he stayed and remains the most trusted friend and confidant and advisor of his mother.

"Andre married and he then assumed the parental role of his wife's children and in 1996 had a child of his own named Andrea. And in 1999, when Andrea was three, he decided to seek out his mother because he wanted his daughter to meet her grandmother. He found her rather easily. She was living at the Rockaway Parkway address and then took his child...and while they were there, his mother became visibly upset. The defendant Madeline Carmichael pointed to the three-year old who looks like Andre did at the age of three and said 'don't ever bring that three-year old around here again.'

"One or two visits later with Sabrina on or about October 12th, 1999, Sabrina finally unburdened herself of the secret she had carried for twenty years. She told Andre don't bother with the investigator, your twin sister, my younger sister dead, killed by our mother and our older brother, put in a trunk and then last seen at the Rockaway Parkway address." Mr. Schreiber paused to scan the judge's face. He was good, natural. I hoped he was drawing the judge in. "She even swore Andre to secrecy that day, actually prepared what in effect was a written   contract that Andre would later rip up saying that he would not tell anyone about the secret she had kept for twenty years. As I told you, the ties were never broken between her and her mother during the period. But Andre, after he left, basically ripped it up.

"Andre started reaching out for law enforcement on October 13th, 1999, found himself talking to the Cold Case

Squad. He told the Cold Case Squad that he had information regarding the disappearance and the death of a young child and an appointment was arranged for the next day on October 14th, 1999, in which the Cold Case Squad arranged to pick up both Sabrina and Andre at Sabrina's address and take them down to the Fiftieth precinct to discuss this matter.

"Sabrina had meanwhile independently decided, having unburdened herself with this secret, finally that she was going to the police. So both of them went on that October 14th date. At that point, Andre told the police what his sister had told him regarding the defendants' involvement in the death of the child and the concealment and cover up. And Sabrina told them all about what she had seen on that fateful day in 1979 and told them additionally that she remembered that in front of the closet, that she had last seen baby Latanisha put in a trunk, that there was now a wardrobe closet in front of it.

"Also, I said despite the fact that she was torn by the fear and the horror and the mixed loyalty, she finally cooperated and finally unburdened herself and told all. Even so, as suggested, that relationship with her mother exists to this day.

"After that, Your Honor, the Cold Case Squad found these revelations bizarre, even for them. But eventually Sabrina's coming forward after all these years, I believe you will see, Your Honor, that without her help Latanisha's remains and the story of her murder would still be buried.

"When they heard what she had to say, they didn't run out looking for the remains of Latanisha. They first started investigating to see whether or not there was such a child and, in short order, found out that there was a child born to Madeline Carmichael named Latanisha in 1976. She would have been twenty-five this February. And now, after they checked that out and had become more of a believer, they then went to the District Attorney's Office with a view towards getting an application for a search warrant for the Rockaway Parkway address after they confirmed that Madeline Carmichael still lived at that address.

"Judge Knipel, Lawrence Knipel, authorized the issuance of a search warrant for the apartment on November 5th, 1999. When a team of detectives knocked on the door and the defendant Madeline Carmichael living at the apartment asked what they wanted, they said they were looking for a lost child. She then said, 'I have two grown children, Sabrina and Gregory.' And they said, well, the search warrant is to look for Latanisha, and she replied, she's a grown woman, twenty-three years old, I haven't seen her in years."

The courtroom was pin-drop quiet, as if all knew the horror awaiting. "The search then continued. Madeline Carmichael tried to stop them from executing the warrant, claiming that she had pee-pee pads laying in the next room for which she was embarrassed. She was escorted into the living room, would later fall to the ground and was taken to Kings County Hospital where she was later medically cleared the following morning and then taken to the sixty-seventh precinct.

"The police searched on at 8:20 p.m. They discovered that there was a large wardrobe closet right in front of the other closet, the bedroom closet, just as Sabrina had said. You will hear in detail, Your Honor, about the opening of that closet, the documenting and photographing of what was found, but suffice it to say that at 10:20 p.m., at the end of the search, inside a plastic bag was a blue trunk with metal edges, this just as Sabrina had described. Inside were several newspapers, the most recent one being November 4th, 1979. There were moth balls just as Sabrina said, and a series of brown cloth – excuse me, plastic bags, inside which there was a brown cloth and inside that was the skull and skeleton of a small child dressed in a diaper, just as Sabrina had said."

An audible murmur rose as if of pain.

"You will hear how everything was packaged and how the remains were wrapped and about the baking soda and the moth balls and the incense sticks used to help conceal the odors in the closet over those many years.

"Late that night, the defendant, Madeline Carmichael, was charged with murder in the second degree and other charges." Mr. Schreiber administered the zinger. "The skull and the skeleton and remains recovered were taken to the Medical Examiner's Office where they were seen by the examiner, a radiologist and anthropologist, and determined to be the body of a two-to-four-year old child - cause of death being violent homicide; manner of death being homicide. You will hear a medical expert explain how and why these conclusions were reached, conclusions which merely confirmed what Sabrina saw and what she told to Andre and the police and will tell to you.

"The medical examination, in light of the body's deterioration over twenty years, was difficult. The odors were gone, but the defendants' actions concealed that body, but common sense will tell you, Your Honor, I suggest, that the cause and manner of Latanisha's death will prevail. She died just the way Sabrina said so, and I point to Gregory Carmichael's statement as against him in which he confirmed the manner in which she died."

Modern DNA testing offered more evidence, and at this point, Mr. Schreiber called on it. "Recently the United States Armed Forces conducted DNA testing, Mitochondrial DNA, which is DNA inherited solely from the mother. It was used to identify the remains of Jesse James, the Unknown Soldier and Czar Nicholas II. And in this case they took a blood sample of Madeline and compared it to remains of the humerus bone of the body found in the closet and found to be a match, mother and daughter, excluding approximately ninety-nine percent of the population, confirming what I think Your Honor will already know, it was Latanisha's remains that were recovered from the trunk, exactly where Sabrina said they were placed." I looked away, fighting tears.

"Finally, the Cold Case Squad learned that the defendant Gregory Carmichael was up in the Cape Vincent Correctional Facility on an unrelated case and they went up there to speak to him on November 6th, 1999, the day after remains of Latanisha were found in the closet and the morning after Madeline Carmichael was placed under arrest. And he told investigators over the next few days, after first omitting any mention of Latanisha, saying that he hadn't seen her in years and talking about how an enraged Madeline Carmichael beat Latanisha unconscious because the child vomited after being force fed in front of company and how he helped his mother put the body in the trunk, put it in the apartment and helped move the trunk when the family moved."

Mr. Schreiber was taking his time but moving closer. His voice was like a bar tone bell. "I suggest, Your Honor, though in evaluating Gregory Carmichael's statements, and those obviously are admissible against him and Madeline, that they are significant in two major other respects: One, he corroborates Sabrina Carmichael by confirming she was present at the time Latanisha was murdered; and two, he confirms that Latanisha was beaten to death. This wasn't an accidental death, this wasn't a natural death, and the common sense findings of the examiner will let you know that that was so.

"Lastly I suggest, Your Honor, who will have to evaluate both statements introduced against each defendant respectively, that you will see how similar they are in so many respects. Both originally denied that there is a Latanisha. Then they admit but alibi, saying they haven't seen her in years. And then, despite the extraordinary contradiction between them, they then both try and absolve themselves of any blame in the child's death and basically blame the other, pointing fingers.

"I point out, Your Honor, that Gregory Carmichael put the entire blame for striking Latanisha on his mother, denied striking the child himself, although admitting on occasion he disciplined his younger siblings. So, too, Madeline Carmichael with her actions and words volunteered information about her son's violent tendency, how he used to leave bruises on the children's heads, moaning out loud about *how could a mother let a child hurt a child* and also talking about at the same time demonstrating how she wanted to choke Gregory while then talking about how she feared the cops would come one day, how Gregory kept their secret and how it was she who was the devil, she who was ashamed, she who didn't deserve to live.

"I just wanted to spend one brief moment about the charges if I may, Your Honor. I know I have been long and I appreciate the court's indulgence.

"After the grand jury reviewed the evidence, the

defendants were charged with acting in concert with one another for causing Latanisha's death and charged with murder in the second degree on the two theories, intentional and depraved, but concealing her body in the closet which continued until it was discovered on November 5th, 1999, tampering with physical evidence and for in connection with the concealment of her body and the cover-up that followed, whether it's the efforts of each defendant to tell people where Latanisha was to throw them off, or whether it was the affirmative efforts to try and keep her alive. But the bottom line is that I suggest to this court, because there will come a point I believe when the court will have to consider this, that we contend those two charges, the latter ones, are continuing crimes, not barred by the Statute of Limitations, but rather cases which begin the running of the statute when the body was discovered in November of 1999, not when it was put in the closet back in 1979.

"We will supply at the appropriate time for the court, cases which have dealt with this issue of continuing crimes in the area of bail jumping and endangering the welfare of a child, as well as criminal prosecutions under the General Business Law, under the Social Services Law and the zoning ordinances as well. But suffice to say, and now it's at least a part of our argument, that concealment can constitute a continuous crime and the cases that basically held the law should not be held up to ridicule by rewarding a defendant for excellence in successfully and creatively evading its process. And I particularly point out that, in this case, twenty years that child was in the closet and, as Your Honor will hear, each and every day the evidence in that closet deteriorated while it was concealed until it was discovered. These are continuous crimes.

"These cases are truly about the actions of these defendants, Your Honor, not the inaction of an eight-year-old child. Because once Sabrina Carmichael finally came forward, those responsible for the investigation in this case wasted no time. They quickly investigated and solved the crime, bringing the defendants to justice, locating and gathering the evidence, most importantly Latanisha's remains so that she can have a proper burial and that they can have their just reward."

He looked over to see that the newspaper reporters were taking down his words.

"The only verdict I suggest, Your Honor, at the end of this case that will satisfy justice, will be guilty as to each defendant on each count with which they are charged: murder in the second degree, tampering with evidence and hindering prosecution. No lesser count should be considered by this court of murder in the second degree, and certainly not unless the defendants expressly on the record waive the Statute of Limitations.

"I cite now for the court should it become an issue later People v. LeGrand, 61 AD2d 815, a Second Department case and leading case in this area for the authority of the court to exact that waiver should such a request be made by the defendants to consider any lesser included of the murders because as LeGrande said, otherwise it would be a useless gesture because the only homicide the defendants can be convicted of in the absence of a waiver is murder in the second degree.

"Your Honor, back in 1979 when Latanisha Carmichael was three years old and these defendants were twenty years younger and healthier, they showed no sympathy, mercy compassion or sense of decency when they killed that child and unceremoniously buried it in the closet. And now as you are about to decide their fate twenty years later, they are deserving of no sympathy, mercy or compromise from you." His words echoing in the courtroom, Mr. Schreiber took a deep breath, uttered "Thank you," and sat down.

They showed no sign of sympathy, no compassion, no sense of decency when they buried her in a closet, he said. These words echoed in my mind and reassured me that I had finally done the right thing in coming forward.

I looked at the judge's face for a response, but her face was inscrutable; obviously she was too experienced to show emotion. After Mr. Schreiber sat down, she nodded to Joshua Horowitz and Jeff Adler, signaling that it was their turn to speak.

It was now Mr. Horowitz's turn to plead Mama's case. He was experienced and resolute but I felt the prosecutor's opening had been strong. She looked over at Mr. Horowitz, waiting. Time froze.

"May it please the court, Your Honor," he said in a deep sonorous voice. "I represent Madeline Carmichael in these proceedings.

"Your Honor, there are times when events that so shock the human conscience and psyche happen that it becomes hard to fathom just what happened. And there is even less of a desire on the part of anyone to find out exactly what it is that happens.

"There are situations where a person is so vilified, demonized and eventually dehumanized that we lose sight of the idea that it becomes the trier of the fact, the court's responsibility, to determine what exactly happened at the time of the event.

"People are put on trial in court and they are convicted in the court of public opinion for being different, feared, sick, being involved in chilling and frightful incidents. People are indicted with words, but must be convicted with facts and with evidence. That is another thing altogether.

"We are going to prove to you that when the hatred, the shock, the prejudice, all of this story of what happens ten years later, fifteen years later, twenty years later is stripped away from this case as it should be, that we are going to find a horrified, panicked single mother, living with her children in a dangerous environment where the street is just outside of her door, living in fear, who makes a terrible decision. She tries to save the only thing that she has, which is her family." Mr. Horowitz was poised, calm and composed. There were no fireworks, only his compassionate tone and look of unabashed sympathy.

"Unfortunately for Madeline Carmichael, she's not like everyone else. She was married at seventeen, abandoned with children, and has physical and mental ailments. She made some unorthodox decisions. She brought up children and physically abused them. We don't deny it.

"We will not put in a defense to the fact that Madeline Carmichael applied for benefits from the government, from the child welfare, from the SSI, and she got whatever money they gave her for the existence of another child and then spent it on her other children. We will not put in a defense that she led a variety of agencies and people on a wild goose chase and covered up what had happened that day in her apartment.

He shook his head and sighed. "She made a terrible choice, but the choice was not a choice of whether to kill her own child. The choice was to cover up whatever it is that had happened in their apartment, and whatever it is that had happened in the apartment is all that's important in this court. Collecting benefits, putting a child in the closet, lying to administrators of agencies are all not good things, they are also not elements of murder.

"She is the one that lived with her horrible secret and she is the one that lived with it every single day for twenty years, just feet away from her head when she slept. She is the one that lived with it, with the terror, the anxiety, waiting for the day, she said, when detective D' Alessandro was going to come knocking at her door. And you will see that she had not one, not two, not ten, not a hundred chances to discard the evidence if she wanted to finish this case, to bury it once and for all. She could have done it and been home free. She had hundreds if not thousands of chances to finish all of this, and we wouldn't be here taking the remains of the child and putting them somewhere else, anyplace else, other than where they were. She chose not to destroy the evidence, but she, in fact, preserved the evidence in this case, not destroyed it.

"She may be looked at as different. She may be looked at as weird. She may have done things over the course of time which the agencies don't approve of, that she may have taken whatever money they give out to parents who are bringing up children. She may have done these things and she may be guilty of the cover-up. She may be guilty of the story that has been told by the prosecution as far as the cover-up, but she is not guilty of murder.

"This child died in a tragic accident. That tragic accident, while not brought to the attention of authorities immediately and put into the closet for all of that time, takes on an ominous tone. However, the court will see that despite the allegations that two adults are pummeling a young child with fists, that there were no broken bones discovered in the autopsy. The bones were furthermore sent for further examination and there were no prior fractures, no healing fractures, no bones ever broken in this child."

I sat idly by in the chair as if perched on the edge of a cliff. "So as to the event itself, we have a child who is eight years old at the time who has twenty years to allow life to enter into this memory as it does and now recount what she saw, but we don't have medical evidence which is going to corroborate that this child was beaten to death. No snapped neck, no crushed skull, no broken ribs, no broken arms, no breaks at all.

"In fact, the physical evidence, despite the common sense opinions of anybody, there will not be any medical opinions I submit that will render with any degree of medical certainty that this child was beaten to death."

His voice, almost evangelic in its sincerity, slowly continued. "We are not asking that murderers should go free. Murderers should not go free. But we are asking that she should not be convicted because of a cover-up, because of taking money from agencies, because of things like this. A person has a right in a court to be judged on the facts and the evidence of what happened at the time that the crime was allegedly committed, not on nice stories or not nice stories of fifteen years later and things like that. She's guilty of a cover-up, not of murder.

"And when the police did what they did and executed

their search warrant and arrested her, they didn't bring the defendant to her final justice. For that she comes here to the court for justice, for a decision that will reflect what happened on that horrible day in her apartment but, it's not murder.

"Thank you, Your Honor."

Mr. Horowitz sat down and Jeff Adler, Greg's lawyer, stood toward the front aggressively. A reaction rippled though the spectators. "May it please the court, counsel, co-counsel, Mr. Carmichael, Ms. Carmichael.

"It's certainly no surprise, Your Honor, that we heard from Mr. Schreiber, a very emotional, very dramatic opening statement a few minutes ago." He waved his hand behind him in the direction of the prosecutor but kept his eyes on the judge. "I for one cannot match the emotion and the drama that you heard and, quite frankly, don't want to. That's the reason why we are here having, Your Honor, decide this case, not a jury. Because when, as Mr. Horowitz just suggested, Your Honor, when we strip away the drama, the emotion of what happened here, what I suggest to you, you will see from the evidence, Your Honor, is that what's left here is a one witness case against Gregory Carmichael, one witness describing an incident that happened approximately twenty years ago, one witness who was approximately eight years old at the time of this incident, one witness who said absolutely nothing about what she now says that she saw twenty years ago, saying nothing about it for twenty years.

"And so obviously what we are here to do, Your Honor, is to ask you to look closely at this one witness which, when all is said and done, is the only direct evidence that I expect the People to offer that Gregory Carmichael is guilty of murder.

I'm going to ask you to look at that one witness in light of the factors I just pointed out to you. I'm going to ask Your Honor to evaluate her testimony and decide for yourself, is she really pure of heart when she comes in here or is there some bias that she has against Gregory Carmichael? Ask yourself, is her story – does her story make sense as she will describe it? Does it really have a ring of truth to it that this beating happened that she is going to describe? And, of course, compare it to what she has to say in the case to see if it's consistent."

He stepped back, assuming a more relaxed pose for a moment. "Mr. Horowitz got a little bit more into the issue of the examiner than I had planned to right now, but let me point out as Mr. Horowitz suggested that the medical evidence here, and you will hear presumably from Dr. Macajoux who per-formed the autopsy, I suggest to Your Honor that what you will see is inconsistent with what Sabrina Carmichael is going to describe happened inside that apartment. For Mr. Schreiber to stand up here and say to you a few minutes ago that the med-ical examiner found that it was death by homicide or homici-dal violence, Dr. Macajoux to draw the same conclusion to a degree of scientific certainty, I don't see, Your Honor. I suggest that when you hear the evidence you won't see it either. I think that certainly you can draw an assumption and specu-late that it might have been homicidal violence, but we are talking about proof to a medical certainty, scientific certainty. I didn't hear anything compelling and I have yet to see any-thing compelling on that point. And I suggest when all is said and done, when you review the evidence you will too, will have certain very, very strong reservations about that conclusion. But we'll explore that further when the medical examiner, Dr. Macajoux, is here. So when you compare what Sabrina Carmichael has to say to this other evidence, factor in all the things that I just suggested to you. I suggest to you that it's certainly not as clear cut as might seem at first."

He leaned forward, pausing for a good long beat, and his face was now grim, serious. "Now, these prosecutors are taking on the burden, Your Honor, of proving to you, of fully convincing you beyond a reasonable doubt that Gregory Carmichael committed murder inside that apartment. And I suggest to you from the evidence that in that endeavor they will fail; that there are certainly some areas where they will succeed in proving what Mr. Schreiber suggested to you. This business about the cover-up, you know, like Mr. Horowitz, I don't expect there to be any dispute in that Mr. Carmichael assisted his mother in placing the body inside the trunk and putting it inside the closet in order to cover up what had happened inside that apartment. To draw the conclusion from that, therefore he was involved in causing the death of this child, I suggest, Your Honor, was purely speculative. Again, there was no direct evidence of that other than the testimony they will offer from Sabrina Carmichael."

The tension in the room was palpable. Mr. Adler went into the attack mode. I felt he was shooting daggers at Andre and me. "There are certain statements that Gregory Carmichael allegedly made to police. You are familiar to some extent with the circumstances leading up to those statements from the Huntley hearing that we had, but I suggest to Your Honor that it is the third statement, the one that's actually on the audio tape, that was by far the most telling. And to suggest to you exactly what happened inside those interview rooms on the two previous days as well, when you hear Lieutenant Dove participate in the questioning here in the interview, when you hear how he asks questions that run on for paragraphs at a time, essentially putting words in Gregory Carmichael's mouth, you can get an idea that there really is some question about how specific Gregory Carmichael could have been or was in those initial two interviews.

"I suggest to you it's more of a case of Gregory Carmichael giving yeses, uh-huh, that's-what-happened-type of answers, not the type of specificity there that might be suggested from the original two statements. And realistically that's what's to be expected. Just as I suggest to you, common sense says that Sabrina Carmichael at age eight was not really in a position twenty years later now to give an accurate, realistic assessment of what happened inside that apartment."

Like a skilled boxer, he jabbed all the while seeking to inflict heavy damage to the prosecution's case. "I suggest to you Mr. Carmichael had similar difficulty and although Mr. Schreiber will certainly attribute the modus of lying, covering up the murder, he did. That's why the statement came out the way it did. I'm asking Your Honor to draw a different conclusion, not to speculate, which is what I suggest Mr. Schreiber and the prosecution is asking you to do in this regard. So in that area there's also going to be testimony certainly about beatings that my client allegedly gave to his siblings at the request of his mother on different occasions."

When Mr. Adler repeated the word "suggest" for the third time I felt vulnerable, as if assaulted. "I suggest to you the one reference to the beating of Andre over money may well have happened. There was a dispute about the belief that Andre had taken rent money from the apartment, and that led to whatever happened at the schoolyard. Again, Judge, this is maybe eight years or so after the fact. It has absolutely nothing to do with proving how Latanisha was killed inside that apartment or how she died for that matter. For as Mr. Horowitz suggested, we are not even sure from the evidence that we have here that she was killed. There were equally plausible explanations that this child could have died accidentally and that the parent went into cover-up mode as Mr. Horowitz suggested. So, again, Your Honor, the crux of the case, the reason we are really here, is to decide the issue: can the DA support beyond a reasonable doubt their accusation of murder against Gregory Carmichael?"

His voice was sharp. Mr. Adler made his plan of attack clear. "I believe during the half hour or so that Mr. Schreiber addressed you, he spent maybe twenty seconds speaking to you about the actual direct evidence that Gregory Carmichael had anything to do with this. And that's no surprise either, Judge, because there really isn't a whole lot of evidence to back up this accusation. In that area, Your Honor, in the area regarding the accusation that Gregory Carmichael in any way caused this child's death, I suggest to you that the prosecution's evidence is woefully lacking. And you will see it for yourself because on that point Gregory Carmichael is not guilty." Looking purposeful and serious, Judge Feldman now intervened, rapping her gavel.

In both their opening statements, Mama and Greg's lawyers essentially said that there was no conclusive medical evidence that Latanisha had been beaten to death because the autopsy, they said, had been "inconclusive." They both argued that what happened to Latanisha had been a terrible accident – although neither one of them offered an explanation for how they though Latanisha might have died.

Mama's lawyer, Joshua Horowitz, kept saying *she may be guilty of a cover-up but she is not guilty of murder*, and that the murder case against Mama *has been built solely on the family childhood memories of Sabrina, who was only eight years old when it happened.*

As soon as the lawyer said that, Andre moved his hand slowly over his knee, took my hand and squeezed it gently. We both kept looking straight ahead of us, aware of Mama's family suddenly looking at us for a reaction, but it was if Andre had just whispered in my ear. I squeezed his hand back.

When Mr. Horowitz talked about how Mama had been treated since her arrest, about how she had been "demonized" in the media. The way he said that, it was almost as if he was accusing the district attorneys of intentionally spreading lies about Mama and Greg just so the reporters would print them. I wondered if that was how Miss Dwimoh took his comments too, but from where I was sitting I couldn't see her face.

When the shock, the hatred and the prejudice is stripped away from this case, Mr. Horowitz had said, *we are going to find a horrified single mother who makes a terrible decision to cover up an accident.*

And then, Ama Dwimoh called me as her first witness.

chapter 14

A Sister's Testimony

If you have ever looked through the fish-eye lens of a door's peep-hole, you will understand how the courtroom looked to me as I walked toward the witness stand. Maybe I felt so dizzy and disoriented because I hadn't eaten for so long, maybe it was because of how frightened I was, but whatever the cause, suddenly the entire room seemed to recede as if I was seeing it through the wrong end of binoculars. My heart was thudding as I took my seat and held up my hand, which I was certain Mama and Greg both could see was shaking.

I swore to tell the truth, the whole truth, and nothing but the truth, so help me God.

So help me God, I repeated to myself.

Miss Dwimoh stood up and walked close to where I was sitting. She looked attractive and professional, dressed in a dark suit with her long hair pulled back. Behind her there were several legal pads on her desk, but as she approached me her hands were empty. Obviously she knew our story backwards and forwards and didn't need any notes. She stood a little bit off to my left, blocking my view of Greg, but Mama was still in my line of vision. She was sitting very straight, staring right at me. Mama looked completely different than just a few days earlier when I saw her in prison and handed her the shoes; her forehead was furrowed, her eyes were squinted, and her entire expression was scrunched, as if she was daring me to say anything against her.

I forced myself to look away from her and focused only on Miss Dwimoh.

Miss Dwimoh began by gently but firmly asking me to describe what happened that day when I was eight years old, what I had seen. I repeated everything exactly as I had to Andre, to the police, to the prosecutors – except that this time I used another word to describe Mama and Greg.

They were both devils, I said, the word escaping from my mouth before I could even consider whether I wanted to use it or not. But the second I said it, I realized that was how I truly felt about them both. Maybe sitting there on the witness stand and having just sworn to tell the whole truth before God, had done something to me I didn't fully understand. All I knew for certain was that suddenly fear seemed to have left me, and words came flowing out of me like a river that has been dammed up for years and years before it finally gets to run free.

I described how I saw both Mama and Greg standing over Latanisha and beating her that day, and how Latanisha started screaming in pain.

They hit her over and over, and then she fell silent. I'll never forget watching them put her in the garbage bag like she was trash, or how they had put her in the trunk right in front of me and then dragged it into my mother's closet.

Miss Dwimoh asked me if Latanisha's beating that day had been an aberration, if it was something completely different than what normally went on inside our home. I shook my head.

It was the worst episode in a lifetime of abuse, of anything that had come before or after. But it certainly wasn't an aberration. I was beaten terribly as a child by both Mama and Greg, and I still have the physical and emotional scars from it.

Now, Ms. Yaw, do you remember why your baby sister was being beaten?

No, ma'am, I don't.

Do you remember who started the beating?

I remember my mother starting it.

What did you do while this whole thing was going on?

Andre and I sat there in shock.

Who used to hit you more often, Miss Dwimoh asked – *your mother, or Greg?*

Whichever one got to you first.

Miss Dwimoh took a few steps toward me. Instantly from the corner of my eye I saw Greg sitting at the table with his lawyer. He was glaring at me with such hatred, with such fury, that I was certain he would have been capable of wrapping his hands around my throat if given the chance. The anger on his face sent a chill down my spine. I looked back at Miss Dwimoh.

She asked me questions such as why I never told anyone about Latanisha's death, and what happened after we moved from one apartment building to another on Rockaway Parkway. I explained how everything from our old apartment went to the new one—beds, lamps, tables and the trunk that contained my sister's remains. Out of the corner of my eye, I saw the judge write something down.

Now, Sabrina, when you and your family lived at 96th Street, did you ever get any visitors?

None that I can remember, no.

Did you have any friends while in school?

I had friends, yes, but they weren't allowed to visit.

Did any family or relatives ever come by East 96th Street?

No.

What about when you moved to Rockaway Parkway. Did you have friends then?

Yes, I had friends, but they never came to visit.

Miss Dwimoh then began asking me questions about Sonny, if I remembered him and who he was. I answered that he had always been like a stepfather to us, or even more like a father, and that he used to visit our mother at 96th Street and later at the apartment on Rockaway Parkway.

When Sonny would come to your house, what would your mother do?

Maybe I should have said that it was what she wouldn't do–that she never beat us in front of him – but instead I thought about how Mama used to be whenever Sonny was there.

She would be happier and treat us better. She would cook and play music, not that she wouldn't cook all the time. She was always cooking, but she was happier.

After more questions about the closet, and the times Andre got curious and tried to open it, I was surprised when I saw a piece of furniture from Mama's bedroom brought into the courtroom. Miss Dwimoh asked the judge to enter it into evidence, and then she turned to me and asked if I recognized it. Seeing it there, right in front of me, I couldn't help thinking that it was the one object that was the symbol of our family's secret–that nothing else could have represented any better how Latanisha's death had been hidden for all those years.

My answer came out almost as a whisper. *This was the armoire that was placed in front of the closet.*

The judge then asked Mama's lawyer if he had any objection to entering the wardrobe into evidence. Mr. Horowitz said he didn't, but then he said, *I just ask that the witness keep her voice up a little louder.*

Miss Dwimoh went back to the subject of the beatings I said I had received over the years. *Did you ever tell any school teacher or authorities what was going on inside the home?*

Yes, I did.

What, if anything, happened when you told them?

Nothing.

Did you ever tell anyone at the school about what you observed happened to Latanisha, your baby sister?

No, I did not.

When you told people at the school about abuse, what did you tell them?

Well, they would question me about the marks I had on my body, the bruises, black and blue, or welts and scratches. I would tell them that my mother and older brother did it.

Miss Dwimoh then said she wanted me to talk about when I was fourteen years old, and asked me, *What was going on in the home at the time?*

But Mama's lawyer, Mr. Horowitz, objected to the question, telling the judge that whatever happened to me six years after Latanisha died wasn't relevant. Gregory's lawyer, Mr. Adler, said he joined in the objection too, but Miss Dwimoh told the judge that I was going to talk about the circumstances under which I was placed into foster care, and so the judge said she would allow it.

Miss Dwimoh began by asking me if I remembered the first time I went into foster care, and I answered that it had been before I got pregnant with my daughter Madeline, when I was about fifteen.

Now, when baby Madeline was born – and I want to direct your attention to when you were at the hospital – what, if anything, did you tell people at the hospital?

Again, I was questioned how I got the marks on my body, and one of the nurses asked me what happened. I told them that my mother and brother did this, and the next thing I knew I was going home without my child. I was going back to live with my mother and older brother Gregory.

So, to the same home that you described to the people at the hospital?

Yes.

Where did baby Madeline go?

She was placed in foster care.

It meant a great deal to me that Miss Dwimoh took the time to let the judge understand that part of my life, to help me explain, even if I didn't do a very good job of it on the witness stand, how betrayed I had felt for so many years. Looking at Miss Dwimoh standing in front of me, I had the feeling, for the first time in my entire life, that someone was actually standing up for me, that she was letting everyone inside that courtroom know that I had truly tried to get help, to get someone to understand what was going on inside our home.

She then asked more questions about when Andre was placed in foster care, the ten years we didn't see each other after that, and then about the day in 1999 that he had showed up at my apartment trying to find his twin sister. I described how I had finally told him what happened to Latanisha and how she was murdered. Miss Dwimoh also asked me about any contact I had with my mother since her arrest, and I explained that I often sent her clothes and money orders for various amounts.

The Miss Dwimoh asked, *Did your mother ever send you anything?*

Yes.

What kinds of things did she send you?

Cookies, I said, *and bibles for my children.*

Judge Feldman leaned forward and spoke to me. *She sent you cookies?*

I turned to face the judge. *Yes.*

Miss Dwimoh continued. *When was the last time you received a package from her?*

Approximately four weeks ago. Again, cookies and a bible for my son.

Miss Dwimoh stepped toward me, and it seemed to me that her voice became softer. *Ms. Yaw, were you ever planning on telling anybody about what happened to your baby sister?*

I shook my head. *Never.*

If Andre would never have asked you about what happened to Latanisha, would you have told him?

Never.

Ms. Yaw, what made you finally break your silence?

Well, he was determined to know whether he had a sister. And it was time for him to know.

In the last twenty years, Ms. Yaw, have you ever told anyone what happened?

Never, I said. *I never had the ability.*

What do you mean by your statement that you didn't have the ability?

I didn't answer right away. How do you tie up twenty years of silence into a neat little answer, one that would make any sense?

What I mean, I said finally, *is because of my own childhood, what had happened. I lost my daughter to the system, and then there were no family or relatives coming around to be able to tell them. Then, I was scared to tell anyone. That's what I mean.*

Miss Dwimoh thanked me, gave me a reassuring look and sat down. Now it was Mama's lawyer's turn to cross-examine me.

He was a thin, intelligent looking man of medium height, with salt and pepper hair and glasses. As he approached me, I glanced over at Mama, and for a second it felt as if my stomach flipped. She had exactly the same expression she used to get right after she'd tell Greg all the mistakes I had made, or all the disrespect I had given her, and then she'd wait for Greg to start wailing on me. The only difference was, this time it was her lawyer who was going to do the wailing.

Mr. Horowitz greeted me very politely, and then started off by asking me about my relationship with Mama.

Ms. Yaw, during the time that your mother was in prison since she was arrested, you and her got along pretty well. Would you say that's true?

Yes.

She sent your children cookies and a bible and other things, and you sent her back things while she was in jail, too?

Exactly.

You sent her many letters when she was in jail and she answered you with letters, too?

Exactly.

And you, in fact, told her to call you? In your letters, you wrote that she should call any time of the day or night, that you wanted to hear from her as much as possible, that you were concerned about her health. Is that true?

Yes, exactly.

Now, your childhood relationship with your mother wasn't the same as it is now, would that be true?

It's...My voice trailed off for a second or two. *It was much different.*

And in fact, you've testified that you were hit on a number of occasions by your mother. And punished by her as well?

Exactly.

And certainly, when you reached the early teenage years, would you say that your relationship further deteriorated?

I would say so, yes.

He took a step closer to me. *And at a certain point, you wanted to go out with your friends, with boyfriends and things like that, and your mother was very against that, wasn't she?*

Yes, she was. She was very strict.

You would call your mother a strict mother as you were growing up?

Too strict. To an extreme.

By strict, he asked, *would you say that she wanted you to always finish the food that was on your plate?*

Yes.

Was that a particular thing with your mother, that the food not go to waste and that the children finish all the food that's on their plates?

Yes it was.

Now, the food that you mentioned before, when you were growing up, she would cook the food.

Yes.

And you said she used to cook special things when Sonny was coming over, but even when he wasn't? There was always a meal for all of you?

Exactly. We never went to bed hungry.

And your house...In fact, you had people come into your house, you know, from agencies. They always found your house neat. Would that be true?

That's true.

He asked me several more questions about how neat and clean the house had always been, and then about the clothes I wore to school. I told him they had always been clean. Then he changed subjects. He asked me if Mama had been extremely upset when she learned I was pregnant.

Yes, I said.

And that's the point that you went to live with somebody else in foster care?

I was starting to feel upset now; as if my words were all coming out wrong, that only tiny slivers of truth were being told. *That's not the point*, I said. *The point is the house was abusive. That's why I left.*

Mr. Horowitz asked, *You have a daughter named Madeline, don't you?*

Yes.

That's your daughter's name, isn't it?

Yes.

And didn't you name your daughter after your mother?

Yes.

And your mother is the one who delivered your baby?

Right.

And that was in the living room of her house?

Right.

Again, Judge Feldman leaned forward and spoke to me, as if she wasn't certain she had heard correctly. *Yes?*

I turned, met her eyes and nodded. *Yes.*

Occasionally touching the bridge of his nose when he was looking at his notes, Mr. Horowitz continued. *And hadn't you also made several trips to visit your mother since her arrest? Hadn't you sent her gifts like money orders and clothing, and didn't you even give your mother the pair of shoes she is wearing in court today?*

Yes.

I glared at the lawyer and thought: *And Mama is the only one who could have told you that.* Was that, I wondered, what she had been trying to do the whole time – get me to give her money and clothes and food, to write letters to her, just so her lawyer could stand up there in front of the judge and basically say that it was obvious I still loved her and cared about her? Had that been Mama's goal all along–to make the judge figure that if I still loved her, then could Mama be the devil I was describing? Did she want the judge to think: How could it be reasonable to believe that I would still love her, even bring her the very shoes she was wearing that day in court, if Mama really did murder my little sister so brutally right in front of me? Had Mama been trying to manipulate the judge's opinion?

Mr. Horowitz turned slightly, as if he wanted to make sure that the judge could get could get a good look at Mama's shoes – the ones I had brought her. And then he started hammering away some more, asking me questions about what a good mother Mama had been while I was growing up.

Isn't it true that as a child you never went hungry?

Isn't it true that the apartment on Rockaway Parkway was always neat?

Isn't it a fact that the clothes you wore were always clean?

I didn't deny any of those things. They were all true, I said.

* * *

Finally, Mr. Horowitz said that he had no more questions of me at that time. He had a satisfied expression. I felt he believed he had successfully thrown my entire credibility into doubt. Had he? I didn't know the answer to that. And I didn't have time to think about that anymore, either, because as soon as Mr. Horowitz took his seat, Gregory's lawyer, Jeffrey Adler, stood up.

He was younger than Mr. Horowitz, perhaps in his mid-thirties, and I instantly got the sense from his aggressive manner and stance that he was going to be even fiercer on me than Mama's lawyer. His voice reminded me of a growling dog, chained to a post, that can't wait to have at you.

Mr. Adler began by asking me about the day Latanisha died. Did I have any idea how it started? Could I remember any problem that had been going on before the incident? Could I remember anything that anyone said? Did I remember what time of day it happened? Did I recall how many feet away I was from where Latanisha was sitting? To each of his questions, I said that I didn't remember. In fact, I answered that way to practically every question he asked me. It was the truth.

How about your mother – do you recall at all what she was doing inside that room before this started?

I don't remember, no.

How about Gregory? Do you recall at all what he was doing inside this room before you first noticed Madeline start hitting Latanisha?

I don't remember anything.

Was there any food around inside that room at that time?

I don't remember that.

And this happened about twenty years ago, so it's a little bit difficult for you to remember the details. Is that true?

Exactly.

But there was one point where I was able to answer Mr. Adler's questions with certainty, when I could tell him exactly what I remembered. He asked me several questions about where Mama and Greg were standing while they hit my sister that day, and I answered that they were on either side of her, with Tish sitting in the middle. And it was both of them that were hitting her, all over her body.

Can you be sure, as you sit here now–his words came out slow and staccato-like–*whether every time one of them swung, they actually made contact with Latanisha? That every single time they swung they hit her?*

Oh yes, I answered. And then I said it one more time. *Yes.*

Mr. Adler asked me about the child abuse complaints I had made over the years. *Wasn't it true that even though those complaints were investigated, you had never been taken from the family home?*

Yes.

One of these times, back in 1982, where they investigated and found that you weren't in danger, didn't you, in fact, tell them that everybody at home was always looking out for you and you disliked that?

I don't remember that.

Is that how you felt?

No, that's not how I felt.

Perhaps if I hadn't been so scared, been quicker on my feet, I would have told him that it wasn't my fault that child welfare workers never properly investigated what was going on, because if they had, they *would* have taken me out of the home. I felt the way he was saying it, it almost seemed like one of those do-you-still-beat-your-wife type of questions—any way you answered, it still would come out wrong. Still, it seemed to me that Mr. Adler was trying to get me to admit I had exaggerated the pain I suffered all those years, and that the reason child welfare workers had dismissed my claims was because there wasn't any truth to them. And if I had exaggerated the beatings I got over the years, he seemed to me to be implying, why I wouldn't make up other things as well?

But the toughest part of Mr. Adler's cross examination came when he tried to question me as to whether I had really seen what Mama and Greg did to Latanisha that day. Further, if I had really witnessed them beating her to death. He stepped close to me.

The truth is, he said, emphasizing the words, *that you don't really know what happened that day, do you?*

I stared at him and shook my head in disbelief. I was not going to let fear overcome me or make it seem like I had lied; and I sure was not going to let it seem that black looked like white, and white looked like purple, as it might have in his questions about the child welfare workers. What if the judge believed that? What if the judge believed that I exaggerated everything that happened to me and Andre? And what if she believed that Mama really was the loving, caring mother her lawyer described, a person very different from my memories?

If the judge decided I was a liar, she might also believe that Greg had never laid a hand on me, either. And if she believed that, it wouldn't be a long stretch for her to decide that Greg had probably never laid a hand on Latanisha, or that maybe I was a pathological liar who, for unknown reasons, was now trying to put my own mother and brother in prison.

I looked at Mr. Adler and said in a loud, clear voice: *I know what happened! And I'm not going to sit here and have you tell me otherwise. I know what happened.*

Mr. Adler gave a little shake of his head as if he'd made his point.

That's all I have for this witness, he said to the judge.

* * *

Finally, I was allowed to go back to my seat. As I walked toward Andre and Bronsetta, I felt my knees buckle a little bit beneath me, almost as if I was walking on the deck of a ship being tossed around at sea. Andre must have seen it, because he stood up and took my arm as I sat down.

When the court went into a short recess, Andre asked me if I wanted to go into the hallway with him for a few minutes. The only time I had been happier to get out of anywhere was when I had finally left home, at fifteen.

"You were strong in there, Sabrina," Andre said. "I'm so proud of what you did. You stood up to both those lawyers."

I started to say something back to him, when suddenly Mama's relatives came walking up to us.

"You're the one who should be in jail, not her," the first said, pointing her finger in my face.

The other shook her head with an expression of utter disgust. "How can you do that to your own mother?" she said. "To your own *mother.*"

As they walked away, Andre saw me start to collapse against the wall. He took my arm and led me over to a nearby bench.

"They can't hurt you," Andre said. "They can't do anything to you. It's too late for them. If they had really wanted to protect our family, they should have done it years and years ago. Don't let them get inside your head, Sabrina."

Just then, Ama Dwimoh walked past a group of reporters that had just come out into the hallway. She shook her head when they asked her something, and then approached Andre and me.

"Are you okay?" she asked reassuringly. I nodded and smiled weakly. "Good," she said.

She told us that the rest of the day would involve some procedural issues, and that if we wanted to, Andre and I could both go home. Of course, she added, she would be sending another town car for both of us early the next morning, when it would be Andre's turn to testify.

As soon as Andre and I began walking toward the door, the reporters and photographers instantly surrounded us, walking on either side of us while taking pictures and yelling questions.

"Sabrina! How do you feel about your testimony?"

"What kind of punishment do you want for your mother and brother?"

"Sabrina, are you confident they'll both be convicted?"

I shook my head as I walked, refusing to say one word. I had spoken to the press before, but everything I had to say to them now already had just been uttered inside that courtroom.

In the car going back home, I stared out the window at the brownish-blue skyline, at people in cars driving alone, at homeless people with backpacks made from sheets. Did those homeless people, I wondered, once have husbands or wives who loved them, kids who loved them, a place that once felt safe? Did something happen to them one day – did they wake up one morning and find out that the world as they knew it, or had imagined it, no longer existed? Did they have secrets they couldn't tell anyone, or secrets that had been told about them, or secrets that had suddenly reared their heads and destroyed everything they had once built for themselves?

"Sabrina?"

I turned and looked at Andre. The car had stopped in front of the apartment building where I lived and the driver was waiting, his eyes looking at me in the rearview mirror.

"See you tomorrow morning?" Andre asked. I nodded, stepped out onto the sidewalk, and then watched as the black car drove away and disappeared.

I knew my kids would be waiting for me, but I wasn't ready to go back inside yet. I wasn't ready to talk to Chris or to pretend inside my apartment that the trial did not touch my life there, or to act as though I had split myself in two – one life for the outside world, one for my family, just so Chris wouldn't have to deal with what was happening to me.

I wasn't ready to go inside and lie about how fine I was doing.

I walked over to the apartment building's small playground and sat down on one of the benches near the sandpit and swing set. I was alone; except for the cars, the only sounds I heard were occasional voices coming out of open balcony doors. Some were loud and angry, others laughing or patient.

And then, I heard a much quieter voice, almost as if someone was standing right behind me, talking into my ear.

Don't be afraid of being alone, Sabrina, the voice said. *You never really are.*

I did not turn my head; I just clutched my purse tighter to my chest as tears streamed down my face. It was the same voice I heard when Andre showed up at my apartment the second time, demanding to know where his twin was, the same voice that had said to me that day, *He's got to know, Sabrina. He's got a right to know.*

"Tish," I whispered.

chapter 15

A Brother's Justice

Andre did not look nervous as he walked to the witness stand the next morning. Maybe he was – maybe he was as frightened as I had been the previous day – but if so, he didn't show it. He held his head high with his shoulders pulled back and his posture completely straight. He reminded me of pictures I had seen of people in India who can walk over hot coals without feeling a thing or even getting burned in the slightest. I had seen many expressions on my brother's face over the years, but I had never seen the quiet strength of this one.

I had expected that Miss Dwimoh would be the prosecutor who talked to him, but instead it was Mr. Schreiber.

After he was sworn in, Mr. Schreiber led him through all of the questions that he and Miss Dwimoh had previously asked Andre in the district attorney's office. Andre told the judge that he had no real memory of Latanisha, and that his memories only went back as far as six or seven, three years after his twin died. He testified that the first time he suspected he had a twin was when he was about eight years old, after his aunt asked him about her. Andre explained how he had gone home from our aunt's apartment, and then how he asked Mama if it was true what his aunt had told him.

And what was your mother's response? Mr. Schreiber asked.

She didn't really respond to me, he answered. *My mother and Greg then spoke. The next thing I knew, I was being beaten. I was kicked, punched, slammed to the floor.*

As Andre described that beating, I looked over at Mama. Until then, she had been slouched in her wheelchair, looking away from him – at the walls, at the floor, at the ceiling – as if she was infinitely bored, or else didn't care what Andre had to say. But now she was looking right at him. Her mouth was pulled into an expression as if she had just sipped sour milk, and she was shaking her head, as if just the sight of him completely disgusted her. If there had been one of those cartoon balloons above her head that said what she was thinking, it would have read, "How *could* you?"

But Mama wasn't the only one staring at Andre. With the Koran lying in front of him on the table, Greg inspected Andre with an expression that reminded me of a thick shiny knife blade. In his eyes was a look of cold steel, a look that seemed as if it wanted to pierce Andre's gut and slip up under his ribcage.

Andre, I saw, looked right back at Greg. And I was so proud of him at that moment. There was not even a flicker of fear in Andre's eyes, not even the slightest trace of intimidation. The little boy who once had been so terrorized by Greg, the little boy who used to tremble and run whenever he heard Greg's keys in the door, was gone. Andre was a grown man now – a strong, good man – and I think he realized right then that Greg's hold on him finally was broken.

Mr. Schreiber asked Andre if that was the only time he had ever been beaten by Mama. Andre shook his head.

I was never allowed to go out of the house or to have any friends. My mother was a very strict disciplinarian. I was beaten very frequently. Everywhere I went in the apartment, she was there; everywhere she went, I was there. My mother basically beat me with anything she could get her hands on – canes, extension cords, you name it.

Was your mother the only one who beat you?

Sometimes it was just Greg who beat me, Andre answered. *Mama used Greg as an enforcer. Many times Greg would obey Mama's orders to beat Sabrina, too.*

Mr. Schreiber asked, *Gregory Carmichael was directed by Madeline Carmichael to do the beating in your presence?*

Yes, he said.

Now, do you know a guy named Sonny?

Andre answered that he did and described Sonny as Mama's boyfriend.

How often would you see him at the Rockaway Parkway address, if at all?

Very often, Andre answered.

Mr. Schreiber didn't ask him anything else about Sonny, and I wasn't sure why Andre had been asked about him at all.

Mr. Schreiber then asked Andre about the closet inside Mama's bedroom, and what memories he had of it.

Andre told the judge how he used to like to play with doorknobs when he was a child, and also how Mama was always adamant about keeping him away from that closet. He explained how Mama and Greg would sometimes beat him to keep him away from the closet, which he said often had a bookcase or bed in front of it. He also described how it happened that he ended up in foster care – Mama and Greg thought he had stolen four hundred dollars in rent money – and how, about a year later, on his thirteenth birthday, he had seen Mama and Greg one last time in a restaurant. It was there, he told the judge, that he asked Mama for a second time whether or not he had a twin. But again, he said, she avoided answering his question directly.

At that point, Mama's lawyer objected. Mr. Horowitz said he didn't see the relevance of asking Andre about how often he had seen Mama while he was living in foster care, but the judge apparently didn't agree with him.

I find it relevant, Judge Feldman said. *I will overrule the objection.*

Andre was allowed to describe what happened on his birthday at the restaurant in Brooklyn. But again, he said, she avoided answering his question directly.

She said to me: When you get old enough, I will tell you. I know someone who looks like you, talks like you, sits like you, Andre testified.

Just then, Mama leaned over and whispered something in her lawyer's ear. Mr. Horowitz nodded and took some notes. I wondered what Mama possibly could have been reacting to – if she was whispering that Andre was lying or what he'd said wasn't what she had said at all or something else that might possibly discredit him. Most of all, I wondered what Mr. Horowitz really thought of Mama. Every accused person has a right to a lawyer, I knew, but was it possible that he really believed that his client truly was a victim of panic, a frightened single mother who now was being vilified for a horrible, tragic accident?

Now, prior to the time you went into foster care, Mr. Schreiber asked, *did Sabrina ever approach you and speak to you about a twin brother or sister?*

No, he said.

While you were still living at the Rockaway Parkway address before you went in foster care, were you attending school?

Andre said that he had been, but not always regularly. He said he remembered going to a Catholic school whose name he had forgotten, and later to a public school. When Mr. Schreiber asked him about the type of classes he had taken, Andre said that he had been placed in Special Education because, as far as he had heard, he was hyperactive and had a reading problem.

Did you have many friends during the time you were in school?

No, I didn't.

Did you have any friends over at the house?

No, he said.

Andre was asked about the years he lived in foster care, and whether or not he had been asked by social workers and caseworkers or psychologists about his family. Andre said yes, that he had been.

Were you asked about the composition of your family, who were the members of your family?

Yes, I was.

Why don't you tell us what you told them.

Well, I basically told them what happened in the home. I told them who was in the home, and I also indicated about my twin.

What precisely did you tell them about your twin?

I said, I think I have a twin out there, and I told them what my aunt told me.

And did you tell them where you thought your twin sister was?

No.

Did you have any idea where your twin sister may be?

No.

Then Mr. Schreiber asked Andre to describe how he found out definitively about his twin.

In a measured voice, he described how he had come to my apartment one day in 1999, my initial refusal to tell him the truth, and then, later, how I had broken down and described Latanisha's final beating. But first, Andre said, I had made him sign a confidentiality agreement and promise not to go to the police, because I was afraid that our lives would be in danger if the truth ever came out.

After they were finished beating Latanisha, Andre testified that I told him, *Mama tried to resuscitate her, but it was no use.* Andre then described how, so many years later unable to forget he had broken his promise to me, torn up our written agreement and gone to the police.

Let me ask you something, Mr. Schreiber said. *After you spoke to members of the Cold Case Squad, did you tell your sister that you were going to be meeting with the police?*

Yes, I did, Andre said. *I gave her a call and told her what I already did. But by then she was already agreeing with me to go to the authorities.*

Mr. Schreiber thanked him, and then sat down at the prosecution table. Now it was Mama's lawyer's turn to ask him questions.

Like Mr. Schreiber, Mr. Horowitz also asked Andre about any recollection he had of his twin, and Andre once again said that he had no memory of her or the day she died. But then, just as Mr. Horowitz had done to me, he started asking Andre about what kind of mother Mama had been to him while he was growing up. Andre described how Mama beat him regularly, and with objects within reach – canes, extension cords, belts, you name it.

You say that you were beaten by your mother, Madeline Carmichael. And you say that she beat you with anything that she could find.

Yes.

And when she beat you, was it hard? Did she hit you hard with things, or did she just tan you?

It was hard enough to bust me open, he said.

You were hit by hard objects.

Yes.

Like a cane?

Yes.

This is a cane that could support a person, and not a children's bamboo cane?

A cane, Andre said. His voice was getting lower and stronger now, probably because it must have seemed to him that he was being asked the same thing over and over.

And you were hit hard with these.

Yes, Andre repeated.

Didn't your mother always feed you?

Yes.

You never went hungry as a child?

No.

And she always kept you in nice clothes? Clean clothes?

Yes.

You never went to school in rags?

No.

And yet you sit here saying she was a bad mother?

Andre's jaw clenched at that question and his hands balled into fists. Anyone looking at him could instantly tell that Mama's lawyer had gone too far, that he had pushed Andre over the edge. I expected Andre to raise his voice – the same way I had done when I shot back at Greg's lawyer that I knew what I had seen that day – but Andre didn't.

He kept staring at Mama's lawyer, who had just taken a few steps away to glance at his notes, almost as if he had no response to what Andre had just said. Then Mr. Horowitz turned around again and approached Andre.

Mr. Carmichael, did you ever suffer any broken bones because of the alleged beatings?

No.

Were you ever hospitalized for any of your alleged injuries?

Andre's jaw clenched again. Maybe he was thinking the same thing I was – that it was another one of those do-you-still-beat-your-wife type questions. If Andre said yes to the lawyer's question, it would be a lie; but the same thing, in a way, would have happened if he said no. Just because Andre didn't end up in the hospital didn't minimize the truth of what he was saying.

No, Andre said slowly. But then he added, emphasizing each word: *But that doesn't mean she didn't bust me open plenty of times.*

Did you complain to anyone about these beatings?

I did not complain until I left and was out of the home.

So your testimony is, you never said anything about Greg or those beatings for all of those years?

Mr. Horowitz didn't seem to react to Andre's heart wrenching replies. He pressed on.

Isn't it also true, Mr. Carmichael, that you never reported any of the alleged beatings to anyone at school?

Andre looked down at his hands and gave a frustrated shake of his head. *Yes,* he answered. *But that was because Mama never let me speak for myself. I was always with my mother.*

Mama's lawyer shook his head slowly, as if he wanted those last words of Andre's to sink in. In the silence that followed, I felt it was almost as if he was asking the judge to think about that: was it really reasonable to believe that a child would never report child abuse to school officials because his mother never let him speak for himself? I felt he was asking if it was reasonable to believe that any parent would be capable of exerting that kind of constant pressure or influence.

I looked over at Greg to see if he had any reaction to what that lawyer was saying. Did it bother him at all, I wondered, that Mama's lawyer seemed to be suggesting that whatever beatings Andre might have gotten over the years, they couldn't have been very severe? Did Greg have any memory of everything he had done to Andre and to me – or had he, perhaps, conveniently chalked up everything bad he had ever done to an "old" Greg, the one before his religious conversion? As I watched my older brother–his head and eyes were lowered–I wondered what thoughts were going though him, if he had any remorse whatsoever for what he and Mama had put us through, or for what they both were putting us through right now.

Mama, unlike Greg, had been staring at Andre during most of his testimony, rarely taking her eyes off of him. Was she trying to intimidate him? Was it one last, desperate attempt to exert some kind of control over him? Or was it, perhaps, something else: was Mama listening to Andre's voice – the measured, controlled voice of a man who was revealing "all of her business" – and wondering whether her lawyer had been able to cast a long-enough shadow over Andre? If her lawyer was going to be able to save her?

Well, now, this business about being always with your mother in your house, Mr. Horowitz went on. *From the time that you remember, did you live in a neatly kept house, or was it a mess?*

It was a neatly kept house.

Was your mother, you know, taking drugs all day?

No, he said.

Was your mother smoking drugs or using drugs, to your knowledge?

I never saw her.

Was she drinking all day? Was she drinking around the house?

I never saw her drinking or taking drugs.

Mr. Horowitz then asked Andre about the type of neighborhood it had been while he was still living at Rockaway Parkway, and whether Andre would describe it as safe or rough. When Andre called it the latter, Mr. Horowitz asked him if Mama had wanted him to stay inside, to which Andre said yes.

She didn't want you out on the streets by yourself. Is that what you're testifying to?

Again, I saw Andre's jaw clench. *I'm testifying that I went nowhere. Nowhere! I didn't have friends. Nobody ever...*He stopped talking for a second, and I could see him struggling to find the words. *I had no friends come over to my house. I went nowhere.*

Andre said that last word so loud, and so forcefully, that it seemed to me that "nowhere" was echoing inside the courtroom.

Now, during that time, Mr. Horowitz went on, *was your home ever visited by any workers from the child welfare agencies?*

Yes, Andre said.

And these workers came to your home?

Yes.

And you are telling us that you had been beaten severely, or you had been beaten hard a number of times with different objects. When these workers came to your home, did you show them your injuries?

Andre said no, he hadn't, because by the time the welfare workers arrived, his injuries already would have healed. That, he said, or else Mama would tell the caseworkers that he had fallen off the bed, or had been playing too rough, if they did happen to see any marks on him.

But nobody took you out of the home?

Nobody, he said.

The caseworkers didn't see any injuries that caused them to take you out of the home?

None.

Mr. Horowitz then said he wanted to go back to the time when Andre was still attending the Catholic school he had described earlier. He asked Andre if the school was affiliated with a church that Mama belonged to, and also whether Mama used to go to that church. Andre answered yes to both questions.

Okay. And did you ever go to that church?

Yes, I did, Andre said.

And your mother used to take the family to that church?

Yes.

And could you estimate, if you remember, how often you used to go to that church?

Pretty often.

Mr. Horowitz went back to the issue of the private Catholic school. *Isn't it true,* he asked, *that that school was paid for by your brother Gregory, who worked and paid for your schooling in that first year out of the money he was making?*

I took a deep breath and looked carefully at Andre's face. Was he going to tell Mama's lawyer about the way we suspected that Greg had made that money, or perhaps point out that possibly any so-called job my older brother had back then certainly didn't involve any employer's weekly pay stubs?

But Andre didn't say a thing about that. *Yes, that's true,* was all he said.

The subject of money, though, wasn't over. Mr. Horowitz asked Andre about his earlier testimony, when he had described the day Mama and Greg showed up at his public school, and Greg turned him upside down looking for $400 in rent money that he and Mama both thought Andre had stolen.

Mr. Horowitz said, *That money was saved in a special place, because it was needed in order to pay for the apartment so that everybody had a place to live. Isn't that so?*

Yes, Andre said.

And they–Gregory and your mother–came to school one day when the money was missing, and you had taken the money. Isn't that true?

Yes.

And the money was needed to keep a roof over the whole family's head. Isn't that true?

You just said that, Andre shot back. *I answered that already. Yes, that's true.*

Is that true? Mr. Horowitz went on. *And you took that money.*

There was no doubt in my mind how frustrated and upset Andre was getting. Maybe people in the courtroom, people who didn't know him, wouldn't have known that; but Andre's mouth was working side to side, the same way as when he stood in my doorway back in 1999 and told me that he wasn't finished looking for his twin sister, that it wasn't over yet.

I did not take the money, he said emphatically. *I removed the money into a different area. Not so they couldn't find it, but so my mother could find it.*

But she didn't find it, Mr. Horowitz said. *She came looking for it at school. She came in front of everybody at the school, and she was looking for the money.*

Right.

Gregory even turned you over because they thought it. Held you upside down because they thought you would have the money in your pocket.

Right.

Now, understandably at the time, you denied taking the money? Is that true?

I saw Andre opening and closing one hand, and then he took a long, deep breath. *I did not deny taking the money. What you asked me is two different questions. Yes, I deny taking the money. This question you had asked me – you had not asked me where I placed the money or where I put the money. It's like two questions!*

Even though it seemed to me that Mama's lawyer was trying to rattle him, Andre was holding up so well. I was so proud of him for not getting tangled up or confused or backing down.

So your testimony now is that when they came and asked for the money in front of the teachers, in front of the school, and the lunch room and the principal and everybody is looking, that you said, yes, just go home and you will find the money, and you told them where the money was?

Yes, Andre said.

That's what you are telling us?

Andre looked Mama's lawyer straight in the eyes and didn't flinch. *Yes,* he said. *That's what I am telling you.*

Mr. Horowitz gave a little nod of his head and then said, *Do you know that that money was never found by your mother, or anyone?*

Mr. Schreiber objected to the question, but Judge Feldman said Andre could answer it if he knew.

Andre said he didn't, that he had never known that. Mr. Horowitz went on with his questions.

That wasn't told to you at any time by them that that money, that $400 that you had removed from where it belongs, was never found where you said you had put it?

No, Andre repeated. *I never knew that.*

Mr. Horowitz then asked him about what happened later, after Mama and Greg left his school. *That was the day, in fact, that you were placed in foster care?*

Yes.

And you were placed there – your mother had voluntarily placed you in foster care?

As soon as Mr. Horowitz asked him that, I wondered if that had been what Mama had told her lawyer. Had she made it sound as if the reason Andre went to live with Mrs. Lewis was because she thought Andre had been a thief and she had no other option?

No, she did not, Andre answered. *When they asked me, did I want to go back home, I voluntarily said no.*

If Mr. Horowitz was surprised by Andre's answer, he didn't show it. *So you didn't want to go back home?*

Right.

Okay. Mr. Horowitz went on. *Would it be fair to say that your mother didn't want you to come back home?*

Andre looked over at Mama in her wheelchair, and so did I. Her face was stony, like something carved out of petrified wood.

I don't know what she wanted, Andre said, looking back at Mama's lawyer.

Mr. Horowitz only had a few more questions to ask him. They concerned the time when Andre initially went to live with Mrs. Lewis. He asked Andre if it was true if he had ever stolen anything when he first went to live there. I assumed that Mama's lawyer, along with the prosecutors, had already talked to Mrs. Lewis before the trial and that she must have described to them Andre's behavior when he first arrived there.

That's true, Andre said.

Mr. Horowitz also asked if Andre had constantly cursed in the foster mother's house when he first went to live with her. Again, Andre said yes.

And eventually, when you stayed in the Lewis's house for a while, then these things abated and you didn't steal from them anymore? Is that true?

Yes, Andre said.

And when you first came you used to curse at them, and after a while you didn't curse at them anymore?

For the first time, I saw a little smile on Andre's face. And I was pretty sure I knew exactly what he was thinking, too: about how angry he'd been when he first went to live there, about how much pain he'd had inside of him, and then how Mrs. Lewis's love and kindness saved him. Andre had already told me that, too – that if it hadn't been for the blessing of his foster mother, he was certain he would have turned into a completely different man.

Yes, Andre said. *That's true.*

But Mr. Horowitz didn't seem focused on that part of what happened to Andre.

But at the time that you were initially placed there, you were stealing from them? That's true?

Andre nodded. *Yes*, he said. *I did answer that.*

Mr. Horowitz had a satisfied expression on his face. *That's all I have for this witness*, Mr. Horowitz said, returning to his seat.

Judge Feldman asked the lawyers if they wanted to take a break before Greg's lawyer questioned Andre, but Mr. Adler said he was planning to be very brief – just five minutes. The judge said that was fine then, and that he could go ahead.

Good morning, Mr. Carmichael, Mr. Adler said.

Good morning.

Mr. Adler was extremely polite to Andre. His questions were mainly ones that had already been asked, such as about the time that Mama and Sonny went to Atlantic City when he was about eight years old and Andre stayed with his aunt; whether I had ever told him what was inside the closet before he went into foster care; and the times he had attempted to pry open Mama's bedroom closet with various objects, like a knife or spoon. He also asked Andre if he had ever asked me about having a twin sister before he went into foster care. Andre said he never had.

Mr. Adler then turned his attention to the day in 1999 when Andre came to my apartment and I finally told him what had happened to Latanisha.

And that meeting actually was the second or third in a series of meetings you had. You had about two or three meetings leading up to that day, right?

I believe so.

And in fact, it was during those meetings, leading up to this day, that you had mentioned to Sabrina that you were going to start getting serious about finding out about this twin of yours, right?

Andre agreed that was true.

Right, Mr. Adler said. *But it was in these days, in these meetings leading up to the one in 1999, that you specifically told Sabrina that you were going to go out and get investigators possibly. Right?*

Yes.

You made clear to her that you were real serious about it. You were going to start taking specific steps to find out about what happened to your twin sister, right?

Yes.

And it's only after that, for the first time, that Sabrina Carmichael told you what she knew?

Yes, Andre said.

Mr. Adler nodded his head, and then said to Andre, *Okay, that's all. Thank you.* Then he turned to the judge and said, *Nothing further, Your Honor.*

As soon as Mr. Adler took his seat, Mr. Schreiber told Judge Feldman that he only had one or two follow-up questions.

May I, Your Honor?

Mr. Schreiber then asked Andre about Mama's closet, and whether or not any changes were made to it after he or I had tried to get into it. Andre didn't seem sure about what he meant, so Mr. Schreiber then asked if there ever was anything blocking the closet while he was still living in the home.

Mr. Horowitz objected to the question – he didn't say why – but the judge said she would allow it.

Besides clothes, Andre said, *maybe a dresser. But that's about it.*

Okay, Mr. Schreiber said. I have one last question. *Why did you move the money?*

Why? Andre asked.

Yeah. Before you were in foster care. We had a whole discussion about this incident and the fact that you moved $400 reserved for rent. Is there any particular reason you took it from one spot and put it in another?

Yes.

Had you ever moved money before?

No.

So why on this particular occasion did you move it?

I thought it was going to be stolen from the home, he said.

Andre did not name any names and probably didn't have to. By that time I was already living in foster care, and so Mama and Greg would have been the only ones, besides him, with access to the money. It certainly didn't seem likely that Mama would have stolen her own rent money.

I have no further questions, Mr. Schreiber said.

chapter 16

The Verdict

At the request of the district attorney, Andre and I left the courthouse that day before a medical examiner took the witness stand. For reasons that were never explained to us, it wasn't the same medical examiner that had performed the actual autopsy on our sister; it was, instead, an expert who formerly had worked in the King's County Coroner's office and who now worked in Washington, D.C. From what we read in the newspapers the next day, he had analyzed the autopsy report, and from it concluded that Latanisha's death had been a "homicide." Still, there remained the problem of explaining precisely how she had died, which he couldn't do. Due to the decomposed state of our sister's body, the medical examiner was unable to testify to the cause of death with certainty.

I wanted to ask Miss Dwimoh how it had been possible to determine that Latanisha's death had been a homicide without also knowing what had killed her, but I didn't. Neither did Andre. Even though that didn't make sense to us – and it seemed as though Mr. Horowitz and Mr. Adler had a good reason to jump on that inconsistency, the way we later were told they did in court that day – Andre and I both decided to just let things play out, to not bother the district attorneys with our questions.

For the next few days, as the trial reached its close, Andre and I sat inside Miss Dwimoh's office and waited for updates about what was going on inside the trial. The hours inched by long and slow; we flipped through magazines, stared at the walls, tried to talk about our kids, or Andre's job, or his new apartment, or anything else to keep our minds off the clock ticking as if in slow motion.

Most of the time, though, we were both silent and still.

When we found out that Mama's former boyfriend, Sonny, had been called as a witness, Andre and I both wished we had been able to be there, to see him again. He was sixty-eight years old and in poor health now, and apparently he had just gotten out of the hospital the day before, where he was being treated for cancer.

Sonny, we learned, explained how and when he originally had come to the United States from Jamaica, and how he met Mama about a month later while we were all still living at the St. John's apartment. He testified that Mama had four children living with her at the time – Greg, me, and "two little small twins." After our family moved to 96th Street, he said, he used to come see us about once a week. He then described, in his heavy accent, one of the last times he had seen our sister.

It was a day when Mama was "coming up the staircase," he said, and "she held the little girl with her hand."

And then came a day, he said, when he no longer saw that little girl, whom he called "Tisha." About three weeks later, he said, he asked Mama where she was. Sonny said that Mama just looked at him – we were told that Sonny made a grimace or a scowl on the witness stand, as if to show the way that Mama had looked at him – but that she didn't answer him. About three months later, he said, he asked Mama once again where "Tisha" had gone, but he said she gave him the same response: a scowl and silence. Finally, after asking her a few more times, he stopped asking about our sister.

Sonny was asked by Mr. Schreiber about any assistance he gave to Mama when we all moved from 96th Street to Rockaway Parkway, and Sonny had a clear memory of having a rented truck. Mr. Schreiber, we learned, then handed Sonny a piece of paper and asked him if he recognized it. Sonny said he did; it was the receipt for the rental truck he had used to help us move after "Tisha" disappeared. He knew that was the same receipt, he said, because it was the only truck he had ever rented in his whole life.

I imagined there probably were plenty of people in that courtroom who must have been amazed that the district attorney's office could have tracked down a receipt that was nearly twenty years old, but I wasn't. I knew exactly where it probably came from: Mama's "filing cabinet" under her mattress.

At one point, we were informed that Detective Daniel D' Alessandro had testified about Mama's reaction when he and other members of the Cold Case Squad went to her apartment.

After Mama cracked the door and they pushed their way in, Detective D' Alessandro said she fainted when he and other detectives headed for the closet. But when she came to, Detective D' Alessandro allegedly testified that the first thing she said was, "I'm glad the truth is out now."

When Andre and I were left alone again, I saw him shaking his head. Then he stood up and started pacing back and forth.

"What's the matter?" I asked.

He shook his head again.

"Andre, tell me what's wrong. Is it about what Mama said about the truth being out now?"

He stopped and looked at me, as if he was trying to decide whether to say it or not. And then he finally said what was on his mind.

"Why are we in here, Sabrina? How come we're sitting here and getting everything told to us through a filter? How come we're not in that courtroom, hearing it for ourselves? Does it bother you that Aunt Dorothy and Aunt Barbara can hear everything that's going on in the trial, but we can't?"

I started to remind him about how Miss Dwimoh had thought it would be too painful for us, but he cut me off.

"Sabrina," he asked, "do you ever get the feeling that people can turn anything into a secret with just a wave of their hands? Or that you and me just keep coming up against one secret after another? Do you ever wonder why that is?"

* * *

On Monday, October 23, Andre and I were invited once again to come inside the courtroom. This was the day that closing arguments were going to be made in the case, and also when the judge was expected to give her verdict. I don't think either one of us had slept a wink the night before; Andre told me in the town car on the way over to the courthouse that he knew exactly how many cracks were on his bedroom ceiling.

We both took a deep breath as we opened the courtroom door and walked inside. Everyone from the first two days was there – members of Mama's family, Greg's ex-girlfriend and Greg's grandson on her lap, the detectives – but there also was another woman we hadn't seen before. Later we found out that it was Miss Dwimoh's mother.

The reporters also were there, except there were more of them, filling the two back rows. Many of them had been writing about our family's case since Latanisha's body was first found, and I suppose this was the moment they had been waiting for – to find out what kind of justice would get handed down. They couldn't have wondered that more than Andre and I did.

But there also was something in the room that hadn't been there before, something whose presence struck both Andre and me the second we entered. We both knew immediately what it was, even before we actually set eyes on it.

The odor inside the courtroom was pungent and musky, a smell like no other I'd ever encountered. It was as if an archeologist had just moved a huge stone from the mouth of a long dark tomb, as if this was the smell of time itself. And then we saw the source of it: the blue metal trunk that had been inside Mama's closet. Someone had placed it right in the middle of the courtroom, directly in front of the judge's bench and just a few feet away from where Mama and Greg were sitting.

Mama, her wheelchair pushed up near her lawyer's table, was looking away from it, almost as if she was focusing on a fly on the far wall. Greg, too, kept his eyes diverted from the trunk, with his head bent down and his eyes on his Koran on the table in front of him. I saw that the reporters were all scribbling in their notebooks.

After Judge Feldman called the court to order, she asked if the prosecution was prepared for final arguments.

We are, Your Honor, Miss Dwimoh said, rising from her seat. She walked around the table and stood next to the blue metal trunk. I did not have a tape recorder with me, and I wasn't scribbling notes the way the reporters were doing. Then in her strong, resonant voice full of feeling, she began talking of the horror of the day of Latanisha's death and its meaning.

When Madeline Carmichael and Gregory Carmichael beat Latanisha to death, that beating was not an aberration. It was not a one-time event that had tragic consequences. The evidence in this case has shown that both defendants had a long history of abuse and that, indeed, their abuse lasted for years after Latanisha died. On that day, however, their beating proved fatal.

You have heard the medical examiner's testimony that Latanisha's death was a homicide. And you have heard the powerful eyewitness account of Sabrina, who saw what her mother and brother did that day, and has carried the memory of it for the rest of her life. There was no doubt in her mind, no hesitation. "I know what I saw that day," she told you. She knows, because she was there.

You also have heard the detective's testimony that Gregory stated to investigators that the reason Latanisha was beaten that day was because she had vomited. This was the terrible sin the child had committed – and this was what caused Madeline and Gregory Carmichael to beat her to death - because the child committed the sin of vomiting.

And then, what did they do? Did they call 911 for help? No. Did they call for anyone else to help them? No. Madeline Carmichael performed amateur CPR on her daughter, and then she and Gregory stuffed the child's body into a trash bag. Was there a chance that Latanisha might have been saved if an ambulance had been called? Was Latanisha still alive then, was she still breathing when her mother put her into that garbage bag and placed it inside this metal trunk, the same one you see right in front of me today?

We will never know the answer to those questions. We will never know what the last few moments of Latanisha's life were like, if she knew what was happening to her. We will never know if she was aware that she was inside a trunk in her mother's closet.

But there are two questions that have been answered in this case, two things we do know. Did Madeline and Gregory Carmichael kill Latanisha Carmichael? The answer to that question is yes. And should Madeline and Gregory Carmichael have to answer for their crime, in addition to concealing for more than twenty years what they did? Again, Your Honor, the answer to that question is yes.

After Miss Dwimoh sat down, Mr. Horowitz stood up and addressed the judge. He was brief, but spoke in a confident and compelling voice.

This is a highly emotional case, but the evidence presented has not proved that Mrs. Carmichael intentionally killed Latanisha. The evidence has not risen to the level required, that would prove culpability beyond a reasonable doubt. The medical examiner's report was inconclusive, and the district attorney's office based its entire case on the faulty memory of a child who was eight years old at the time. Mrs. Carmichael was a strict but caring single parent, and her only offense was concealing a tragic, accidental death that haunted her.

Greg's lawyer essentially said the same thing. His client had been charged in the case only because of my "faulty memory," and based on the evidence that had been presented the judge had an obligation to find his client not guilty.

As soon as both lawyers were finished, Judge Feldman cleared her throat. You could have heard a pin drop it was so quiet in the room. The judge was looking at Mama, but the blue metal trunk was right in her line of vision. And then she issued her ruling, in words to this effect:

Mrs. Carmichael has been charged with murder in the second degree. It is the court's finding –

Andre reached over and took my hand.

It is the court's finding that Madeline Carmichael is guilty of second-degree murder.

The judge then turned to Greg.

It is the court's finding that Gregory Carmichael is guilty of criminally negligent homicide, as well as hindering prosecution.

The rest was a roar in my ears. There was murmuring all around me, but I did not hear another word of what was said. They both had been convicted.

* * *

One week later, on November 2, Mama and Greg came back to court to hear Judge Feldman hand down their sentences.

As soon as the courtroom was quiet, Judge Feldman said, *Are the defendants ready for sentencing?*

Madeline Carmichael is ready, Mr. Horowitz said.

But Mr. Adler first wanted to say one thing. He said he wanted to make a motion to set aside the convictions because they were legally unsupported by the evidence, and also because the evidence did not prove guilt beyond a reasonable doubt. He also said that the charges should have been barred by the statute of limitations.

Mr. Horowitz then said that he would join in Mr. Adler's application.

But Judge Feldman did not agree with them. She said, *I found the evidence ample to support the conviction of both defendants on the counts dealing with the concealment of the child's body. As to the statute of limitations, I believe Mr. Schreiber is correct. This is an offense that the statute starts to run when the evidence is discovered, so that would be my ruling. As to the adequacy of evidence on the other grounds, I found it is adequate to support the verdict.*

Mr. Adler nodded. *With that*, he said, *we're ready for sentence.*

Judge Feldman then asked the prosecutors if the People wished to be heard. Mr. Schreiber said, *Yes, Your Honor*, and then Miss Dwimoh spoke to the judge.

Your Honor, what we will have is Andre Carmichael to address the Court before the People's remarks. She motioned to Andre and then said, *Mr. Carmichael.*

Andre stood up and faced the judge. From where he was standing he could look directly at Mama and Greg, too. He had no notes in his hand, nothing written down. He told me earlier that he just wanted to speak from his heart.

I come here today before everybody in court to say thank you, to the D.A.s and the judge, for finding my sister and bringing her name to light, he said. *As for your judgment, whatever you judge today, Judge Feldman, and as far as my brother, I understand. But in a way, I don't. I feel like this: If I was the oldest, this wouldn't have taken place. I hope in God's eyes that God will forgive him, just as God asked me to forgive my brother and mother.*

*As far as my mother, there's nothing on this Earth...*He stopped, shook his head and seemed to search for the right words. *I'm a father of five children. I have a fourteen-year-old son, to a four-year-old daughter. I could never take any of my children's lives, no matter what. Many times I haven't had any food, any place to go. But that's no excuse.* He turned and looked at Mama. *I'm just saying that I hope God will forgive you, just like He asked me to forgive you in my heart.*

And then he looked out at everyone in the courtroom.

Everybody in this room has a person to answer to, and that's God Himself. So that's all I have to say. Thank you.

As Andre sat down, Judge Feldman nodded. *Thank you,* she said.

And then Mr. Schreiber rose. He spoke very passionately about his belief that the maximum sentences should be handed down in this case.

I say that, Your Honor, because I think there are certain crimes that by their very nature are so heinous, so callous, so egregious and so depraved and so utterly devoid of conscience, humanity, morality, compassion and decency that they are in and of themselves worthy of the maximum penalty that our law allows...Neither of these defendants, Your Honor, in conclusion, showed any mercy, compassion or decency twenty-one years ago when they violently took that young child's life and discarded her remains like yesterday's clothing...

After Mr. Schreiber was finished, Mr. Horowitz rose to address the Court. He said he wanted to bring to attention some facts about his client's life that had been brought to his own attention by her and members of her family.

My client comes from an abused background, Mr. Horowitz began. *She took care of her siblings herself from the age of fourteen, fifteen and sixteen when her mother was gone, both sick and not in the household...This family had no money. She took care of the siblings. She sent them to school, took them to church every single week when there was no food in the house, as there most often was not. She sent her siblings on the street to beg for bones from the butcher, which she made into stew. This was a family who grew up without food. Is there a connection between missing meals and trying to feed four or five other children with some sort of obsession?*

Mr. Horowitz then shifted from talking about Mama's siblings to her own children, and how Mama had treated us while we were growing up.

She took care of every single child in this family that had any problems, and never was there a report that any child was abused, that any child was hurt, that any child was anything but well fed. Even the testimony here was that everybody was well fed. The house was well kept. The children were sent to school in proper clothing to the best that they could afford...There has not been a word adduced at trial or anywhere about her treatment of anybody before the tragedy which happened on that day.

Mr. Horowitz then talked about what Mama had done by hiding Latanisha's body for all those years, and the reason for it.

It also seems that in a world where people dispose of remains in so many different ways, where people were buried at sea, where somebody wants this, somebody wants that, that for a mother's desire to stay close to her child and to keep her family intact should not be looked at as the callous throwing away of a child, but should be understood for what it was – a tragedy had occurred for which the Court has found her responsible, and her desire to stay close to her family and to her child as long as she could.

With that, Mr. Horowitz finished and sat down.

Judge Feldman said, *Mrs. Carmichael, do you want to say anything about the sentence in this case? Do you want to speak to the Court?*

No, Your Honor, Mama said.

You have a right to say to something, Judge Feldman said.

No, Your Honor, Mama repeated, looking at her lawyer. *He has well said it for me.*

Now it was Mr. Adler's turn to speak to the judge. He seemed to have great praise for the way the judge had conducted the trial, especially since he pointed out that she not only was the judge, but the finder of fact.

We knew full well the risks involved – that you might be introduced by any other human being by sympathy for the family, by the emotion of the situation, by the trunk that was propped up in front of you during final arguments and that you might take the easy way out, Your Honor, and simply find both defendants guilty of murder. Well, you did not do that. In fact, you did exactly the opposite of that, Your Honor. You obviously gave this case a great deal of thought, a great deal of consideration before reaching your decision, and for that more than anything else, Gregory Carmichael and I thank you.

Mr. Adler then spoke about the prosecution's case, and how it had relied to some extent on sympathy and emotion. He told the judge he did not think it was necessary to talk at length about Gregory's difficult upbringing, or how Gregory also was abused and mistreated by his mother throughout his life. And then he talked about Gregory's role in concealing Latanisha's body.

Certainly, my client did at times give a false account of where Latanisha was, in terms of being in a foster home or down south, but as you heard from the evidence, Sabrina did the very same thing, Your Honor. And I certainly don't think that that really was the basis for your verdict of guilty on the hindering count. The basis for that, really, is putting the body in the closet.

Mr. Adler then said that because of those reasons, as well as others he had mentioned, he was asking the judge to give Gregory a concurrent sentence – which I learned later would mean that if the judge sentenced him to jail time for different crimes, he could serve both sentences at the same time.

When Mr. Adler finished speaking, Judge Feldman asked Gregory if he wanted to say anything about the sentence.

Yes, Your Honor. Yes ma'am, Greg said. *May I stand?*

Yes, you may, Judge Feldman said.

I want to thank my attorney, and my mother's attorney, and even the D.A., and my sister that this has come to light so that this burden can be relieved off our family. Because it's true, I love my brother, and true, I never even got to really function with my brother or sister. We touched base from time to time, but it wasn't like an ordinary family in a household real strong, you know, even despite our secrets with Latanisha's death.

He looked over at Andre and me, and then back at the judge. *My mother would have taken this to her grave*, he said.

And today, if it wouldn't have come to light, it never would have been heard from me, Your Honor. Thank you.

And then he sat down.

Now there was only one person that everyone in the courtroom was waiting to hear from, only one person who hadn't yet spoken – Judge Feldman.

* * *

She sentenced Mama to fifteen years to life in prison, and then said that based on medical information that had been provided to her, it was likely that Mama would die of bone marrow cancer within a few years. She said the minimum sentence – Mama had been facing twenty-five years to life – ensured that Mama would not walk out of prison.

I don't think the maximum sentence will do anything more than make a headline, the judge said.

Greg was sentenced to consecutive sentences - not concurrent - of three to four years for a criminally negligent homicide, and one to three years for hindering prosecution. Mentally, I calculated how long he would be in prison. If he served the minimum, it was possible he would not be in jail that long.

One day, he would get out again. But I would not think about that day until I absolutely had to.

The trial was over. I saw a bailiff walk over to Mama and prepare to wheel her out of the courtroom and take her back to her prison cell.

"I'll be right back," I said to Andre, as everyone rose and the reporters began walking out in the hallway.

I went over to Mama, reached into my purse and pulled out two small gold boxes. The bailiff peered inside the boxes before he handed them to Mama.

Mama didn't say anything; neither did I.

Afterward, in the town car on the way home, Andre asked me what I had given to her.

"Earrings," I said. "And a wrist watch. Mama said she wanted to be able to tell how long it took the time to pass."

chapter 17

A Reporter's Search for Andre

The first time I ever came across the names of Madeline or Gregory Carmichael was when I read about their conviction in the *New York Times*. It was a short news item, but nevertheless the story touched and stunned me, just as I later learned that it had thousands of other people. It wasn't necessary to be able to read Spanish or Portuguese or Italian to understand headlines like "MAE ESCONDE CORPO DE FILHA POR 20 ANOS" or "UCCIDE LA FIGLIOLETTA E LA TIENE NACOSTA PER 20 ANNI" to realize that the gruesome discovery of little Latanisha Carmichael in the Brownsville section of Brooklyn had reverberated all around the world.

To me, what was shocking not only was that a mother had killed her own child and then concealed that child's body in a

closet for two decades; it also was the idea that Mrs. Carmichael's other children had grown up in the midst of that horrible
secret, suffering because of the deed. Then I was moved by the
incredible courage it must have taken for Andre and Sabrina to
finally come forward with the truth so many years later.

I had no way of knowing the extent of the monstrous
brutality Andre and Sabrina Carmichael had been forced to
endure at the hands of their mother and older brother to ensure
that the secret never came to light, and I also was not aware of
how long, or how many times, Sabrina and Andre had both tried
to get someone to help them. Indeed, it wasn't until a week after
Madeline and Gregory's conviction that I read *Newsday's*
in-depth investigation of the role that child protective services
had played—or rather, failed to play—in the Carmichael case.

In my opinion, the *Newsday* story was a powerful indict-
ment of how the city's child welfare agency, currently called the
Administration of Children's Services, had failed the Carmichael
children. According to the article, family court and confidential
city records obtained by the newspaper showed that dozens of
ACS caseworkers and supervisors had had contact with the
Carmichael family for more than a decade after Latanisha died,
but no one ever bothered to confirm Latanisha's whereabouts.
Indeed, the story detailed how numerous caseworkers had
made home visits, and then stated in their reports that they had
visited Mrs. Carmichael and her "two daughters," or that
"ten-year-old twins, Andre and Latanisha, share a back room"
with their twenty-four-year-old brother, Greg. By that time,
Latanisha had been dead at least seven years.

But the *Newsday* story also included caseworkers' numerous concerns about Mrs. Carmichael's behavior. In June 1986,

for example, when Sabrina was fourteen and Andre was nine, one caseworker allegedly described Mrs. Carmichael as "incoherent" and "contradicting herself." Two days later, the language of another alleged report became even more   alarming and urgent: Mrs. Carmichael was described as   "obviously agitated and paranoid," and switching "on and off from compliant to hostile." The situation, the caseworker reportedly wrote, was felt to be "volatile."

But even more heartbreaking were the documented instances in which either Andre or Sabrina had literally begged someone to help them. According to the *Newsday* article, on March 23, 1984, for example, school officials reported that they saw a gash over twelve-year-old Sabrina's eye and that she told them she was "afraid to go home." Three months later, on June 22, Sabrina allegedly reported that she was "hit by her mother and kicked by her brother" and that her mother beat her "regularly." Less than two months later, on August 18, 1984, Sabrina reportedly called social workers "from a store, saying her mother and brother beat her."

There also were distress calls made from "confidential" or "anonymous" sources. According to one alleged report on July 17, 1985, an "anonymous caller" said that Sabrina was "being beaten at home" and the caller was "too frightened to go home." Less than three months later, on Halloween, another "confidential source" allegedly reported that "Sabrina has been hit with a hammer and requests immediate intervention."

Had no one, I wondered, been on the other end of those phone calls? Had no one heard those desperate cries for help? What possible explanation could there be for not immediately responding to such pleas?

In the wake of the disclosures, a spokeswoman for ACS, Jennifer Banks, issued a statement which said, "We are sorry that the services in place in today's child welfare system were not there for the Carmichael children twenty, ten or even six years ago. The only thing that we can do now to address the tragedy is to continue our mission to strengthen the system so that this will not happen again."

The agency, however, did not discuss what might be done to directly address its long record of sins of omission in the Carmichael case. No amount of money, of course, could ever compensate Andre and Sabrina for the years of terror they had experienced, and nothing could give them back their childhoods, either. But did the city nevertheless have a moral, ethical or legal obligation to them? Would the city, I wondered, do anything to try to atone to Andre and Sabrina for the years and years it had failed them?

In the beginning, when I first began reading about the Carmichael family, the first question I asked myself was: How could a young child simply disappear from the face of the earth, and not one soul ever sought to discover where she had gone? Several of the articles mentioned, for instance, that Mrs. Carmichael had told various people over the years that she had sent Latanisha to live "down south" because she couldn't care for her daughter. According to other reports, Andre had told numerous social workers after he went to live in foster care that he thought he had a twin sister.

What perplexed me was, had there been no one else in the Carmichael family—no other relatives of Mrs. Carmichael, for example—who ever wondered where, exactly, "down south" was? Had social workers simply accepted everything Mrs. Carmichael told them, even though there was a long history of child abuse complaints against her? Was it possible that Mrs. Carmichael had been such an excellent liar that she had been able to hoodwink everyone, including trained social workers?

As I poured over the numerous distress calls made by Sabrina and most likely a young, terrified Andre, I also began to wonder about something else. Was it possible that the answers perhaps lay in something even worse to consider: that every person in a position of responsibility had looked at Mrs. Madeline Carmichael and seen a poor, African-American single mother living on welfare, a woman whose children had been raised in the projects, and then, even if no one ever had been conscious of such a thought process, they all had decided that tracking down the whereabouts of one more of her children was not of particular importance? If Latanisha had been white, if she had been a cherubic-looking little girl with blond hair and blue eyes, would her disappearance have mattered more? If Sabrina and Andre had been white, would their repeated distress calls have been answered?

I did not want to believe that decades after Dr. Martin Luther King, Jr. talked about his dream, race could have played any role in the city's failure to protect Andre and Sabrina. Although I worked on other things, the story of Sabrina and Andre and their deceased sister would not leave me. At night and in the day when I least expected, it sprang to my mind. Finally, I decided to call the district attorney's office.

* * *

Frank Urzi, Kings County assistant district attorney in the Crimes Against Children Bureau, was polite but not particularly encouraging. Ever since Madeline and Gregory Carmichael's conviction a few days earlier, Urzi said his Brooklyn office had been swamped by calls from journalists and television producers across the country, some even internationally. All of them wanted the same thing: to get in touch with Andre Carmichael.

I, apparently, was going to have to get in line.

"I'll tell Andre you called," Urzi said. For confidentiality reasons, he said he couldn't give me Andre's unlisted phone number or address. "I can't promise anything, though," he added. "I don't know if Andre wants to talk to the media anymore."

Urzi listened patiently as I proceeded to plead my case, to try and distinguish myself from the rest of the journalistic pack. I was not the media, I told him, although at one time I had been. I used to be a reporter for the *Los Angeles Times*, I said, but now I was a freelance magazine writer and author. My first nonfiction book, about a woman who successfully sued her dead stepfather's estate because of his decades-long sexual abuse of her, was due out in just a few months.

"Well, as I said, I'll give Andre your message and—"

"I'm also a fraternal twin," I interjected. "When you talk with Andre, would you mind telling him that for me?"

There was a rather long pause, and then Urzi said that he would. Only after I hung up did it occur to me that Urzi had probably heard multiple variations of the same simpatico claim from others who had called. Indeed, much later, Sabrina told me that after her mother and brother's guilty verdict, she and Andre had both been "amazed by how many reporters had twins out there."

"Establishing the bond" was what some journalists called the technique of offering up so-called "personal information," or else of adopting the patina of warmth and sympathy in order to get subjects to open up. From anecdotal experience, it had been my impression that many reporters often revealed stunning amounts of information about their own lives in order to gain an interview subject's trust—regardless of whether that information was, indeed, true or not. Immediately I recalled a former colleague whose news beat had included interviewing newly-arrested rapists and murderers down at the county jail.

"If you want them to open up to you, you've got to be sincere," he had said to me one day. "If you can fake sincerity, you've got it made." He had not been smiling when he said it.

Urzi, of course, had no way of knowing that I wasn't faking anything, that I truly did have a twin brother. He also had no way of knowing that something had genuinely grabbed me by the throat about Andre's story. In the beginning, I assumed it had to do with our shared twin-ness, with my ability to envision even a sliver of what Andre must have gone through during his search for his missing sister. After all, I thought, who else except another fraternal twin could truly understand how that twinned "other," that mismatched bookend of your birth, was perhaps even more necessary for your sense of completeness than any identical twin ever could be?

Identical twins, to my thinking, were more like photocopies of each other. Nowhere between them existed the yin and yang of the fraternal bond; nowhere was there that unifying quality that made one a half of the other, and both dependent on the other for a sense of wholeness and symmetry. When Andre told one television reporter that on the day Sabrina revealed that Latanisha had been murdered twenty years earlier it felt to him as if half of his heart had died too, I knew instantly what he meant.

In my own life, that same sense of symmetry, of connection with my twin brother, had imprinted itself upon me very early. Whenever I tried to locate myself in memory as a young child, my twin was always there right beside me: Bernard and I standing on a limb of a loquat tree when we were perhaps two years old, the sticky rust-colored juice dripping onto our bellies; Bernard and I, daredevils before we had even started preschool, speeding down our long steep driveway on tricycles; Bernard and I sitting in my parents' koi pond when we were three, the light through the pine branches falling in gray-green shafts onto the glinting water.

And it also was that early sense of symmetry, I suppose, that led me to believe that once a person has experienced that feeling, it never can be totally forgotten. Even if I had never seen Bernard again after, say, the koi pond—even if my three-year-old twin had simply vanished into thin air one day and no one in my family had ever spoken his name again—I was certain that the burnished memory of him always would have remained imbedded within me.

Remained imbedded, just as it obviously had for Andre Carmichael.

That, then, is what I attributed to the feeling I had only experienced a few times in more than two decades as a journalist: the imperative that I absolutely had to talk with Andre, that he simply could not turn me down. Something about his hunt for his twin sister felt as though someone had dropped a pebble down my inner well, and that after a long fall that pebble had finally landed with a deep, resonant *plunk* within me.

A few days went by before I called Frank Urzi again. He repeated what he had said to me in our first conversation that

Andre would contact me if he wanted to talk to me. I waited another week before I called the prosecutor once more, and this time I got his recorded greeting. I left a message, imagining Urzi rolling his eyes behind his desk as he heard my voice, but I did not care. Even though I began to feel a bit like a stalker, for the next several weeks I made it my ritual to call him and leave messages every Tuesday morning and Friday afternoon. There was a not-so-subtle subtext to all my calls: If you want to get rid of me, then get Andre to call me.

By the third week of November, Andre still had not contacted me, and I was losing hope that he would. Nevertheless, I continued to make my regular phone calls to the district attorney's office. By that point, the voice on Urzi's answering machine was almost beginning to sound like an old friend.

"Hi Frank, sorry to bother you again. But if you hear from Andre Carmichael, will you be sure to tell him I'm really hoping to talk to him? Thanks a million. Oh, and by the way, I hope you have a nice Thanksgiving."

And then something happened in my own life that put Andre out of my thoughts.

Two days before Thanksgiving, my parents flew out from the San Francisco Bay Area to spend the holidays with my husband and me. Both my parents had been professional symphony musicians all their lives, and even though they were both retired, just the week before, they had performed a recital together in San Mateo. Another recital already had been scheduled for January.

But that January concert was not to be. Shortly after her arrival at my home in Tampa, my mother was rushed into surgery after experiencing a heart attack. She survived just long enough for all five of my siblings, including two of whom who flew in from Europe, to be by her side and tell her how much we all loved her.

My mother, I believe, died in peace. She was surrounded by her husband of fifty-two years and all six of her children, along with her most beloved music, played softly on a small boom box inside the cardiac care unit: Brahms, Mozart, Beethoven's Violin Concerto, a piece she had performed as a soloist early in her career.

But just like Andre and Sabrina Carmichael's mother, she, too, had carried a dark secret for most of her life, one that had haunted her, unbeknownst to anyone, for more than forty years. My mother had never spoken of it—not until just a short time before her death.

The last time I had flown out to California to see her had been sometime in early spring, 2000. I did not know it would be our last real visit together, that we would never have the chance to talk of those things again. It was then, though, that she told me that she needed to admit something "horrible" and "monstrous" that she had done long ago.

"I cannot carry this secret anymore," she said.

* * *

Toward the end of December 2000 and beginning of January 2001, I left a few more messages on Frank Urzi's answering machine, and I also wrote a letter to Andre Carmichael in care of the assistant district attorney, telling Andre as honestly as I could why I wanted to meet with him. I wrote that I also was a fraternal twin, but I did not mention anything about what my mother had revealed to me nearly a year earlier. I do not know whether that omission was a conscious or unconscious one—if I had not yet come to terms with my mother's death or what she had confided to me; or if I was unable to dare think of my own mother and Mrs. Carmichael connected in any way. To link them—even if it was only in thought—seemed a great betrayal.

By the time Christmas had passed, I no longer actually expected an answer from either Andre or Frank Urzi. Still, I kept calling because of what I knew would happen if I did nothing. Unless I tried to work again—or at least, unless I tried to give myself the illusion of working—I knew I would end up doing the same thing I had for the last several weeks: curling up on my office floor, reading my mother's old letters to me, fingering the shoes she left behind when we took her to the hospital, and crying.

During that interval, I re-read every one of the letters and notes my mother had ever sent me, which for reasons unknown to me I had kept, ever since I moved away from home at age fifteen, in a large silk bag inside my closet. Over and over, though, I kept returning to my mother's last letter to me, written in a shaky script and dated just a few days before my last visit to see her in California.

When you come, I will tell you something you may not want to know. But I am ready to tell it to you now. I hope you will be able to find it in your heart to forgive me.

And then, in the same way that my parents' arrival at my home had put a temporary end to my thoughts about Andre Carmichael, one day a blinking light on my answering machine temporarily interrupted my thoughts about my mother.

It was Frank Urzi's voice. He had been in contact with Andre. "He says he'll talk with you," Urzi said.

Immediately I punched in the phone number Urzi had left for me. After several rings, a deep voice answered and then called out for Andre to pick up. From the acoustics, I gathered it was not a typical office—immediately I thought of a large stockroom—and it turned out that Andre was working as a security guard at a Manhattan post office, double shifts, four days a week.

I have no idea what Andre must have thought of me when I immediately burst out, "Oh, Andre, I can't believe I'm really talking with you! I've tried for so long to find you!"

The voice at the other end was soft, gentle. "That district attorney who called me? Frank? He said you've been trying for three months to get hold of me. It's hard to believe someone would try that long."

We talked for nearly an hour. I could sense Andre's innately trustful nature, along with a part of him that had learned to be cautious. "It's nothing personal," he said at one point, "but I really don't want to get played, as they say in New York."

"Andre, I would feel exactly the same way."

And then finally he agreed to meet with me. It was a Tuesday; his only free day, he said, was Friday. For a brief moment I considered waiting another week—the airfare would be horrendous on such short notice—but suddenly it didn't matter. If I didn't go right away, I was afraid Andre might change his mind.

"I'll be there," I said.

At 1:45 p.m., when Andre still had not arrived at my Manhattan hotel, I took the elevator downstairs and paced the sidewalk, smoking one cigarette after another in the rain. He was nearly two hours late. *At least you remembered your umbrella,* I thought. I had left my home that morning at 5:00 a.m. with no coat—even in late January, Tampa's "cold snap" was in the mid seventies—and stupidly I was wearing only a thin blazer with cotton slacks. By the time I went back inside the lobby, I was frozen.

But at least Andre was there. Somehow I had missed seeing him arrive.

He was so sorry, he said. He had gotten caught up in—I didn't catch the rest. Immediately I sensed he wasn't so great about time, something that would turn out to be correct on one level. But my assessment of him also would undergo a significant change: Andre's sense of time apparently was only affected as far as the present was concerned. When it came to the distant past, his memory often seemed almost photographic in its detail and vividness.

Ten minutes after greeting each other in the hotel lobby, Andre and I were in the back seat of a taxi headed over to the office of a lawyer Andre told me he had come to trust. The lawyer, he explained, was not exactly representing him—that is, he had not yet formally agreed to take his case—but the lawyer was "interested" in Andre's situation, particularly in the possibility of suing the city of New York on Andre's behalf.

"I don't know whether you'll believe this or not, but I'm not doing this for money. What I really want are answers," Andre said as the taxi sped along. "I didn't find out until after the trial that the caseworkers had been coming to our apartment for years and then writing in their reports that Latanisha was still alive. Another report even said that Sabrina called up and said, *Please send someone to help me.* What else was Sabrina supposed to do? Shoot fireworks off the top of our apartment building? They had to know that all kinds of abuse was going on in our home. What I want to know is, how could our whole family get ignored all that time?"

The Administration for Children's Services clearly had been asked similar questions by reporters. In one statement, ACS spokeswoman Leonora Weiner said that the agency now had stricter supervision of caseworkers who had smaller caseloads, and that ACS also now required verification from teachers and neighbors for information provided by the family. "Whatever lapses might have happened then," Weiner said, "we have many more safeguards against something like that happening today."

Andre stared out the taxi window. "But I also want to know, how can I be sure it's not happening to some other family out there, right now? How do I know there aren't kids out there right now, pleading for help just like Sabrina and I did, and getting ignored? But no one from the city has even bothered to contact me or apologize. Someone from ACS basically said to the newspapers that they're sorry the system wasn't good enough back then, but I feel that doesn't mean the system is fixed. And it's also not the same thing as an apology. So getting this lawyer—it's the only way I know to get the city's attention."

"I don't know what to say to you, Andre. I don't understand how any of that could have happened, either."

We rode a block or two in silence. Then I asked, "Have you asked the city for an apology?" The moment I said it, I regretted it.

"The way I see it," Andre said, turning to me, "it's as if a woman asks you to buy her flowers. You can go out there and do it, buy her a big giant bouquet, but it still doesn't mean the same thing as when you decide to make that kind of gesture all on your own. You know what I'm trying to say?"

I nodded. I knew exactly what he was trying to say.

"Tell me about this lawyer we're going to see," I said.

Even though Andre said he had already contacted "a bunch of lawyers" about representing him, including O.J. Simpson's lawyer, Johnnie Cochran, all of them, he said, had essentially told him the same thing. Even though they had all agreed that Andre had suffered a grievous wrong and that there had been something very wrong with the child protective services system in New York, it still did not matter.

"They all said it was too late to do anything against the city because too much time has gone by. It's called the statute of limitations. I tried to tell them that wasn't right. I said if I didn't know what happened twenty years ago or ten years ago or even five years ago, how could that legal time limit already be over? But even Johnnie Cochran finally hung up on me."

The lawyer we were going to see that day, Andre said, was the only one who had told Andre he might still have a chance, that there might be a way around the problem of the statute of limitations. I wondered if perhaps the lawyer was considering invoking something called "delayed discovery," a legal strategy that had been successfully used in California by some victims of sexual abuse. Originally used in cases such as asbestos exposure, where victims do not realize until many years later what caused their current illnesses, cases of sexual abuse that occurred as long as thirty years earlier had successfully been prosecuted in both criminal and civil courts.

"Oh, I forgot to tell you," Andre said as the taxi driver wove dangerously through lanes of traffic. "We need to pick up my sister at 34th Street."

"Your sister?"

"Sabrina," Andre said, in a tone suggesting I should have known it all along.

And he was right, too. Except that, until that instant, I hadn't realized it. I should have known it all along—should have realized that Sabrina was just as much a part of what had happened as her younger brother, just as much a part of their terrible family secret as he was. Secrets don't just affect the person kept in the dark; they also affect the people who keep them. Until that moment, though, it hadn't occurred to me that in chasing "Andre's story," I had been behaving just like virtually every other journalist who had written about the Carmichael family. In practically every published account to date, Andre's search for his twin had been the main focus, with Sabrina treated almost as a footnote.

And I had been guilty of doing exactly the same thing.

The taxi stopped near Penn Station. Sabrina was not at her appointed spot. "She said she'd be here," Andre said, as our taxi drove off into a sea of red tail lights and rain. He looked perplexed.

"What time were you supposed to meet her?"

"One o'clock," he said, looking around.

I looked at my watch. That appointed time had been more than two hours earlier.

chapter 18

Connection

At the address Andre gave to our second taxi driver, we were met by a thin, gray-haired man wearing a light gray suit and red bow-tie. Immediately he reminded me of Orville Redenbacher of gourmet popcorn fame. This was the lawyer Andre had entrusted to ensure he wouldn't get "played." But the man, who carried a thick manila envelope with the word "Carmichael" written across the front, quickly explained that he would not be sitting in on our meeting. Instead, he said, it would be handled by a retired judge who was "an expert in literary contract law." The lawyer assured Andre he would be in good hands.

Andre smiled and nodded politely as we were ushered into a small conference room with a long oval table and chairs on rollers. A severe-looking woman, who had an uncanny resemblance to that popular television jurist, "Judge Judy," rose from her chair and stiffly held out her hand.

"Please, take a seat anywhere," the judge said.

Only then did I notice the pleasant looking African-American woman in a corner chair behind the door. With her hair piled in loose curls on top of her head, her tasteful earrings and casual business attire, she looked as if she could have been a secretary. She was also very pregnant, due to give birth to her seventh child, I learned later, in less than a week.

"Sabrina?" the judge said. "Would you like to join us at the table?"

Sabrina remained seated and shook her head, smiling shyly.

"We stopped off to get you, but I guess you'd already gone," Andre said to her. Again, Sabrina just shook her head and smiled demurely. I introduced myself, shook her hand, and told her how glad I was to meet her. And then I took my seat at the conference table.

After a few brief pleasantries, the judge got down to business. From the manila envelope she pulled out a thick document and leafed through it, peering over the half-sized reading glasses perched on the edge of her nose.

"Of course, there will need to be a paragraph inserted, which assures that Sabrina will first clear all of her memories with Andre," she said.

I waited for someone to say something, but no one did. "Excuse me?"

The judge peered at me over her glasses. "There will have to be a clause that stipulates a course of action in the event that Andre and Sabrina are not in concordance regarding certain occurrences," she said.

I looked at Andre, who appeared to be staring at something on the floor. Sabrina was sitting behind me; I could not see her face.

"And of course," the judge continued, "there also would need to be a paragraph permitting me to vet the book for Andre in order to protect him."

"Vetting," I knew, was a term used by publishers to make sure nothing was printed that might embarrass, disgrace, defame or otherwise cause a libel action to be filed.

"Thank you very much, judge," I said. "But what if Sabrina remembers things differently from Andre? And what if Andre remembers things differently from Sabrina? Andre has to be free to tell things his way, from his own experience and memory, but so does Sabrina. This isn't just about Andre. It's about Sabrina, too."

The judge flipped through the document. And then she said something about how Sabrina's memories might be in conflict with Andre's, and how it would be her duty to protect Andre.

"I am very sorry," I said. "I realize you are looking out for Andre's best interests, but there is no possible way I could agree to your terms. People remember things differently." She looked at me as if I had slapped her.

"Thank you for your time, judge," I said. I stood up and shook her hand. Then I turned to Andre, then Sabrina, and thanked them both for meeting with me.

Downstairs, outside on the sidewalk, the wind cut through my thin jacket like someone was stabbing me with icicles. My hands were so cold I could barely feel the cigarette I was holding. *What I would do for a pair of gloves right now.* And then, suddenly, I thought of my mother. Just a few weeks before she flew out for Thanksgiving, I had called her and told her about Andre, about how much I wanted to reach him.

"Put it in God's hands," she had said to me.

I looked upward, but all I could see were patches of gray above office buildings. *Well, Mama, I've really screwed things up. Something about that judge just made me so angry—and now it's all over. Now what?* I took another puff on my cigarette and looked around for a taxi.

Just then there was a voice behind me. "I didn't know you smoked."

I turned around. It was Andre. Sabrina was standing right beside him, unsuccessfully trying to wrap her parka around her belly.

"You don't look like someone who smokes," he said, grinning.

"Well, Andre, I hope it won't be my fatal flaw."

"I hate to ask you, but do you have an extra cigarette? I ran out."

I fished in my purse, trying to extract just one, but my fingers were so numb that I finally gave up and handed him the entire pack. He lit up, inhaled and handed the pack back to me.

"You were pretty strong in there. That judge didn't know what hit her."

"I'm sorry," I said. I looked at Andre—he had such an incredibly kind face, such a gentle face—and then at Sabrina. Immediately I thought of that old term from English novels for a shy, timid woman: church mouse. "I truly didn't mean to insult the judge," I said. "I'm sure she was only doing what she thinks is best for you.

"But you know what, Andre? I firmly believe that no one has the right to control another person's memories. It would be great if we all remembered everything that ever happened to us exactly the way it really happened, if there were some huge video camera in the sky that we could rewind and then say, 'Oh! I was wrong about that date!' Or, 'Gee, I was wrong about what happened first!' But that's not how memories work.

"We don't always remember things in a precise timeline—first A, then B, then C," I went on. "And we can't look back into someone else's heart and know what they were thinking when they acted the way they did. We can't always understand why someone did something, even if we think we do, either. I guess what I'm trying to say is, sometimes we remember things wrong. But even if we do, that doesn't mean we shouldn't be allowed to remember whatever it is we really remember."

I looked at Andre and then Sabrina. "And you, Sabrina? No one has even talked to you about what happened, have they?" She looked down and gave a tiny shake of her head. "I came here to New York and I was just about to make the same mistake. But you know what? This happened to you, too. I don't know exactly how, or what it did to you, or what you went through. But I do know that everything that happened to Andre had to affect you, too. And even if it's not me who ends up telling your story, I hope you won't forget that. I hope you never let anyone do what that judge was trying to do. Because no matter what anyone says, you matter, too."

A taxi pulled up to my outstretched hand. "Good-bye," I said to them. "And God bless you both."

I slid into the backseat, trembling. I could not tell if it was because of the cold or because I had just lost something I had believed so deeply, and for so long, was destined for me. I gave the driver the name of my hotel. Only then did I notice a pair of gloves on the seat beside me. They were ladies', made of fine Italian leather, and had a beautiful mink trim at the cuffs.

"Lady," the taxi driver said, glancing in his mirror, "consider them a gift. No one ever comes back for that kind of stuff."

I slid them on; they fit perfectly. And it was the strangest feeling: as if my mother was sitting right there on the seat next to me.

* * *

There was not much to pack. It only took a few minutes to fold up the stupidly planned thin cotton blouses from my hotel closet. And then there was a knock on my door. It was Andre's face I saw through the fish-eye lens.

"Do you mind if we come in for a minute?"

"Please," I said, opening the door wider. Sabrina was with him. I saw them look at the open suitcase on the bed. I could not put my finger on it, but something about Sabrina seemed different, as if, en route to my hotel, some of her timidity had been brushed off like snowflakes off a sleeve.

"Sabrina and I have been thinking about what you said. And talking it over," Andre began.

I shook my head. "I'm really sorry, Andre. I never should have—"

Sabrina took a step forward. "I want you to know, Miss Mackey, that I feel so much better now, after what you told that lady. And also after what you said on the sidewalk because up until then, I was feeling pretty bad. I really was."

I did not know what to say to them.

"We talked it over, and we both decided we don't want any lawyer messing in this," Andre said. "We just want to tell you what happened, however we remember it. We're not doing it for money or anything like that. We're doing it for our sister."

"That's the only promise we ask of you," Sabrina said. "The only thing we want is for you to give us your word that you'll tell everyone that this isn't Andre's story, and it's not my story, either. It's Latanisha's story. It's the story of a child who should be alive and with us right now."

I did not know why my eyes suddenly welled with tears or why my throat grew thick with emotion.

"I promise you," I said.

We talked about how we would be in contact with each other—by phone, by recording their thoughts into hand-held tape recorders, by what I expected would be numerous trips to New York. Afterward, Andre and Sabrina took the hotel elevator downstairs and walked outside onto the sidewalk. I did not learn until several years later what they said about me that day.

"Did you see her face when we were talking about Latanisha?" Andre asked.

"I sure did," Sabrina said.

"She's got something in her life too—there's some kind of ghost back there, I can just tell."

"You got that right," Sabrina said. "It's like she understands."

South El Monte Library
1430 N Central Ave
South El Monte, CA 91733
(626) 443-4158

Title: The lost boy : a foster
child's search for the lo
Item ID: 0112436380540
Date charged: 3/18/2017,
12:04
Date due: 4/25/2017, 23:59

Renew items online.
Log in to: www.colapublib.
org

chapter 19

The Shadow of Doubt

People often talk about "closure," as if life were a book: you finish the last page and then the story is over. But life does not always work that way. And in the months following the trial of Madeline and Gregory Carmichael, it was not what happened for Andre and Sabrina.

One of the most important tasks still left untended was laying their sister to rest. Ever since detectives from the Cold Case Squad had discovered the blue metal trunk, Latanisha's body had been held at the Kings County morgue in Brooklyn. Andre and Sabrina wanted to hold a proper memorial service for her, but they had known that nothing could be done until the trial was over.

Unfortunately, however, they soon discovered that they would have to wait even longer.

"We keep calling to find out when they will release her body, but it's starting to feel like we're getting the runaround," Sabrina said to me. "No one seems willing to give us any answers."

Andre said he understood that there "probably is a process they have to go through before they can let us give our sister her memorial service." Nevertheless, he hoped it would be soon.

"Every day that goes by, every day I know my twin is still waiting for us to set her free," he confessed, "it hurts me inside. This is difficult to describe, but it's really like my heart actually *hurts*."

Meanwhile, Sabrina continued to receive letters on a regular basis from her mother, along with poetry written from Mrs. Carmichael's bed inside the prison's infirmary. Most of the letters contained meaningless tidbits of news, such as how the flu bug was going around, or how no stamps could be sent to inmates by relatives because some had been found to have drugs on the stamp glue. Sabrina nevertheless read each communication carefully, looking for some sign of remorse or regret that might be hidden between the lines.

There was only one time that Sabrina thought she might have received a hint of that. For Valentine's Day, 2001, Mrs. Carmichael sent Sabrina what appeared to be an original, untitled poem:

Whenever February comes over the Hill
She spills her red and gold at will.
She covers summers flowerly days
With copper-colored leaf displays.
She Autumn dresses every tree

In cloaks of crimson artistry.
She skips among the trees and then
Spreads golden Sunshine on the glen.
February days are bitter sweet.
Too soon they leave on padded feet.
So my cup of red and gold I'll fill...
Whenever February comes over the hill.

"Andre and Latanisha were born in February," Sabrina said to me, "and right away when I read that, I thought that she was expressing how difficult that month was for her. Even if she wasn't aware of it, even if she wasn't conscious when she wrote it, for her to pick that month seemed as though, deep down, maybe she was remembering what was missing."

All through 2001, Sabrina continued to travel a few times each month to visit her mother in prison. Neither of them ever talked about Latanisha's death or Sabrina's testimony when she had referred to her mother and brother as "devils," or the role Sabrina had played in putting her mother behind bars. Instead, Mrs. Carmichael confined her conversations to items she needed Sabrina to send to her, often providing her daughter with long lists of things. More importantly, however, she also continued to tell Sabrina over and over how much she loved her, and how God blessed her by giving her such a wonderful daughter.

For the first time in her entire life, Sabrina was getting affection from her mother. For the first time ever, love was being expressed to her. And so Sabrina kept traveling up to the prison, waiting and hoping that her mother would finally say the other things she had waited so long to hear.

"I keep thinking she'll bring it up when she's ready," Sabrina said. "I keep telling myself that she knows what she did to my sister, and she'll talk to me about it soon."

But as her mother's bone cancer worsened, Sabrina began to fear, perhaps, that time might never come. During early 2002, she traveled to the prison even more often—for medical reasons, Mrs. Carmichael had since been transferred from Riker's Island to the Bedford Hills Correctional Facility— aware that time, for her mother, was running out.

"She's in a lot of pain," she said, "and it's pretty obvious that she's not going to serve out her whole sentence."

During one of those trips Mrs. Carmichael, now heavily medicated, told Sabrina that she wanted to tell her a story, one she had never heard before.

"You've got a right to hear it," Mrs. Carmichael said to her.

Sabrina leaned forward and took a deep breath. Maybe this, she thought, was going to be what she'd waited for her mother to say.

Mrs. Carmichael started out by telling Sabrina that she was born in 1939 in South Carolina. She grew up in Orangeburg, a small town where "everyone knew your busi- ness." Her own mother and father worked hard to give her and her thirteen younger siblings a good Catholic upbringing; they all went to church each Sunday, confessed their small sins, and went home again. When she was in her late teens, she married a "good man" named Joseph Carmichael. They were "so happy, we loved each other so much," she told Sabrina. But then, she revealed, she committed a life-altering sin.

"She told me that she had been trying to have a baby with her husband for years," Sabrina said, "and then she had an affair with her best friend's husband and got pregnant." Mrs. Carmichael felt that there was no reason for her husband to know the truth. If she kept the secret to herself, she thought, she and her husband could both simply raise the child as their own. Why reveal a painful secret if it wasn't necessary?

However, when she revealed she was pregnant, her husband confessed a secret of his own. Long before they were married, he had known he was sterile, but he had never had the courage to tell her.

"Soon everyone found out what she'd done—her family, her friends from church, the whole town—and she was turned into an outcast. It was impossible for her to live there anymore. She had to leave everyone she loved and everything she had ever known and start all over."

Mrs. Carmichael moved north to the anonymity of New York, where she gave birth, alone and friendless, to Gregory. Until she was assaulted and injured her back some years later, she apparently had supported herself and her child by working as a nurse—Sabrina was never able to determine what level of training or licensing her mother had received—and nine years later she gave birth to Sabrina, whose father was Chester MacLean, a merchant seaman who was light-skinned and had freckles.

As she talked to her daughter about these events long before, Mrs. Carmichael did not mention to Sabrina that Latanisha had the same coloring. She only said that "even though Mr. MacLean only showed up now and then, whenever it suited him," she nevertheless had come to love him very much. One day, though, he simply disappeared, for good.

"He had another family," Mrs. Carmichael told Sabrina.

Sabrina waited to hear something more from her mother, but that, apparently, was the end of the story. Whatever it was that her mother felt Sabrina "had a right to know" was apparently contained within their short conversation that day. After that, her mother became quiet. Sabrina thought perhaps all the medication her mother was under had interrupted her train of thought and she forgot what she had intended to say.

Sabrina was disappointed, but she still held out hope that her mother would talk to her, finally, about something meaningful and "real"—about Latanisha, about what happened to their family, about what the secret had done to them all.

She already had thoughts about what the secret had done to her mother.

"I told Andre one time that if it had been me who had done what she did, if I had been the one who had to carry around that dark secret, it would have eaten me alive," Sabrina later said to me. "And now I really think that's what has happened to her. She's still hanging onto the secret, she's still not talking about anything that happened and the bone cancer is literally eating her alive."

Still, for many months after the visit in which her mother talked about her extramarital affair, Sabrina struggled to understand what her mother had gone through in those early days, or what the disappearance of Chester MacLean might have done to her mental state right after the twins were born. Sabrina thought back to the loving mother she had once known when it was just her, Greg and her mother at the Castle Hill projects, and she wondered: Did her mother, perhaps, suffer from post-partum depression? Could the long-term stress of having four children and living on welfare perhaps have magnified that depression? Was it possible that her mother's contact with child welfare workers during her pregnancy—when she told them she was "too sick" to care for Gregory and Sabrina, and they both were then temporarily placed in foster care—was a failed attempt to let someone know what deep emotional trouble she was falling into?

Now Sabrina also began to think about something else, something that began to torment her: What if she had false memories and had been wrong about everything?

During the months leading up to the trial, Sabrina had been unswerving in her memory of what happened that day when she was eight years old. As Andre had pointed out, even during repeated questioning, she never once had changed any aspect of her story. It was that same certainty that Sabrina had shown on the witness stand when she refused to allow her mother's attorney to intimidate her, and it also was the same certitude that later caused prosecutors in the district attorney's office to call her a "spitfire" because of her responses under cross examination.

However, that doesn't mean that prosecutors were always completely certain that Sabrina would be able to withstand such pressure. To the contrary, Ama Dwimoh told me later that prior to Sabrina's testimony in court, she had been concerned whether Sabrina would be able to hold up on the witness stand, particularly since Sabrina was receiving affectionate letters from Mrs. Carmichael and also making regular trips to visit her mother in prison.

"While we were preparing [to go to trial], I knew that Sabrina had conflicted loyalties between what we were doing on behalf of Latanisha and her mother," Ms. Dwimoh said, adding that in the types of child abuse cases she prosecutes, "it's not uncommon that the victims are still connected to the perpetrators."

The unknown factor, however, was whether Sabrina's mother was attempting to "sway her to silence," and also whether Sabrina, at the eleventh hour, might not be emotionally capable of providing her vitally needed testimony.

"I understood this was not going to be easy for Sabrina," Ms. Dwimoh went on. "This was her mother. No matter who you are, you always want your mother's approval. Sabrina had held onto the dark secret for so long and paid such a huge price, I didn't know what kind of manipulative power Madeline Carmichael would have over her."

But as the trial neared, the prosecutor must have felt relief that Mrs. Carmichael's outpouring of affection "never changed [Sabrina's] willingness to testify."

"Did I have concerns about its impact in court?" Ms. Dwimoh asked. "Yes. It's hard for people to testify against people they know, people they love. And when it's your mother, the situation is very trying. It would not have been unreasonable for Sabrina to say, 'I've done all I can do.'"

Ms. Dwimoh seemed to have little doubt about what the trial's outcome would have been if Sabrina had done that at the last moment.

"I never would have been able to convict [Mrs. Carmichael] of the murder," she said. "Sabrina was the critical piece of evidence in this. Everyone knew it, too—Madeline knew it, Gregory knew it. The body had decomposed, and so from a forensic perspective, all I would have had was a badly decomposed body."

But Mrs. Carmichael, Gregory and the prosecutors weren't the only ones who realized that it was Sabrina's testimony that had been the "critical piece" in the trial. Now that the trial was over and Mrs. Carmichael was incarcerated, Sabrina seemed to realize it, too. And that, I think, is when she began to agonize about what she had done, when the weight of that knowledge began to sink down heavily inside her.

Over the course of several conversations with Sabrina, I grew increasingly worried when, for the first time, it seemed as though Sabrina was now doubting her testimony and tormenting herself with the possibility that she had made a terrible mistake. Several times, Sabrina told me that she was asking herself "all sorts of questions":

What if Joshua Horowitz, her mother's attorney, had been right after all? What if Latanisha's death really had been a terrible accident, just the way he said it had been? And what if her mother had been filled with such a terror of discovery after the accident that it eventually pushed her already fragile mental health over the edge?

Sabrina began to be haunted by the idea that what she thought she had remembered—and more importantly, what she had testified to in court—actually might have happened differently, that her "faulty memory," as her mother's lawyer had said during the trial, was responsible for her mother now being forced to die a horrible death in prison.

"I told my therapist that I couldn't let go of the guilt, that it feels like it's eating me up," she said to me. "I told him that was why I was going up even more often to the prison to see my mother, because I'm the one who put her there and I keep asking myself *what if I was wrong?* I can't get rid of that thought."

Ama Dwimoh, it seemed to me, had been correct to worry about whether Mrs. Carmichael held a "manipulative power" over Sabrina and might "sway" her. Perhaps overlooked, however, was the possibility that such manipulation might occur after the trial, and not just before it. As just one example, in one letter to Sabrina, Mrs. Carmichael wrote "I love you Babe" on one side of the paper, along with a list of items she needed Sabrina to send to her. This list was relatively short, compared to some of her requests in previous letters:

Four tee-shirts, size extra large
Pre-cooked chicken wings
Canned tuna
Canned shrimp
Salted peanuts
Chef-Boyardee
Prunes-Dry

On the other side of the paper, however, Mrs. Carmichael had made an altogether different kind of request.

"Sabrina, here is the appeal address," she wrote, along with the mailing address for the Office of the Inspector General in Albany, New York. Mrs. Carmichael had even been thoughtful enough to write the letter she wanted Sabrina to copy by hand and then send out on her behalf:

"To whom it may be of concern,

"My name is Ms. Sabrina Yaw. I am the daughter of Ms. Madeline Carmichael #0190364 whom resides now at Bedford Hills Correctional Facility...I am requesting of you to please grant my dear Mom, Mrs. Carmichael, [an] appeal application. Thank you again, N God Bless."

I asked Sabrina if she was planning to send the letter. There was a long pause before she answered.

"I don't know," she said. "I'm still thinking about it."

It was no wonder to me that Sabrina was confused and tied up in emotional knots; her testimony had been responsible for ensuring her mother and brother's conviction—and now Mrs. Carmichael was attempting to manipulate her into filing an appeal on her behalf. It struck me that Mrs. Carmichael was using every wile to gain sympathy and trying to get Sabrina to recant. And from the way Sabrina kept talking about her new uncertainty about what happened that day when she was eight years old, suddenly I did not think it was impossible that Mrs. Carmichael—the same woman one investigator had called "crazy like a fox" —might succeed in her efforts.

Andre, meanwhile, had no desire to contact his mother. He didn't hate her—"that word is too strong, it's something else," he said—but he also was afraid of what he might say to her if he saw her again.

"I don't trust myself to go there," he told me. "I want to forgive what she did, but I just can't. I keep thinking about my family and our fight to survive. Still, nothing in the world would make me beat my kids like they were stray dogs or take my frustrations out on them. That's the difference between us. People talk about how abused kids grow up to be abusers themselves, but I'm here to say that it's not always like that. I'm living proof of that."

There also was another reason Andre did not go to the prison. Over the course of the last year or so, he had single-hand-edly pulled his entire family out of desperate living conditions.

Now they had a comfortable apartment of their own. With five children to support, Andre told me he could not afford to take more than one day off each week, and that day was reserved for his family, which included being able to occasionally visit Sabrina on Sundays.

"I want my children to grow up with the things I didn't have," he said to me. "I'm not necessarily talking about *stuff*— about material things—but I want them to grow up feeling loved and cared about. I want to come home after work and be with them, maybe just listen to what's going on in school or things like that. I guess what I'm trying to say is, you can have a lot of kids, and even if they only have one white bear that they all have to share, if you're giving them love and showing them that they matter to you, I think they'll grow up and be good people."

Andre said he didn't blame Sabrina for visiting their mother—"Sabrina needs to do whatever she needs to do," he said—but it disturbed him to listen to Sabrina talk about how their mother still had never mentioned Latanisha's name even once.

"Sabrina still has hope that she's going to talk about it. For our mother's sake I hope she does, I hope she doesn't carry it to the grave with her. But I'm not holding my breath."

One area of Andre and Sabrina's life, however, remained unchanged. Even after more than two and a half years had passed since Mrs. Carmichael's arrest, Latanisha's body still remained at the Kings County morgue. Andre and Sabrina had been told that their sister's remains were needed as evidence in the event of an appeal, and later that there was a bureaucratic problem involving red tape. Regardless of the reasons for the delay, however, Sabrina and Andre grew increasingly upset as the months went by.

"My twin sister was in a trunk for twenty years, and now she's in the morgue for another two years? To me, that means that my twin sister is still alone, that she's still being forgotten," Andre said to me in March, 2002. "All Sabrina and I want to do is give her a proper funeral so she can finally rest in peace. Is that too much to ask?"

"It's like a nightmare that just won't stop," Sabrina said. "It's like she's still inside that closet."

Finally, in early June, 2002, Latanisha's body was released to the Frank R. Bell funeral home in Brooklyn. Sabrina called to tell me about the memorial service she had planned for the following Saturday, June 8, as well as to let me know about the attempts she was making to allow her mother to be able to attend. She said she had been told that, in extremely rare cases, prisoners could be granted such requests "out of compassion."

"The way I see it, she's dying," Sabrina said. "Hopefully that will make them have some kind of compassion and let her come. I know she killed my sister, but I also think the least she can do is come say good-bye to Latanisha."

I wanted to ask Sabrina if I could come to the service as well, but something stopped me—something, I should add, that flew in the face of all my experience as a reporter. What it boiled down to was, I did not want to intrude upon her family at such an emotional time. Sabrina must have sensed that immediately, because as soon as I began talking about being in touch after the service, she interrupted me.

"After all we've been through together?" she said, her voice rising up in mock outrage. "I'll never forgive you if you don't come." She said it in a way that deeply touched me, as if both of us had just stepped over the line that separates journalist from subject, and that we now were turning into friends as well.

But then Sabrina told me that, before the memorial service could take place, there was something extremely important she and Andre had to do. Even though they knew that what they had in mind would be extremely difficult, they both felt a need to view their sister's body, "to look the truth in the face," as Andre said to me.

"I'm not going to lie to you. I'm scared of it, of actually seeing her with my own eyes," Andre said. "All my life, I've just had blurry little pictures of her inside my head. Things like two little feet stuck in my face in the white crib, or another baby's hand with the skin burned off on top. There's this part of me that's afraid I'll look at her, and then that's the way I'll always remember her. I don't want that to happen. I'm scared of that happening. But I also know that I'll never have the chance to do this again. To look at my twin sister and let her know that I finally found her."

Two days later, wearing gowns, gloves and masks, Andre and Sabrina entered a back room of the funeral home holding hands. When they looked down at their little sister, they gripped each other's hands even tighter. It was the most gruesome sight either of them had ever witnessed.

Mrs. Carmichael had used her "nursing skills," as Sabrina put it, and preserved Latanisha's body with various herbs "like an Egyptian mummy." Their sister still had flesh and skin on her legs and feet; the herbs gave off a pungent, musky smell that reminded Sabrina of a field trip she once took with her school as a child to the Museum of Natural History.

But what shocked Sabrina the most was seeing her sister's skull. The injuries, she said, were in the exact place she had remembered—and suddenly the memory of her mother punching Latanisha on the side of her head played out in front of her again.

"On the side of her skull, it looked as though the bones were broken and the back of her head was crushed, too. It was one thing to know how she died," she said, her voice shaking, "but it was another thing to actually see it with my own eyes."

Suddenly, Sabrina felt a rush of emotion she had never felt before.

"All that love I've been feeling for my mother, all that forgiveness, it just flew away. Like someone blew out a candle. Ever since the trial, I've been trying to talk myself into believing that maybe it was an accident like Mama's lawyer said, that maybe Tish really did fall backward on her head. But when I saw that hole in my sister's head above her ear, I knew it wasn't any accident. Right then I thought: *Mama has never once said she was sorry. All those times I've been going to see her, and never once has she asked for forgiveness. All those years she knew what she did, but even now, even at the end of her own life, she's still acting as though Tish never existed.*

"Lord forgive me," Sabrina said, "but I stood there and I hated my mother so intensely like I didn't know you could hate anyone." Her voice was trembling. "After viewing my sister like that I even told my therapist that I hated my mother. But he said something strange to me. He said, 'I've been waiting a long time for you to get angry like this, Sabrina. What you're feeling now is a good sign. The anger means you're coming back to life inside.'"

And Sabrina wasn't alone in experiencing powerful emotions. For the first time in more than two decades, Andre was staring at his twin sister, a little girl who would have grown into a beautiful twenty-six-year-old woman had she lived.

"I stood there looking at my twin and I said a silent prayer," Andre told me a few days later. "I said, *'Oh Tish, I'm sorry I wasn't big enough to protect you, to keep you from harm. And I'm so sorry I took so long to find you. But somehow we've always been together, haven't we? All my life I felt you with me. It was always you talking to me, wasn't it? And it was you looking over me, taking care of me all those years, wasn't it?'*

"I stood there and cried," he went on. "I didn't care who saw me—I just sobbed. I thanked her for being my angel, for staying with me, for not letting me turn into someone else, into the kind of person Mama and Greg would have turned me into. And then I told her I loved her. That I'd always love her, and I'd never forget her."

Afterward, Andre and Sabrina walked a few blocks toward the train station in silence. It was warm out, so they stepped inside a corner grocery to get something cool to drink. Andre opened a glass door and leaned forward for a soda, while Sabrina opened a different glass door to grab a bottle of water. Suddenly, they both jerked upright and looked at each other.

"Do you smell that?" Andre said. It was the same herbal, musky smell from the funeral parlor. The scent seemed as if it was coming out of the cool air of the market's refrigerator and then swirling all around them, engulfing them.

Sabrina nodded slowly, wide-eyed.

They walked to the train station without either saying a word. Neither felt capable of talking about what had just happened.

Later that day, as Andre got off the train and walked up the steps to his apartment building, he froze once again.

"I was pulling my keys out of my pocket and suddenly it just hit me," Andre told me. "It was exactly the same smell, the exact same one from the funeral parlor, like nothing I've ever smelled before. I was standing in front of my door and suddenly it was all around me, like a cloud. It was like Latanisha was right there with me, like she had followed me home."

chapter 20

In Jesus' Arms

On the day of Latanisha's memorial service, Sabrina planned to come to my hotel by train and arrive around 1:00 p.m. I waited in the lobby for about an hour, and then decided to call her. Sabrina is one of the most punctual people I have ever met, and so I was concerned that something might have happened. Her husband, Chris, answered the phone. I was surprised when he told me she had just left their apartment a few minutes earlier, and also that he wasn't coming with her to the service.

"I had to stay with the boys," he said.

At 3:00 p.m., a shiny black stretch limousine pulled up in front of my hotel, and out stepped Sabrina. At the last minute, she explained, the Crime Victims Assistance department, thanks to help from the district attorney's office, had approved the funds for it. Unfortunately, though, Andre hadn't gotten the word in time, and so he and two close friends were already en route by train. We would all meet at the funeral home.

Inside the limo was Sabrina's daughter, who at nearly sixteen was the same age as my youngest son. She was wearing an outfit identical in every respect to her mother's: both in matching silvery blouses with sheer black sleeves, a long black skirt and tasteful black pumps. They both wore their hair the same, too, pulled tight on top of their heads with a ring of loose curls.

"You look more like twins than mother and daughter," I said. They both smiled and gave each other a long, affectionate glance.

Her daughter, I thought, was absolutely lovely. She was quiet but poised, and seemed to possess a strong sense of herself that reminded me of her mother. Sabrina's oldest son was sprawled out on one side of the limo in a blue basketball outfit and wearing headphones. Sabrina explained that he would be changing into a dark suit when we got there.

"God forbid he should have to wear a suit and tie one second longer than he absolutely has to," she said, smiling at her son. He was jerking his head up and down to the music in his headphones, but when he noticed his mother looking at him, instantly he broke into a wide grin. There was an easiness between them, as if they shared a deep understanding.

"You're also going to be meeting someone else today," Sabrina said, turning to me. She had an impish expression on her face now, as if she wanted me to guess who it was.

"Would I be able to figure it out if I tried?"

She shook her head, smiling. "Never."

"Okay, then I give up," I said.

"Remember I told you what my mother said about how my father disappeared right after the twins were born and about how he probably went back to his family?"

I nodded. It was the conversation in which Mrs. Carmichael had told Sabrina that she had a "right to know" about something, and Sabrina had expected her to talk about Latanisha.

"Well, it turns out that Chester McClean had a very big family. Andre and I have three half-sisters and three half-brothers. Can you believe it? We've got ourselves a whole new family."

At the funeral home, Sabrina was greeted by a soft-spoken woman who informed her that Andre, along with several family members, had called to say they were running a little bit late. Sabrina thanked the woman, and then Sabrina, her kids and I went into the chapel to wait.

There was a small organ in one corner, and along the front on a long narrow table were four huge flower wreaths of pink roses, pink carnations, pink chrysanthemums, and pink orchids. Each wreath had a long pink ribbon with the words, "Beloved daughter and sister," and I noticed that beside each wreath there also was a white card that read, "From Mother, Andre and Sabrina."

It did not seem like the right time for me to ask Sabrina why she had chosen to include her mother's name on the cards, especially since I knew how upset she had been just a few days earlier, but the wording also apparently caught the attention of a reporter from the *New York Daily News*, who approached Sabrina and asked if she could speak with her for a few moments. Sabrina explained to the reporter, in carefully worded language that reminded me of a deer stepping gingerly in a forest that is too silent, that she had written it to give some dignity to the service. She said she knew that her mother had killed her sister, but she wasn't a monster.

"She had a sweet side, too," Sabrina said.

The cards suddenly made sense to me, but not in the way Sabrina had just explained them to the reporter. Sabrina might have been trying to humanize her mother, but the cards actually spoke more to Sabrina's character than Mrs. Carmichael's. Just one week earlier, Sabrina had been staring at her sister's body and feeling a rush of fury toward her mother, but already she had transformed that into forgiveness, into understanding. Where, I wondered, had she learned that? And how was it possible for someone to have endured everything she had, and then grow up to be so generous of spirit?

A few minutes before the service was set to begin, Andre arrived. He was dressed in a beautiful black silk jacket cut in a Japanese style with matching silk pants, and he was smiling broadly, joking with his friends and family members about his perpetual lateness. I had never seen him look like that—so happy that he looked lit from within. Later he told me that he had walked into the chapel, seen the wreaths of flowers, and "suddenly I felt like one of those big Thanksgiving Day balloons, like I was filled up with helium."

Right before the minister entered and everyone sat down, I saw Andre glance over to a professionally dressed woman a few rows back. Andre nodded to her.

"That's Ama Dwimoh," Sabrina whispered to me.

How incredible, I thought, that the prosecutor would reach out to Andre and Sabrina, even after more than two years had gone by. It seemed to me that only someone utterly committed, and only someone of sensitivity whose life was interwoven into the fabric of one's work, would do such a thing.

And then everyone fell silent as the organist began playing, and the minister, Rev. David K. Brawley, began speaking.

"We have come to celebrate a life, and to remember," he said.

Even though Latanisha's had been a short life, he said, she was God's creation. She had walked this Earth, and that was why we were gathered there, to celebrate God's creation and her presence among us. And there was a story he wanted to tell to all of us.

There was a passage in the Bible, he said, about how David had fasted and grieved for his little boy, who was dying. But once the child died, David rose, washed his face, and ate. When David was asked why he cried and fasted while the child was dying, but then ate and worshipped after the child had died, David replied that while the child still lived, he could not know whether God would be gracious and spare his child. But now that the child was dead, no amount of fasting would bring the child back. David said, *I shall go to him, but he shall not return to me.*

"David knew the child was now with God," the minister said. "He knew he would never see the child again in this life, but that one day he would go to God and see that child again."

And then the minister began to speak of things that Sabrina and I had talked about in the limo on the way over. Sabrina had told me that she believed in life after death, that she believed there was a world beyond our own that we can't understand.

"Even though we can't see it," Sabrina had said to me, "we can still know it's there, the same way that at night time we still know there's a sun."

Rev. Brawley also was talking about this.

"And you all *know* that this isn't all there is, you all *know* that just because the body dies, the spirit does not die," he said. "Some people might be tempted to ask where God was when this child died? The answer is, He was in the same place as when his own son died. Yes, if it were up to Him, Latanisha would not have suffered as she did, and she would have been protected as all children are meant to be.

"But you *know* that Jesus loves all the little children, and that when Latanisha came to him, he didn't just wave at her or smile at her. Jesus took her into his arms—and you *know* she is protected now."

He paused for a moment.

"Even though Latanisha didn't get love and protection on this Earth, she has it now. And you can be sure that she wants that for the ones she loves. And do you know what she is?"

He peered out at us all, and then let his gaze fall on Andre and Sabrina.

"Latanisha Carmichael is an angel now, and she's watching over you. She's free now. She's finally free. And you, Andre, and you Sabrina, you helped to free her."

Epilogue

It has been more than seven years since I first met Andre and Sabrina. Since then, the three of us have become close friends.

The more I talked with them and came to know them, the more I came to realize they were people I had genuinely come to admire and care about. It mattered to me what they were going through when their mother died in prison of bone cancer in August 2002; it mattered to me how Sabrina was holding up after she and Chris separated just a few months later; it mattered to me when Andre called me up one day in 2004 with the wonderful news that he and his wife had just had a baby girl.

They named her Latanisha.

What has never failed to fill me with awe is Andre and Sabrina's unflagging optimism, regardless of what events are

occurring in their lives. It is the kind of optimism that makes
you feel ashamed not to share it, the kind of positive outlook
that makes you realize that faith and belief and hopefulness
have nothing to do with a person's background or circumstances: they are, instead, choices we make in our lives.

Very often they talk to me about the importance of love,
honesty, forgiveness and their faith in God, although both
express those thoughts differently.

One day, Andre told me that he had unexpectedly lost his
job. My first reaction was to worry about him; he did, after all,
have a family to support. But Andre immediately began talking philosophically about his situation. It wasn't what he
would have chosen for himself, he said, but he had learned
that everything happens for a reason.

"Lots of times you can't see what that reason is until
much later, so that's why you just have to keep putting one
foot in front of the other and doing whatever gets put in front
of you," he said. It was the same way, he added, as it had been
that day when his daughter wanted to go visit her grandma,
and Andre took her just to make her happy.

"I couldn't see around the corner of that day, either," he
said, "but now I know the reason for it."

Sure enough, Andre soon landed a much better job, one
that no doubt utilizes both his easy-going nature and strong
work ethic. Today he is the manager of a busy Brooklyn restaurant. Unfortunately, Andre and his wife also are now separated; the couple's two daughters live with him.

Sabrina, too, has overcome numerous obstacles, and
some of her greatest accomplishments, she believes, have to
do with how well her children are doing. She takes great pride

in the fact that her daughter received her Associate of Arts degree from the City University of New York, and that her oldest son will enter college as well.

Sabrina, like Andre, also has had professional accomplishments. A few years ago she returned to school, attending classes at the Bronx campus of CUNY and became a certified nursing assistant. Her goal is to return to school for an additional nursing degree.

No school, however, could possibly teach the kind of compassion I have already witnessed in her. For example, one day Sabrina called to tell me about a woman whom she and another home healthcare aide had been taking care of for more than a year. She had no children and no family, but she did have many friends and former colleagues who visited her frequently—until the woman became hospitalized and then passed away.

Sabrina said that, at the woman's funeral, she and the other healthcare aide were the only two people in attendance.

"That showed me again that in this world, people need people, but they're not always there when you need them. So you *have* to rely on God," she said. "At the same time, it also reminded me that you never know why God brings certain people into your life. I like to think I was brought into her life for a reason. She was very educated, and so were all her friends, but in the end, it was just two nurse's aides with her."

After I spoke to Sabrina, I turned to my husband and I began telling him something my mother had said years and years earlier, when I was just a small child, about an elderly cousin of my father's.

The man, I told my husband, had been a renowned neurosurgeon, and even in his eighties still wrote brilliant articles for scientific journals. As small children, my siblings and I reluctantly went with our parents to visit him and his equally sharp-tongued wife, where I unsuccessfully tried not to stare at his curved back and misshapen shoes, the results of child-hood rickets. We were all frightened of him, I think; he was a brusque, impatient man, ill-suited to underage company and those without doctoral degrees, and his thick German accent made everything he said sound even more terrifying.

My mother, however, apparently had a similar response to him. In the car driving home from his house one day, she said to my father, fighting back tears, "That man might have one of the most educated minds on this planet, but he has the most uneducated heart of any human being I have ever known."

I stood in my kitchen, shaking my head.

"What made you think of that?" my husband asked me.

I told him it was because of Sabrina and Andre.

"I have known many people in my life with supremely educated minds," I said, "but I cannot remember meeting any two people with such supremely educated hearts."

Afterword

In the course of writing this book, it was necessary for me to ask Andre and Sabrina many extremely difficult questions, ones I knew would force them to go back into their haunted pasts and recall some of the most painful episodes in their lives. There were times when I literally felt as though I could not do this to them anymore; that I could not, for example, ask them to describe the scent of their sister's remains. What I was doing seemed as if it continually was dragging them backward into the murkiest corners of their lives, at the same time that both were struggling so mightily to move forward.

But there also were times in which it was clear they felt the same way, when reliving so many awful experiences simply became too much for them, too overwhelming. Whenever that occurred, the three of us would set our work aside and sometimes weeks or even months would go by before we reconnected. When we did, we began as friends do, catching up on whatever had been going on in each of our lives.

It wasn't until one of our more recent conversations, however, that I realized there was something I had never revealed to them, something that connected us far more than the fact that I, too, am a fraternal twin. For more than seven years, I had sealed it off inside of me, but now, I said, I felt I had to tell them about it. For all those years they had been sharing their most private pasts with me, and I needed to do the same thing with them.

"Okay," they said, and then waited.

When I had a hard time finding the words to begin, Andre said in a gentle voice, "Come on, just say it. Whatever it is, it's okay. You can trust us."

And I knew he was right. I could trust them.

This is what I said to them:

I never told you anything about my mother. She died four weeks after your mother and Gregory's trial. She and my father had come out to my house for Thanksgiving, and she had a heart attack while she was there. That's why I kept calling you the way I did, Andre—I was afraid that if I didn't try to keep working, I'd fall apart or completely break down.

But maybe there was another reason, too, one that has taken me a long time to talk about.

My mother was a professional musician, a very gifted violist in an orchestra, as well as a violinist and pianist. Still, when we were growing up, all six of us kids used to tease her about how she seemed like she was "on another planet," or how she looked as if she was walking around inside a fish tank. Somehow, though, she always seemed to get it together in time to play concerts at night. We didn't know until much later that she'd had scores of doctors giving her tranquilizers. Back then, doctors did that, handed out Valium to housewives like it was candy.

She once told me that most of my childhood was a total blur for her. At one point she'd had five kids under the age of six, and I think she was completely overwhelmed. I once asked her, for example, where the surgical scar on my back had come from—a doctor had asked me about it and said it clearly came from an operation of some sort—but she had absolutely no memory of it. She said, "Oh honey, it's possible you did have surgery, but so much was going on back then." I remember thinking, how could a mother forget something like that?

But my mother's condition got much worse. She attempted suicide several times and went in and out of psychiatric hospitals. Whenever she came home again, she barely ate, she wouldn't change out of the same filthy bathrobe and she wouldn't leave the house. For years she sat in front of the television watching game shows. It went on like that for nearly twenty years.

None of us knew what had happened to her. Nothing the doctors did helped her at all. She was locked inside a private hell with a demon none of us could understand. But in a way, what she was going through got locked up inside our family, too. My father said it was a private matter, that we weren't to discuss her condition, which I suppose was another way of saying it wasn't anyone's business.

And then, something incredible happened.

A few years before she died, she saw a doctor who gave her a new drug. Slowly, she got better: she began eating well, dressing carefully, playing her instruments again. She even started attending the little stone church across the street from where she lived. It was as if she had come back from the dead.

And then, about six months before she died, I flew out to California to visit her. She had written me a letter and told me there was something horrible she had done, and that she couldn't carry the secret inside her any longer. To be honest, though, I had put that letter out of my mind. For so many years, she had said things like that—about the terrible guilt she had, even though she couldn't say why, or what a horrible person she was—and I was afraid she might go back to that dark place again.

The day after I arrived, we walked to a small Italian restaurant a few blocks away. It was practically empty. We both sat on stools against a brass railing of a curved mahogany bar, and ordered a glass of wine.

"There is something I want to tell you," she said.

I took a sip of wine. I was happy. I was thinking about how grateful I was that she had come back, that this was the mother my heart had always remembered. It was just like you, Sabrina, when you told me how loving your mother used to be before Andre and Latanisha were born, and how you always wished that mother would come back to you again.

But then my mother said, "It happened a long time ago, before any of you kids were born." She was holding her wineglass in both hands now, but she did not look away from me.

"I killed a baby," she said.

I do not think I moved. No words came out.

She told me she never meant to do it. She said she had been taking care of the neighbors' baby, they were both professors in Berkeley, and the baby just would not stop crying. She said, "And so I shook it and shook it and shook it—so very hard!—and finally it stopped crying. It just lay there. And then I found out two days later it had died."

I put her wineglass on the bar and took both her hands. I told her that maybe the baby had died of something else, that maybe it wasn't her fault. But she shook her head very forcefully.

She said, "No one knew anything about shaken baby syndrome back then. Babies died for no reason. But I knew the reason, and for all these years I have carried that knowledge inside of me. In my heart, I have always known I was the guilty one, and it has always haunted me. I have asked for God's forgiveness, and now I have been trying very hard to find those professors, to ask their forgiveness."

I had never heard her voice or seen her face as it was in that moment: as if she had finally faced her demon in its face, as if she was fully prepared for whatever price she had to pay. We walked back to her home and didn't talk about it again. And after that day, I never mentioned it to anyone except my husband. Except for him, you are the only ones I have ever told.

Neither of them said anything right away.

"The same as our mother," Sabrina said softly. There was a long pause before she asked, "Did she beat you?"

"Never," I answered. "Actually, it was just the opposite. She never laid a hand on any of us, even when she should have, like the time I lay down in the middle of the street because I was angry about something. It was almost as if she was scared of ever raising a hand to us, or of disciplining us in any way. It makes sense to me now—if she killed a child once, maybe she was terrified of doing it again—but it never made sense when I was younger. Still, maybe it had something to do with why I left home at fifteen, the same as you did, Sabrina."

"I just wish you could have told us this before, so you didn't have to carry that by yourself for so long," Andre said. "Why didn't you tell it to us sooner?"

Now it was my turn to fall silent.

"I'm not sure," I said finally. "For a long time, I think it was because I knew that what happened in my family had no comparison with what happened in yours, or with the suffering the two of you went through. But deep down, I also think I saw the connections between our mothers—the terrible secrets they both carried and how those secrets haunted them—and also how, ultimately, those secrets affected both our families. Even if it expressed itself in different ways, all three of us had a shadow from the past cast over our lives."

"The biggest difference was that your mother confessed," Andre said. "Our mother never admitted anything about Latanisha, right up to the very end. So now it's between her and God. And that's something I believe in my heart—that you've got to make peace with whatever hurtful things you've done before it's your own time to go. We're all human, we all do things we wish we could take back. But I really believe that unless you can confess to what you've done and look the truth in its face, it'll follow you forever – or follow the people you love forever."

"At least your mother finally found her peace," Sabrina said. "Thank God for that."

* * *

When I first started, I thought I would be helping Andre and Sabrina tell their story. But over time, my assumption about who has helped whom has been turned on its head. I did not know, as Sabrina once put it, that secrets can be like diseases we pass along to our loved ones without ever knowing it; that they are like stones tossed into a great lake and which ripple onto the shores of generations to follow.

Secrets do not just affect the ones who keep them; they also affect the ones kept in the dark. It does not matter if your family is black or white, rich or poor, scraping by on welfare or socially prominent. But I did not know that, because I was not yet ready to pry the fingers away from my own family secret, to look the truth, as Andre has said, in its face.

And that has been Andre and Sabrina's great gift to me. Very often I have found myself listening to them and thinking:

If Andre and Sabrina can let go of the past and be joyful, if the two of them can be full of faith and gratitude and courage, then so can I.

So can anyone.

* * *

Imagine that there was a common product—a toy, perhaps, or a car seat that each year caused the deaths of more than 1,300 American children. Imagine, too, that in many instances authorities were aware of the households that had that product: they had the names and addresses of people who bought the product and even regularly checked to make sure that the product was being used safely, but children in those homes died anyway.

In many respects, this is what is happening in the United States. The only difference is that the common household item is not a defective crib or a poisonous toy, but instead something even more lethal: the human hand.

Today, as you read this, at least four children will die as the result of child abuse, something that an increasing number of experts are calling a national epidemic. In fact, numerous states have reported disturbing increases in the number of child abuse fatalities and are now urging that immediate steps be taken to combat a situation that apparently has only gotten worse in recent years.

"Unlike other causes of childhood death, the child homicide rate has increased steadily since 1960. It's a serious public health issue," said Kenneth Chew, a professor at University of California at Irvine who, with Richard McCleary, reviewed more than 30,000 California homicides that occurred between 1981 and 1990. In what was called one of the largest-ever studies of child homicide, Chew and McCleary released a study in 1999 that focused on the five percent of victims who were younger than age fifteen. In the majority of cases, Chew said, "very few parents set out to do murder." Instead, he said, "they (the parents) are under stress; they go too far. In more than half of all infant and toddler homicides, the precipitating event is child abuse—shaken baby syndrome."

Another state that has seen an increase is North Carolina, which in 2005 reported a twenty percent increase in child deaths resulting from abuse. Nearly ninety percent of the children who were killed were under the age of four.

"It is important to emphasize that approximately half—fifty-one percent—of the children who died from abusive injuries showed physical evidence of prior non-fatal abuse," said Krista Ragan, a North Carolina child death investigator

with the Child Fatality Review Team/Office of the Chief
Medical Examiner. One cannot hear that statistic and help but
wonder: If those children already had suffered abuse, why was
it not discovered earlier? And it if was, what—if anything—had
been done to try and ensure their safety?

Unfortunately, however, not even children whose
parents or caregivers already are known to child protective
agencies are guaranteed protection. Many states and cities, for
example, have reported an increase in the number of children
who have died while their parents were being monitored for
possible mistreatment. Nationwide, the U.S. Department of
Justice has determined that thirty-eight percent of all children
who died of abuse or neglect in 2000 had prior or current
contact with a child protective services agency.

Perhaps nowhere is this problem better illustrated than in
New York. In 2007, New York's Department of Investigations
(DOI), at the behest of Mayor Bloomberg, looked into an
alarming increase in the number of children who died while
under the so-called protection of the state's Administration for
Children's Services (ACS)—the same agency that Andre
Carmichael had once considered suing. Over an eight-month
period, beginning in October 2005, eleven children died while
ACS was either in the process of investigating the parents, or
else had already completed its findings.

The DOI report, issued in August 2007, was scathing. It
found that ACS caseworkers had lied in their reports; that they
claimed to have investigated families they actually had not;
and that some caseworkers had even gone back and falsified
reports to make it appear they had investigated prior to a
child's death.

Shockingly, the report also said that caseworkers' determinations often were made solely on the word of parents who were being investigated for possible child abuse, a scenario that is similar to a judge basing his or her verdict purely on the denial of the defendant.

"Caseworkers routinely made conclusive determinations concerning abuse and/or neglect allegations based principally, or even exclusively, on the parents' denial of the allegations," the report said. It also cited supervisors who "repeatedly approved case closings, when the caseworkers had not conducted complete investigations."

Among the deaths investigated were:

Sierra Roberts, a seven-year-old girl beaten to death by her father, who later pleaded guilty to manslaughter.

Dahquay Gillan, a sixteen-month-old boy who drowned in the bathtub of his apartment. His mother later pleaded guilty to criminally negligent homicide and reckless endangerment.

Richard Laboy, six, Christian Gaston, five, and Jocelyn Collazo, eighteen months, who all died in the fire of an illegal cellar after repeated reports had cited prior abuse and neglectful living conditions.

Michael Segarra, a two-month-old boy who was found dead in his crib and whose death was determined to have been from "natural causes." The child had tested positive for cocaine at birth, and ACS had received repeated reports that his mother was using drugs in her older son's presence and neglecting the baby.

Nixzmary Brown, a seven-year-old girl found beaten to death in her Brooklyn apartment. Again, ACS had received repeated reports that Nixzmary and her siblings were being abused and neglected.

The cases, said Rose Gill Hearn, DOI commissioner, revealed a "road map of problems with ACS investigations, the same problems that this city has seen over and over again in the past." As such, she added, "they are therefore foreboding harbingers of the future."

New York, of course, is by no means alone. As other states and cities confront horrific cases of child abuse homicide, the question that most often is being asked is: What can be done to stop it? Beyond adding more trained caseworkers to state child protective service agencies, or cutting the caseloads of those individuals, and ensuring more thorough investigations, how can the epidemic of dying children be halted?

One of the first steps, according to some researchers, is to obtain accurate data in order to understand the full scope of the problem. A study conducted at the University of North Carolina at Chapel Hill, for example, found that vital records in the state poorly reflected the actual number of child homicides, and that the 2,973 child deaths reported from 1985 to 1996 actually was closer to 9,500. In fact, the study, published in the *Journal of the American Medical Association,* found that child abuse deaths nationwide may actually be as much as 60 percent higher than previously believed.

Dr. Marcia E. Herman-Giddens, an adjunct professor with the UNC's School of Public Health, explained that records in other states were likely to be just as inaccurate, since all states use the same international system of coding causes of death. The classification system only takes into account fatalities that stem from a "string of events," and not an isolated episode, which means that three children who are stabbed to death, for example, would not be listed as abuse victims if there had been no prior documented abuse.

Additional study "to determine the reasons for the increasing fatal violence against children would help in determining where to direct prevention efforts," Herman-Giddens said.

Prevention, of course, is a major key. The difficult task, however, is that in order to prevent abuse, one first must know where to look and which parents might be at risk of harming their children. Researchers are quick to point out that there is no single profile of a perpetrator of fatal child abuse—virtually anyone, in other words, has the potential to harm his or her child—although certain characteristics do tend to reappear in numerous studies.

According to the Child Welfare Information Gateway (CWIG), an office within the United States Department of Health and Human Services, "frequently the perpetrator is a young adult in his or her mid-twenties, without a high school diploma, living at or below the poverty level, depressed and who may have difficulty coping with stressful situations." Although this is by no means a definitive profile—caregivers of any age, educational background and socioeconomic level have been known to fatally abuse children—this may partially account for an appeal made in 2005 from pediatric researchers to the Pentagon, calling on the Department of Defense to investigate the alarming rate of child abuse homicides at military installations across the nation. The plea was prompted after a study showed that children in jurisdictions with military bases were twice as likely to be killed by a parent or caregiver than other children in the state.

Other studies have shown that children are most at risk of dying from neglect or "maltreatment," as some researchers call it, during the first four years of life, when caregivers, faced with a young child's persistent sleep problems, feeding and toilet-training may cause them to lose control and assault the child or cause a fatal injury while punishing the child.

"Some caretakers," states one publication issued by the United States Department of Justice, "become angry because they view a child's crying or bedwetting as an act of defiance, rather than as normal behavior for a young child."

And those caretakers, statistics show, can come from any racial background. The U.S. Department of Justice reported that for every year between 1976 and 2005, the last year for which statistics were available, nationwide more white children under age five were victims of homicide than African American children. State to state, however, figures may vary.

Nevertheless, in many instances, the CWIG reports that the perpetrator often "has experienced violence first-hand." In other words, a child who has been abused may grow up to be an abuser him or herself—but this is by no means the only reaction to having grown up with abuse.

Although many people may believe that this is true in the majority of cases, psychologists point out that it is a common misconception. "We simply do not understand why some abused children grow up to be abusers, while others grow up to be well adjusted," said Dr. Peter Cook, chief for thirty years of a rural community mental health center in Marble, North Carolina. "If we knew the answer to that, we would be holding a magic key."

Cook points out that many abused children who later become parents themselves are frightened of ever repeating what they went through. "I have seen parents who have grown up with abuse, and they have vowed they won't be that way with their own children, and then the pendulum swings the other way and they become overly permissive," Cook said. "The problem is, they had no training in the tools of good parenting. When they reach into their tool bag, there is only a big hammer, and they vowed they would never use that on their kids. But they don't have any other tool to use."

So what can be done to halt the frightening nationwide rise in child deaths? One of the most important steps is education. Many researchers recommend prenatal and parenting classes that cover anger management, as well as child development. Parents, they point out, also need some form of respite care, and many could benefit from advice and support from visiting nurses.

"Many (parents) don't know that infants and toddlers are built like tootsie-pops, with oversized heads that make them especially vulnerable to shaking or jerking," said University of California at Irvine's McCleary. "No one tells young parents that anger is normal, and there are ways to manage it safely."

Acknowledgments

Andre, Sabrina and I are indebted to numerous people for helping to make this book possible:

Frank Weimann, president of the Literary Group International, for believing in the book from the start: Dr. Joan S. Dunphy, editor and publisher of New Horizon Press; Justin Gross and Ron Hart with New Horizon Press; Ama Dwimoh, Morgan Dennehy and Rosalie Cenatiempo, with the Kings County District Attorney's Office; Frank Urzi; Rita Ciresi, professor of writing and Dr. Deborah Noonan, professor of English, at the University of South Florida; Heath Mackey for his "vision"; Graham Mackey for his encouragement; and John Gray, who has been there for each word.